ENTERING THE MAZE

Identity and Change in
Modern Culture

O. B. HARDISON, JR.

New York   Oxford
OXFORD UNIVERSITY PRESS
1981

Copyright © 1981 by Oxford University Press, Inc.

Library of Congress Cataloging in Publication Data

Hardison, O. B.
    Entering the maze.

        1. Civilization, Modern—20th century—Addresses,
    essays, lectures.   2. Arts and society—Addresses,
    essays, lectures.   3. Technology and civilization—
    Addresses, essays, lectures.   4. Popular culture—
    Addresses, essays, lectures.   5. United States—
    Civilization—1945–   —Addresses, essays,
    lectures.   6. United States—Popular culture—
    Addresses, essays, lectures.   I. Title.
    CB428.H37   303.4   81–299
    ISBN 0–19–502953–4   AACR2

Printing (last digit):   9 8 7 6 5 4 3 2 1

Printed in the United States of America

Grateful acknowledgment is given to the following for permission to reprint the essays that first appeared in their pages. These essays have been revised for the present volume.

The Journal of the California Classical Association, Northern Section for "America and Europe." This essay was originally published under the title, "George Washington in Marble: Notes on the Classical Tradition in America." Copyright © 1978 by *CCA–NS Journal.*

The Ohio Review for "The Open Society." This essay was originally published under the title, "Culture and Openness." Copyright © 1973 by *The Ohio Review.*

Soundings for "Politics and Beauty." Copyright © 1975 by *Soundings.*

Perspectives in Biology and Medicine for "Medicine and Values." This essay was originally published under the title, "Will the Real Doctor Please Stand Up." Copyright © 1977 by *Perspectives in Biology and Medicine.*

Louisiana State University Press for "Hitchcock's Formulas." This essay was originally published under the title, "The Rhetoric of Hitchcock's Thrillers," in *Man and the Movies,* edited by W. R. Robinson. Copyright © 1967 by O. B. Hardison, Jr.

University of Alabama Press for "The Next Frontier." This essay was originally published under the title, "Attempting the Impossible," in *A Time To Hear and Answer,* edited by Taylor Littleton. Copyright © 1973 by O. B. Hardison, Jr.

Grateful acknowledgment is also given for permission to reprint from works by the following.

T. S. Eliot: Reprinted by permission of Harcourt Brace Jovanovich, Inc. from "Little Gidding" in *Four Quartets* by T. S. Eliot. Copyright 1943 by T. S. Eliot; renewed 1971 by Esme Valerie Eliot.

Wallace Stevens: Reprinted by permission of Alfred A. Knopf, Inc.
From "Anecdote of the Jar," in *The Collected Poems of Wallace Stevens* by Wallace Stevens. Copyright © 1923, renewed 1951 by Wallace Stevens.
From "Notes Toward a Supreme Fiction," in *The Collected Poems of Wallace Stevens* by Wallace Stevens. Copyright © 1942 by Wallace Stevens.

Thomas Hardy: From *The Complete Poems of Thomas Hardy,* edited by James Gibson (London and Basingstoke: Macmillan, 1976; New York: Macmillan, 1978).

Don McLean: *American Pie,* written by Don McLean. Copyright © 1971 by Yahweh Music and Mayday Music.

To Howard and Helen Webber

Preface

The central concern of this book is the relation between contemporary culture and the mental ecology of those who, for better or for worse, inhabit that culture. In the metaphor of the title, contemporary culture is a maze, a tangle of paths that seem to lead everywhere and nowhere at the same time.

The maze was created by modern man's highest aspirations and his most brilliant achievements, not by his failures. Does it have an exit? Is modern man condemned to live "in wand'ring mazes lost," like the fallen angels of Milton's *Paradise Lost*, or is contemporary society like the Nature that Alexander Pope described after reading his Isaac Newton as "A mighty maze! but not without a plan"? Or is the basic problem the persistence in modern thought of the belief that at one time there was an exit? Is the desire for an exit a vestigial survival of pre-technological habits of mind?

Because the following chapters are concerned with the relation of modern man to the world he has created, they are concerned with the past as well as the present. Again in terms of the metaphor of the title, the past is like a thread linking us with the entrance of the maze.

The sense of the quiet but inevitable continuity of the past is nicely expressed in Thomas Hardy's poem "In Time of 'The Breaking of Nations'":

> Only a man harrowing clods
>   In a slow silent walk
> With an old horse that stumbles and nods
>   Half asleep as they stalk.
>
> Only thin smoke without flame
>   From the heaps of couchgrass;
> Yet this will go onward the same
>   Though Dynasties pass.

The title of Hardy's poem is taken from Jeremiah: "Thou art my battle ax and weapons of war; for with thee will I break in pieces the nations, and with thee will I destroy kingdoms." The poem was written in 1915 in the midst of the First World War. It can be understood as an assertion of faith in the continuity of traditional values at a time when all such values seemed in danger of being engulfed in the holocaust of blood and violence known as the Western Front.

By the end of the First World War, faith in tradition was already an anachronism as quaint as gingerbread architecture and hackney coaches. Modern man had, as it were, entered a maze of his own making. The continuity of Western history had been shattered. In the new world that was emerging, old men harrowing clods would not be picturesque objects of meditation but symbols of underdevelopment.

What kind of a world is it? After more than fifty years we still do not know. We probably never will, for we are inside, not outside, the maze. We are a continuing process, not a result, and there is no way of knowing where the process is leading.

The central fact of cultural history is that the mind and the world are mirrors. Sometimes the images appear to be accurate;

sometimes they seem as wildly distorted as images in mirrors in the maze of an amusement park.

At any given moment the self is experienced as a stable center of perception, an identity. This center of perception is the necessary condition of consciousness and without it the world would be unintelligible. It is formed in each individual during childhood by institutions that exist primarily to imprint and sustain identity—family, religion, and education, and, in later life, social conventions, laws, the history of the tribe, and quasi-official literary, artistic, and philosophical classics that equip the inhabitants of a culture with common traditions and angles of vision. Identity seems to be unshakable, but its apparent stability is an illusion. As the world changes, identity changes; and as identity changes, it alters the world along with it. Because the mind and the world develop at different rates and in different ways, during periods of rapid change they cease to be complementary. The images they reflect become increasingly distorted. The faces in the mirrors are unfamiliar, like the faces of grotesque strangers, and the sense of identity of individuals and whole societies is weakened and confused.

During no period of history has the interplay between the mind and the world been more dynamic than in the twentieth century. Men harrowing clods are anachronisms in the twentieth century because the mind has made them so. Technology has replaced the horse with the machine and linked the plowman with every skill and every source of materials, no matter how remote, needed to make the technology work. At the same time, what Jacques Ellul calls "technique"—the rational organization of skills, material, equipment, and money into the most efficient possible configurations—has converted agriculture into an international enterprise in which individuals are functional only as they relate to the larger and mostly invisible group project.

This situation has been repeated—is being repeated—in every

human activity and in every geographical region of the earth. Moreover, humanity appears to be on a rising slope with no plateau in sight. Every apparent equilibrium turns out to be an illusion, a momentary pause in an accelerating process of change. The result is a widening gap between the world as it exists in the mind and the world as it is experienced—between identity formed by tradition and identity demanded by the present. This creates enormous social and personal stress. On the social level, problems accumulate, but the solutions turn out again and again to be irrelevant, as though instead of confronting its real concerns society preferred to wrestle with shadows. On the personal level, the disparity between problems and solutions generates anxiety about the future and an intense nostalgia for a past in which identity and reality were, or seem to have been, more perfect images of each other.

The present volume may be understood as a series of comments and observations made along the path through the maze. Traditionalists, beginning at least with Matthew Arnold in the nineteenth century, have often examined that path and have offered conclusions about its direction ranging from the apprehensive to the apocalyptic. It is quite possible that they are right. Modern society may be moving irreversibly toward disaster. It is also possible that they are wrong and that modern society is the transition phase of a movement toward a new level of human development. No judgment is offered here. Whatever the future, the object of the present book is to try to understand the present. It is thus a reading of contemporary experience, not a warning or a call for reform or a summons to a great leap forward.

The chapters that follow are arranged in four groups. Those in the first group ("Taking Bearings") examine traditions that are part of the deep structure of Western—and especially American —culture: the relation of this culture to its secular past; the anxieties generated in it by its religious heritage; the persistence in it of the ideal of openness in spite of all the arguments for closure; and the curious but apparently intense need of the secular state for authentication in great art.

The second group of chapters ("In Mazes Lost") examines some of the unsettling influences that stem directly or indirectly from contemporary technology: the displacement—even the inversion—of traditional values encouraged by modern medicine; the shift in values implicit in the aging of modern populations, which is a by-product of medicine; the implications of the movement from a value-oriented to a utilitarian system of education; and the movement from a world view based on a theory of knowledge to one based on a theory of information. The chapters in the third group ("Mirrors on the Wall") concentrate on the media art created by technology, using film as their representative example. They ask how film considered as one of the major cultural vehicles of modern society relates to the cultural media of the past, and they explore some of the new values that are expressed by it.

Throughout the second and third groups certain themes recur. These themes point to certain underlying imperatives of technological society: its assumption that man is solely responsible for his own future; its preoccupation with utility as a criterion of value; its increasing use of technology to create a fully technological culture (an expressive impulse) in contrast to the use of technology to transmit the values and cultural forms of the past (a conservative, or imitative, impulse).

The fourth group of essays ("The Thread of Ariadne") is speculative. It does not predict where, or whether, we will escape from the maze, but it does raise the question of whether it will be possible in the future to retain traditions that link modern society to its past, like the thread given by Ariadne to Theseus when he entered the maze of the Minotaur. Is there a possible future for the traditions of Jeffersonian democracy, for the self as an undetermined—hence free—entity, for the idea that education should transmit values as well as skills, for poetry as one of the most expressive and possibly the most precious means of expressing identities that are still rooted in history, language and place?

I have made every effort in the following pages to avoid the grim solemnity that Matthew Arnold called "high seriousness." The tone is serious, but there are playful moments, even moments of facetiousness. I hope they convey some of the pleasures that are to be found, along with the challenges, in the contemplation of modern culture. If any jargon remains, it is present by accident not by intention. I have avoided footnotes in the belief that they distract from the text, but I have indicated sources for important facts, statistics, quotations, and the like when these are not self-evident or commonplace. The absence of an index is also intentional since these essays are meant to be explorations of ideas rather than raw material for a data bank.

I wish to express here my gratitude to Mrs. Patricia Jones and Mrs. June Garner for their assistance in moving from draft to final typescript, and to Ms. Kim Lewis and Mr. Tony Outhwaite of Oxford University Press for their expert editorial work.

Among many other obligations, I take special pleasure in acknowledging my debt to the Rockefeller Foundation of New York and the Aspen Institute of Aspen, Colorado. Without a fellowship at the Aspen Institute, awarded by the Rockefeller Foundation for the summer of 1979, it would have been impossible to shape the material presented here into coherent form. Wallace Stevens refers to "The impossible, possible philosophers' man, the man who has had time enough to think." The reader will decide whether the thought in the present volume is worth the effort, but the time to think it was, for the author, a precious gift indeed.

Washington, D.C.   O. B. H., Jr.
June 26, 1981

Contents

"And found no end, in wand'ring mazes lost."
MILTON, *Paradise Lost*

"A mighty maze! but not without a plan"
POPE, *An Essay on Man*

TAKING BEARINGS

1

America as Europe

"A new order of the ages commences, . . . a new generation descends from heaven." These words are not a salute by the revolutionary poet Philip Freneau to the newly born American Republic. They are not even an exclamation by S. Dillon Ripley, secretary of the Smithsonian Institution, on being informed that eighteen million tourists visited his sales shops during the Bicentennial year. They were written by the Roman poet Vergil in his "messianic eclogue" almost two thousand years before the United States became a gleam in the much-celebrated eye of Mr. Jefferson. They announce the birth of a child. The identity of the child is uncertain, but there is no doubt about what the child will do. He will balance the Roman budget, stamp out crime, create full employment, get the mail delivered on time, and support the army. In short, he will restore what Roman poets fondly called "the Golden Age," even as they admitted that it never existed.

There is a connection between Vergil and America. It involves two Latin phrases. The first is *annuit coeptis* and the second, *novus ordo seclorum*. These are seen daily by every American, and some fortunate Americans see them hundreds of times a day. Both are from Vergil. The first is adapted from his poem about farming called the *Georgics*. The second echoes the line already quoted from the "messianic eclogue." They are inscribed on the American dollar bill, forming part of the Great Seal that appears on the side opposite the portrait of George Washington. They can be translated as the motto: "[God] has favored our beginnings. A new order of the ages [commences]." Incidentally, the most famous of all Latin mottoes associated with the founding of the Republic is also from Vergil. Although its proximate source is colonial America, its ultimate source appears to be a poem in the *Vergilian Appendix* giving the recipe for a cheese ball much favored as a breakfast food by Roman farmers. You put all the ingredients of the cheese ball into a bowl, says Vergil, mix them together, and—presto!—from many you get one. *E Pluribus Unum.*

Splendid. But why inscribe Vergilian quotations on that most sacred of American objects, the dollar bill, and put recipes for cheese balls on revolutionary flags? Were the Founding Fathers unable to express their joy over the new order of things in plain English? Were men who stood undaunted before the massed batallions of Lord Howe and "Gentleman Johnny" Burgoyne so intimidated by the demands of authorship that they had to patch their national mottoes together out of scraps of two-thousand-year-old verse? Or is there something more here than meets the eye?

These are serious questions. They are variations on what has been the central theme of American history since Crèvecœur's *Letters from an American Farmer* (1782): Who are we? The best known of these letters is titled "What Is an American?" Crèvecœur answered that Americans are not creatures of the Old World but are a new breed. They have been made over by their experiences into a superior human type.

The most famous refinement on Crèvecœur's idea is a speech titled "The Significance of the Frontier in American History," delivered at the 1893 annual meeting of the American Historical Association by Frederick Jackson Turner. Professor Turner announced to his enthralled colleagues that the frontier is the central factor shaping American character. It follows that, in Turner's words:

> American democracy was born of no theorist's dream; it was not carried in the *Susan Constant* to Virginia, nor in the *Mayflower* to Plymouth. It came out of the American forest. . . . Not the Constitution but free land and an abundance of natural resources open to a fit people, made the democratic type of society in America.

Well, yes. But if so, what are those Vergilian phrases doing on the dollar bill? They may not have been brought over on the *Susan Constant* or the *Mayflower*, but it is equally certain that they were not murmured to our forefathers by the pines and hemlocks of New England's primeval forest.

Over the years, a great many people have disagreed with Professor Turner's hypothesis. During the Bicentennial year alone, at least three books opposing Turner's point of view were published. Irving Howe's *World of Our Fathers* rode the crest of a wave of interest in ethnic contributions to American history. Howe is not concerned with the frontier but with the Jewish immigrants who transplanted the folkways of eastern Europe to the Lower East Side of New York in the last quarter of the nineteenth century, thus creating an enduring and well-defined ethnic enclave in the midst of the most American of cities. There were not many pioneers on the Lower East Side in the 1890s, and if the melting pot operated there, it was set at a slow simmer. Daniel Bell's *Cultural Contradictions of Capitalism* undermines the Turner thesis in a different way. Bell focuses on the influence of the dour European Calvinists who brought the famous Protestant Work Ethic to America. Bell claims to admire the work ethic. His cultural contradiction is the fact that the more successful the work ethic has been, and the more prosperity it has created, the more it has undermined itself by creating a leisure class that supports a "psychedelic bazaar" of consumerism and eventually degenerates into a "Dionysiac pack" of hippies living off dividends from inherited wealth. The work ethic did not come from the frontier, according to Bell, but from Wittenberg, Geneva, and London. The third Bicentennial assault on Turner was *The Origins of the American Self* by Sacvan Bercovitch. Bercovitch is as interested as Bell in the Protestants, but he concentrates on their sense of manifest spiritual destiny rather than their lust for work. Bercovitch insists that the sense of destiny was brought to New England in the seventeenth century at the same time as the Geneva Bible, double-entry bookkeeping, and the art of distilling.

These books are quite right. America's past did not begin with Daniel Boone or even with Captain John Smith. Why not admit the fact? The only criticism one can make of Howe, Bell, and Bercovitch is that they do not look back far enough. The heritage of American Jews is far older than the ghettos of eastern Europe. By the same token, Protestant America traces its lineage back through the Lutherans and Calvinists and Anabaptists of the Reformation to the late classical period—to the Acts of the Apostles and the primitive church that most of the reformers thought they were reestablishing after a thousand years of Romish darkness.

The debt of America to the Old World becomes obvious in another way to anyone who visits Washington, D.C. After the visitor has adjusted his Neiman-Marcus ten-gallon hat and hitched up his Pierre Cardin blue jeans—both of which proclaim his allegiance to the frontier—he notices that he is not surrounded by sod shanties and long-horn cattle. Instead he sees acres of buildings and monuments that seem to have come from the set of *Ben Hur*. These buildings and monuments are statements in form and space. Their message, the message of men and women who have been at the center of American government for two centuries, is deafening: it is the message of power. Only the powerful can control the design of monumental buildings, and only those who control a government can plan a whole city and make that plan stick for more than a century.

The frontier is conspicuous in Washington by its absence. In spite of the efforts of Andrew Jackson Downing in the early 1850s to romanticize the city's appearance and Frederic Law Olmsted's pastoral landscaping of the Capitol grounds, the spaces and buildings have none of the Edenic wildness associated with paintings of the Hudson River school. Instead, they are trimmed, squared, chiseled, polished, marbled, and manicured. Nor do they have the plainness and functionalism associated with radical Protestantism—with Shaker furniture, for example, and New England Congregational churches. In fact, they flaunt their classicism in columns, capitals, friezes, inscriptions, architraves, and statues. A few buildings in federal Washington are in the Gothic tradition—most notably, James Renwick's original Smithsonian Building. But the Gothic buildings are the exceptions, not the rule. From Benjamin Latrobe's sketches for the Capitol, *circa* 1800, to Dewitt, Poor and Shelton's James Madison Memorial Library, completed in 1980, the architectural program for Washington has been predominantly, even overwhelmingly, classical.

This goes for the map of the city as well as its buildings. Major L'Enfant's grand design for Washington was developed in consultation with George Washington and Thomas Jefferson. Its immediate sources were Parisian theories of city planning, but these, in turn, derived from imperial Rome. At the geographical center of Major L'Enfant's city there was to be a building called the Capitol in honor of the Campidoglio in Rome, housing a deliberative body called the Senate in honor of ancient Rome's chief governing body. L'Enfant called the elevation on which the Capitol would be built "a pedestal waiting for a monument," a metaphor taken from ancient sculpture. One of what L'Enfant persuaded himself were seven hills in the new District was originally known as "Jenkins Hill," but was rechristened "Capitol Hill" in honor of its new destiny. The turgid stream draining the hill—long since converted into a covered storm sewer—was called Tiber Creek. These details have a curious effect. They remind one of what scholars call a palimpsest, a manuscript on which there are two texts, one ancient but still faintly legible and the other recent. The older text on Major L'Enfant's map is Rome. It is obscured but still visible under the surface of the modern city.

Nothing about Washington's official buildings is obscure. The Capitol, the House and Senate office buildings, the buildings in the Federal Triangle, Union Station, and the Library of Congress are all explicitly neoclassical. (Admittedly the Library of Congress speaks Latin with a thick Gallic accent.) Most of these are working buildings, providing space for the day-to-day business of government. More spiritual treatments have been lavished on buildings having the quality of shrines, the dominant style for which is Hellenic rather than Roman. The Lincoln Memorial, the Bureau of Archives, and the Supreme Court, for example, owe more to Greece than to Rome. The Jefferson Memorial and the National Gallery of Art, both designed by John Russell Pope, combine Greek refinement with Roman domes.

One other structure must be mentioned: the Washington Monument. As an obelisk, it has two functions. First, it completes the classical illusion by imitating the fondness of Romans for decorating their city with liberated Egyptian antiques. And second, in addition to being an obelisk, it may be regarded as an overgrown Roman milepost. As such, it reminds visiting taxpayers that in America all fiscal roads lead from the provinces to Milepost Number One in the Capital City, an idea that was presumably as familiar and congenial to Tiberius and Caligula as it is today to the Internal Revenue Service. Is it only a coincidence that the Washington Monument is located close to the United States Bureau of Printing and Engraving?

Those who created today's Washington did so without benefit of the Turner hypothesis. They considered it obvious to the point of banality that America is a child of Europe in the broadest sense, by which they understood traditions extending back in time to ancient Greece and Rome. The architecture of Washington is a way of making this understanding plain. It perfectly complements Jefferson's comment on the sources of the Declaration of Independence: "Neither aiming at originality of principle or sentiment, nor yet copied from any particular and previous writing, it was intended to be an expression of the American mind . . . . All its authority rests then on the harmonizing sentiments of the day, whether expressed in conversation, in letters, printed essays, or in the elementary books of public right, as Aristotle, Cicero, Locke, Sidney, etc."

The sense of continuity implicit in the movement from Aristotle to Cicero to Locke is reflected equally in a plan offered to the president of Congress in 1780 by John Adams to establish "a public institution for refining, correcting, improving, and ascertaining the English language." Since this plan is essentially the thumbnail sketch of a possible Institute for Educational Policy, it is of considerable interest. Adams wrote:

> The admirable models which have been transmitted through the world, and continued down to these days, so as to form an essential part of the education of mankind from generation to generation, by those two ancient towns, Athens and Rome, would be sufficient, without any other argument, to show the United States the importance to their liberty, prosperity, and glory, of an early attention to the subject of eloquence and language.

It would be impossible to make the statement any plainer. America's true roots are in Europe, not the frontier. The Europe of America's capital is the spiritual country symbolized by Athens and Rome, which Matthew Arnold aptly described in 1864: "for intellectual and spiritual purposes, one great confederation, bound to a joint action and working to a common result; and whose members have, for their proper outfit, a knowledge of Greek, Roman and Eastern antiquity, and of one another."

* * *

In *European Literature and the Latin Middle Ages* Ernst Robert Curtius attempted to define Arnold's "great confederation" with the precise instruments of scholarship. He had been driven to this task by the frustration and despair that overwhelmed intellectuals on both sides of the Atlantic on the eve of World War II. He explained in 1953:

> What I have said will make it clear that my book is not the product of purely scholarly interests, that it grew out of a concern for the preservation of Western culture. It seeks to serve an understanding of the Western cultural tradition insofar as it is manifested in literature. It attempts to illuminate the unity of that tradition in space and time. . . . In the intellectual chaos of the present, it has become necessary, and happily not impossible, to demonstrate that unity.

The cause of the "intellectual chaos" that disturbed Curtius was nationalism. While there has always been tension between the idea of Europe and the claims of national sovereignty, it did not become open warfare until the Reformation. Even then the warfare was limited. Not until the nineteenth century did historians and literary scholars, who had previously sided with Europe, join forces with the powers of the state to attack it *en masse*. The great Swiss historian Jacob Burckhardt made a central, though partly unintentional, contribution to the cause through his book *The Civilization of the Renaissance in Italy*, published in 1860 and destined to become one of the most influential historical works of the period. Burckhardt regarded the universal culture of the Middle Ages as narrow, dominated by authority, and opposed to individualism. The agent of deliverance from these conditions was the national state or, in Italy, the city-state. He wrote in the introduction to his first chapter that the state is "a new fact . . . in history—the State as the outcome of reflection and calculation, the State as a work of art." Whatever their faults, the new states of the Italian Renaissance interposed their power between the Church and the citizen. The result was a sudden flowering of creative genius in art, literature, science, and social institutions. From Burckhardt's perspective, the modern state thus becomes an agent of individualism and a prime factor in the movement from the Age of Faith to the modern world. In other words, nationalism is liberation.

A second theory complemented Burckhardt's explanation of the Renaissance. This theory had been advanced by the German Romantics of the early nineteenth century and influenced a broad spectrum of cultural studies extending from linguistics to history. It held that each race, culture, or language (the distinction was vague) possesses a unique quality, a "folk-spirit" (*Volksgeist*), which amounts to its basic identity. Since understanding the *Volksgeist* answers for each people the question "Who are we?," its study and cultivation should be a primary concern of each national educational system, even though this removes the idea of Europe—of a unified and cosmopolitan cultural tradition extending from ancient Greece to the present—from the center of the stage and replaces it with the idea of the uniqueness of each of the various races and language groups of which Europe is comprised. Universal culture thus gave way to emphasis on the national cultures of Italy, Germany, England, France, Spain, and others. The internal imperative of each of the national programs was to explain the *Volksgeist* and trace its history. American Studies, which became a popular curriculum subject after World War II, is only the most recent of these efforts to identify the *Volksgeist*; to take it by the throat, so to speak, and force it to answer the question posed by Crèvecœur: "What is an American?"

By contrast, the essential feature of the European tradition that Curtius sought to define is unity. International and even anti-national in character, it began in the Greek city-states, was absorbed and modified in Italy, and was then transmitted to the heterogeneous collection of races and states that comprised the Roman Empire. It outlasted the Roman legions for the simple reason that in almost every department it was crushingly superior to the local cultures it displaced—in administration, law, economic planning, technology, and education. In one department it was deficient: its religion was amorphous and eclectic and lacked a self-perpetuating central bureaucracy. Consequently, while Rome was conquering the world, it was itself being conquered by Christianity. Edward Gibbon's *Decline and Fall of the Roman Empire* is the *locus classicus* for the argument that that conquest was a cultural disaster, that it destroyed a great civilization and replaced it with a thousand years of tyranny, superstition, and ignorance.

The reply of medievalists has been that ancient civilization collapsed because of its own failures. Far from destroying ancient civilization, they argue, Christianity preserved as much of it as could be saved. The alliance between Christianity and the Roman state became official in the fourth century and ripened into marriage with the coronation of Charlemagne in the year 800, by which time Rome had become Europe. The Empire had been redefined geographically by the separation of Rome and Byzantium and the loss of Africa and Spain to Islam. Its center was no longer the Mediterranean but Europe in the modern sense, and its future expansion would be westward, back into Spain and, eventually, to the New World.

Within these new boundaries the Graeco-Roman tradition was preserved. It existed in two forms—in books and in the Latin language—and was therefore primarily the possession of the educated classes. Unlike a folk culture, it could not be absorbed naturally during childhood; it had to be taught. Whatever other functions it served, its basic effect was to create in the educated classes the sense of being shareholders in an international cultural community. It thus counteracted the pull of national and ethnic ties wherever it penetrated.

As long as it did not clash directly with national interests, the idea of Europe persisted as a viable cultural tradition. It persisted in the habit of tracing political institutions to Greece and Rome, in the imitation of ancient models by sculptors, painters, architects, and poets, and in an educational system that made the study of Greek and Latin the foundation of its curriculum. When it finally did come into conflict with the perceived interests of the national state, it lost. The decline of classical studies in the nineteenth century is a symptom of the process. In 1867, well before the retreat had become a rout, Matthew Arnold complained that instead of studying "the best that is thought and known in the world" university students were being forced to read minor vernacular works—presumably because they illustrated the *Volksgeist*. Underlying Arnold's criticism was his concern that the "great confederation" whose members share "a knowledge of Greek, Roman and Eastern antiquity and of one another" was being replaced by a cultural Tower of Babel. Seen from this angle, the debate about the frontier in American history is a reflection in the New World of a larger conflict in the Old. One side insists that Americans are unique; the other side, which expressed its views in the architecture of the nation's capital, insists that they are members of Arnold's great confederation.

This brief overview calls attention to the central role played by education in preserving and transmitting the European cultural tradition. When John Adams planned his "public institution for refining the English language" he turned, as we have seen, to the "admirable models" provided by Athens and Rome. His choice of models might have been made at any time between the sixteenth and the eighteenth centuries, but it seems particularly appropriate for the time when he wrote. In 1780 the United States was in the process of being created. Educational concerns were thus closely related to political concerns about the future shape of the republic. Since all classical writers on education assume that it should advance the interests of the state, their theories would have been especially congenial to the Founding Fathers.

Quintilian's *Institute of Oratory* illustrates the point. It is the most comprehensive treatise on education that has survived from antiquity, and its object is perfectly clear: the purpose of education is to train leaders. Quintilian insists that the leaders be trained morally as well as practically, for they will become the lawyers, bureaucrats, politicians, and magistrates upon whom the well-being of the state depends. Since ancient society was political rather than technocratic, Quintilian's curriculum is centered on what today would be called "communication arts": grammar, rhetoric, and logic. Of these, rhetoric is by far the most important. It is the technique of persuasion. By using it skillfully the leader can translate his ideas into social realities. Quintilian assumes that the orator will be a good man rather than an evil man—hence his emphasis on moral training—and that public issues will be decided by persuasion in open debate rather than by secret agreement. Both of these assumptions have flaws, but the Constitution and the Bill of Rights show that they were shared, with reservations, by the founders of the American Republic.

Since it is impossible to learn technique without examples, Quintilian's program includes a course of readings in works that he considered literary and rhetorical classics. The authors were chosen for their literary excellence and moral rectitude. They tend to be poets, orators, historians, and moral philosophers. Books on technical subjects like medicine, architecture, astronomy, and engineering are ignored in spite of the considerable achievement of the ancients in those fields. Quintilian seeks to produce generalists, at home in a variety of situations, rather than specialists. Homer, Plato, Sophocles, Demosthenes, Cicero, Livy, and Vergil are included; technicians like Galen and Vitruvius and morally questionable authors like Sappho and Lucretius are excluded. The result is what is usually called a "canon of classics." With the addition of later classic authors like Dante and Shakespeare this curriculum is quite similar to the one advocated by Matthew Arnold in the nineteenth century and is recognizably related to twentieth-century American programs in "general education" and "great books."

During the transition from the classical world to the Middle Ages the ancient curriculum was simplified, but its objectives and central emphasis were retained. The simplification has often been cited to illustrate the cultural decay that supposedly occurred after the breakup of the Roman Empire. Actually, the simplification was only a realistic adjustment to the fact that the curriculum was being exported from regions where Greek and Latin were natural languages to regions where the natural languages were Germanic. Latin had to be taught as a foreign language to Franks and Saxons. Since it had to be learned well enough to be used in conversation, there was little time for Greek in the monastic schools. For the same reason grammar was more important in the medieval curriculum than rhetoric. Comprehension was the first goal. Eloquence, if it came at all, came later.

A parallel adjustment occurred in the medieval canon of classics. Classical Latin authors were retained, but they were supplemented by Christian authors. Moreover, they were no longer classified by subject—oratory, history, philosophy, and the like—but in order of difficulty of comprehension from easiest to hardest, the order in which they were necessarily taught. Finally, although the system continued to regard the training of a professional elite as its object, the nature of the elite changed. Instead of becoming magistrates and politicians, the medieval elite became clerics who served the interests of the universal Church.

This fact is central to an understanding of the idea of Europe. As the boundaries of Europe changed, the educational system ceased to be the servant of a specific state and became the servant of a universal power. In effect, the Church created the idea of Europe and set it in opposition to all local and parochial interests. At the same time, it made the educational system into a method of obliterating the local ties and loyalties of those being trained and subsituting a universal culture in their place.

This happened gradually, of course, and largely without conscious planning. However, by the time that Alcuin of York,

Charlemagne's adviser in educational matters, set up a system of schools throughout the Carolingian Empire, it is fair to say that the curriculum was foreign to the native cultures of most of its students.

The curriculum was a powerful cultural force. An education was the necessary precondition for entering into the administrative establishment. At the same time, to become educated meant surrendering a local and natural cultural tradition and embracing a culture that was artificial, alien, and cosmopolitan: artificial because it was a construct of the educational system and could not survive without that system; alien because it had nothing to do with the native languages or traditions of those who absorbed it; and cosmopolitan because it was shared by all educated persons, whatever their nationality or native language.

Within this system classical culture was idealized. Medieval objections to paganism are so well known that this fact needs to be stressed. "The authors," as they were called, were read, admired, glossed, paraphrased, and endlessly imitated. As a result the term "classical" became synonymous with the term "classic." An intellectual framework was formed within which it seemed natural to look to the ancients for guidance in every area of life, with the single exception of religion. Centuries later, the classical architecture of Washington still seemed to its creators not only right but inevitable.

An illustration of the universalizing effect of medieval education will be useful here. The Venerable Bede was born (*circa* 673) a Saxon. As a child he absorbed the pagan and Germanic cultural traditions of his race along with its language. But the education that he received from the Church and that enabled him to become one of the great representative figures of the early Middle Ages was Christian, and therefore opposed to paganism; and it was Latin, and therefore condescending toward what it considered Germanic barbarism. Its subjects were those of Roman education—grammar, rhetoric, and logic—and, with one exception, its classics were either Roman—Vergil, Cicero, and Horace—or Christian imitations of Roman authors— Prudentius, Dracontius, and Martianus Capella. The Bible was the exception. Since it came from Palestine rather than Europe, it must have seemed to Bede even more alien than Vergil or Horace.

Bede's writings are a faithful reflection of his education. His minor works are simplified redactions of classical manuals on prosody (a part of grammar) and on the schemes and tropes of late classical rhetoric. His major work is an ecclesiastical history of England, the theme of which is the providential triumph of Christian culture over Saxon paganism. Its subtitle might be "How We Civilized England." At no point in the *Ecclesiastical History* does Bede pause to lament the passing of a culture which, whatever its faults, had outstanding virtues. As far as Bede is concerned, Anglo-Saxon poetry hardly exists. Bede also wrote an Anglo-Saxon translation of the Bible. In this he is a precursor of many later humanists caught between their commitment to the classics and their realization that those classics have to be translated if they are to be read widely. Translation carries the idea of Europe beyond the elite and into the popular arena where it can compete directly with national and ethnic cultural traditions.

In all of the above respects Bede is representative of a type that could only have come into existence after Latin culture ceased to be anyone's national property. He is the citizen of a world that is unified in time because in it Vergil and St. Ambrose and the Bible are equally contemporary influences and unified in space because its core elements are the same whether in Italy or Spain or England or (eventually) the New World. It is, to use Theodore Solotaroff's definition of Hebrew tradition, "A shared experience that goes beyond opinion and ideology." T. S. Eliot's definition of the historical sense appropriate to the modern poet makes the point nicely. It is, he writes, "A perception, not only

of the pastness of the past, but of its presence . . . a feeling that
the whole literature of Europe from Homer . . . has a simultaneous existence and composes a simultaneous order."

Here, let us interrupt the argument to indulge in a bit of speculation about the future. Until the mid-twentieth century the
classical buildings of Washington were saying something quite
specific and quite significant about tradition in America. Is the
message still relevant?

In spite of its cosmopolitan thrust, the "great confederation"
that was so admired by Matthew Arnold is regional and not global,
its culture based on a canon of classics that is literary and historical rather than technical. For both reasons the idea of Europe
may be outdated. Is not modern society thrusting beyond regional
traditions toward something like a global tradition? And is this
thrust not carried by technology rather than by a canon of
literary and historical classics?

The public vehicle of the emerging world culture is media
art, made possible by technology. The elite vehicle, which is
creating a global establishment of professional administrators
and specialists analogous to the educated clerics of the Middle
Ages, is the language of science. Like medieval Latin, the
language of science is artificial and alien in the sense that it has
to be taught rather than being learned naturally in childhood.
And like medieval Latin, it is universal: it expresses a culture
that is free of all local and parochial traditions.

The language of science, broadly understood, has already
deeply influenced the educational curricula of Europe and the
United States. Despite the inroads of nationalism in the nineteenth
century, which have already been noted, training in the liberal
arts remained central to elite educational programs on both
sides of the Atlantic until World War II. These programs retained
elements of the ancient curriculum—and even "great books"
that would have been familiar to Quintilian or Bede. Since World
War II the trend has been away from liberal arts and toward the

disciplines created by technology, a category that includes both specific technologies and the array of organizational and procedural disciplines—management, banking, public administration, and the like—that complement technology and are classified under Jacques Ellul's term *"technique."*

A less obvious but parallel development has been evident in art and architecture since the beginning of the twentieth century. Art has moved from representationalism to abstraction, and architecture from historicism to functionalism. The most important new museum in Europe, the Centre Pompidou in Paris, explicitly rejects historical traditions in favor of a style that has been labeled "high tech." Washington's newest museum, the East Wing of the National Gallery of Art, rejects the classicism of its companion West Wing but seems self-consciously "modern" —an imitation of a style—rather than functional.

In accord with these tendencies there has been a good deal of rethinking of the liberal arts themselves. In 1971 the Foreign Policy Association of New York published an analysis of future needs in education under the title *International Education for Spaceship Earth*. The quest for a curriculum that meets the needs of an increasingly global society, which is evident in the title, is also evident in the "International Baccalaureate" program that is now offered by United Nations schools around the world and by several private schools in the United States and Great Britain. The problem is that while the scientific component of an international curriculum is easy to formulate because it is universal by nature, what might be called the "liberal" component is extremely difficult to formulate. "Great books" do not translate easily. Even if the translation problem is ignored, there is the formidable, perhaps insuperable, problem of selecting an international canon of classics from the enormous and culturally diverse mass of materials available. Any selection small enough to be useful will be so limited as to be arbitrary. In the absence of an authenticating tradition like that inherited by Europe from the Middle Ages, the only themes that can be invoked to rationalize an international canon of classics are vague general ideas like "the ascent of Man" or "varieties of experience."

In fact, there are as yet no undisputed classics of world culture. All proposed so far are classics of national or regional cultures. Shakespeare probably comes closer than any other author to being a world classic, but Shakespeare is English in spite of his broad appeal, and some of that appeal is undoubtedly the result of the leadership in world affairs of England in the nineteenth century and of the United States in the twentieth. Evidently, global culture is emerging but has not yet fully emerged. Twentieth-century man is in somewhat the same position as the early Church Fathers, who knew they were creating a new culture but did not know exactly what sort of a culture it would be.

Enough speculation. Our present concern is the relation of America to the past not the future. What *about* the classical tradition in Washington?

In 1841 the American sculptor Horatio Greenough completed a monumental statue of George Washington on commission by the Congress of the United States for the Rotunda of the Capitol. Greenough's Washington weighs twenty tons. Even though seated, he is around eleven feet high. He rests on a Greek chair, a *kathedra*. A toga is draped casually but decorously over his loins. His left hand extends a sheathed sword, handle forward, to the passerby. His right hand is raised, and his index finger points to the sky. He probably feels a little ridiculous—like a garage mechanic in a tuxedo. There are, in fact, so many excellent reasons for not posing General Washington in this manner that only the most compelling motive could have overridden them.

That motive was expression. Greenough did not intend to create an historical portrait in the manner of Jean-Antoine Houdon, whose face of Washington he copied. Instead, he wanted to show Washington's significance for American history. To do this he depicted Washington in apotheosis—a throned demigod purged of all earthly blemishes. The technique recalls Michelangelo's funerary statues of Lorenzo and Giuliano de' Medici in Florence, which is not surprising since Greenough was living in Italy when he created his statue.

In Greenough's program every detail is significant. Washington's nudity expresses the purity of his motives. The sheathed sword tells passersby that through war he brought them peace. He offers the sword because the price of liberty is eternal vigilance. His raised index finger announces that throughout his earthly life he was guided by a higher Providence. All of these details produce the effect of monstrous incongruity, which is intentional. It is part of Greenough's program: by making the familiar unfamiliar, it forces the viewer to reconsider the ties between America and the classical past.

Every culture has myths that explain its origin. Usually they are religious. They explain the beginning of the culture as a sudden eruption of the divine into human affairs. Often they describe an erotic encounter whose outcome is the birth of a hero. Drawing on Hebrew traditions, for example, Milton depicted Creation itself as a sexual event:

> . . . Thou from the first
> Wast present and with mighty wings outspread
> Dove-like satst brooding on the vast Abyss
> And mad'st it pregnant.

Greek history begins with the seduction of Leda by Zeus disguised as a swan, and in Roman history, Venus, having become the lover of Anchises, gives birth to Aeneas, founder of Rome. Romulus and Remus are begotten on Rhea Silvia, a vestal virgin, by the god Mars. They are nurtured by a she-wolf that becomes the symbol of the Roman republic.

The myths that establish the origin of a culture are the source of the values by which the culture defines itself. As Milton knew, one answer to the question "Who are we?" is "Listen to the story of how we began." The later history of a culture can thus be understood, in part, as a progressive unfolding of the values implicit in its beginning. But while those values unfold, the culture moves away from its beginning. This process is symbolized by William Butler Yeats's image of a spiral constantly widening as it moves out from its point of origin. Eventually the spiral becomes so wide that it cannot be supported by its link with the beginning. The culture loses its identity and collapses: "Things fall apart; the center will not hold;/Mere anarchy is loosed upon the world."

Perhaps because cultures share Yeats's fear of "mere anarchy," they attempt to slow down the spiral movement of history. They do this through institutions that are innately conservative, including sacred texts, rituals, monuments, museums, libraries, school curricula, and, of course, statues of their Founding Fathers.

Horatio Greenough's Washington is a consciously fabricated culture myth—a myth of origin that answers Crèvecœur's question, "What is an American?" Greenough knew exactly what he was doing. The classical inspiration for his statue was the Zeus of Phidias. Zeus was not only a god but a rebel god who overthrew the tyranny of an older order, a defender of liberty and a savior of men. Nineteenth-century American patriots, including Greenough, regarded Washington in the same light. He was the father of his country, hence the hero with whom the myth should begin. He had overthrown the tyranny of King George III, he had defended liberty, and he had saved his countrymen at a time when their cause seemed lost. There is even a hint of heroic sexuality in the athletic nudity of Greenough's image.

All this symbolism, grotesque though it may seem, is intensified by the planned location of the statue. The Rotunda of the Capitol building stands at the center of America's symbolic space. The street signs of Washington proclaim that the four directions of the world—north, south, east, west—and the integers of the real number system—1, 2, 3, 4,—begin at the center of the Rotunda. This identifies the Rotunda as a sacred place, an *omphalos mundi*, a point of contact between the visible and the invisible worlds. Washington's finger points upward to the cervix-like eye of the dome. Through that eye he passed to his immortal birth among the gods, and through that same eye his influences will enter—and redeem—the imperfect world of history.

In 1841 the dome of the Rotunda was flat, an imitation of the Pantheon, "the home of all the gods." The implications of this are emphasized by the chair—the *kathedra*—on which Greenough placed General Washington. With the statue in place, the Rotunda becomes in Greenough's metaphor the precise center of American space, the seat of American government, the Cathedral of Democracy, and the home of its presiding god, Zeus–Washington, in the city that bears His name. From this position Washington's influence radiates outward in invisible beams that end, ultimately, in the pockets where Americans carry green talismen of their protector. The potency of the talisman is guaranteed on one side by a sacred image of Washington and on the other by the two Vergilian mottoes: *annuit coeptis* and *novus ordo seclorum*—"[God] has favored our beginnings. A new order of the ages [commences]."

This is powerful magic, and one gropes for language adequate to its implications. Its technique is both ancient and modern. The medieval churches in Rome, for example, were deployed to recall the geography of the holy places in Jerusalem in the same way that the spaces of Washington echo the geography of ancient Rome. In the twentieth century James Joyce superimposed the story of Leopold Bloom, citizen of Dublin, on Homer's story of the wanderings of Odysseus. T. S. Eliot explained:

> In using myth, in manipulating a continuous parallel between contemporaneity and antiquity, Mr. Joyce is pursuing a method which . . . is . . . a way of controlling, of

ordering, of giving a shape and significance to the immense panorama of futility and anarchy which is contemporary history.

Probably all history seems to its participants to be an "immense panorama of futility and anarchy." The classical architecture of the nation's capital and the classical symbolism of Greenough's statue can be understood as complementary efforts by those at the center of American power to give a sense of order and coherence to the immense anarchy of nineteenth-century American life. They are "myths of origin." They define the American identity and thereby tell Americans who they are. The need for such myths is continuous. In fact, it may be greater today than it was in 1840 when Greenough created his statue simply because the sense of futility and anarchy is so widespread in modern society. Myths offer something permanent to hold on to during a period of accelerating change.

In the midst of such curious thoughts, the fate of Greenough's statue is instructive. It was installed in the Rotunda in 1841. Two years later public outrage over the nudity of the statue reached such a pitch that the statue was removed. (It was also too heavy for the floor, and, in any case, Greenough disapproved of the lighting in the Rotunda.) In 1908 it was given to the Smithsonian Institution. Today Washington rests in the Museum of American History and glumly contemplates the eternal swing of a gigantic Foucault pendulum. A better emblem of the contrast between the glories of the past and the realities of technological culture would be hard to imagine.

In the Rotunda, the center space reserved for Washington is empty. This, too, is an emblem, although its meaning is obscure. The empty space could be saying, simply, that Greenough's statue was too heavy for the floor. Or it could be saying that, having been brought face to face with a past far older than Professor Turner's frontier, Americans rejected it. Or it could be saying that the spiritual origin of American democracy is, indeed,

Europe. What if Europe is more than its "great books" and its classical architecture and its educational systems? What if it is concealed as much as revealed by these material symbols?

At the beginning of the history of Europe, Jehovah forbade his followers to worship Him in graven images. Both the iconoclasts of the sixth century and the Puritan fathers of the seventeenth century believed that images imprison the spirit. The absence of Greenough's statue from the Rotunda of the Capitol may be saying that, true to their heritage, Americans honor a hidden god. Such a god may have favored their beginnings, as the motto on the American dollar suggests, but will not be fully revealed until the end of history.

2

Necessary Fictions

The most pathetic character in Friedrich Dürrenmatt's play *The Visit* is the Schoolmaster. The play tells the story of a town bribed by an enormously wealthy lady (the "visitor" of the title) to murder her former lover. That, at least, is the surface plot. The real plot is the reenactment by the townspeople of the archetypal ritual sacrifice that is the subject of Sir James Frazer's study of primitive religion, *The Golden Bough*, and that classical scholars such as Gilbert Murray and F. M. Cornford have found at the root of Greek tragedy. The play thus moves on two levels. On one, it is the story of a judicial murder for money, an indictment of materialism. On the other, it has nothing to do with motives in the conventional sense. It is a play about religious impulses that are independent of the ways people explain them.

Dürrenmatt's Schoolmaster is a key figure because he represents the liberal and rational heritage of Western culture. He is "Headmaster of Guellen College, and lover of the noblest Muse." He sponsors the town's Youth Club and describes himself as "a humanist, a lover of the ancient Greeks, an admirer of Plato." He is a true believer in all those liberal and rational values that Western culture has inherited from antiquity.

In keeping with these values, Dürrenmatt's schoolmaster is horrified by the plans of his fellow townspeople, whom he has tried to inspire with visions of nobility, to commit murder. As the climax approaches, however, he crumbles. Not only does he know of the murder plan, he knows he will become a part of it:

> I know something else. I shall take part in it. I can feel myself slowly becoming a murderer. My faith in humanity is powerless to stop it.

The Schoolmaster has discovered that the apparently absolute values of "the ancient Greeks . . . and Plato" have limits. Other values, hidden and irrational, are at least as powerful. Are the latter true and the former nothing more than lovely and venerable fictions?

The Visit brilliantly explores one of the most ancient paradoxes in Western experience, a paradox that appears in the Old Testament in the contrast between the Gentiles who worship graven idols and the Hebrews who worship invisible truth: "Thou shalt not make unto thee any graven image, or any likeness of anything that is in heaven above, or that is in the earth underneath, or that is in the waters under the earth." The same paradox recurs in the conflict between pagan learning and Christian revelation in the early centuries of the Christian era, and again, in the high Middle Ages, in the debate between Thomistic rationalism, which sees the world as an intelligible and orderly expression of divine reason, and the mysticism of St. Bonaventure's *The Mind's Road to God*, which sees the world as a delusion and turns from it to suprarational experience. In the seventeenth century the paradox is embodied in the conflict between science and revelation, a conflict that was renewed in the nineteenth century by the publication of Darwin's *Origin of Species*.

It is still with us. No one could be more devoted to humane

values—or more knowledgeable in the field of biology—than Jacques Monod, co-recipient of the 1965 Nobel Prize for medicine and physiology. In a much-admired essay, "On Values in the Age of Science" (1969), Monod proclaimed the end of the Age of Faith:

> modern nations . . . still teach and preach some more or less modernized version of traditional systems of values, blatantly incompatible with what scientific culture they have. The western, liberal-capitalist countries still pay lip service to a nauseating mixture of Judeo-Christian religiosity, "Natural" Human Rights, pedestrian utilitarianism and XIX Century progressivism. . . . They all lie and they know it. No intelligent and cultivated person, in any of these societies can really believe in the validity of these dogma.

While a great many "intelligent and cultivated persons" undoubtedly agree with Monod, many others do not. Dürrenmatt is a case in point. What he shows through his Schoolmaster is that a rational and secular value system of the kind proposed by Monod is a delusion that may crumble as soon as it is subjected to stress. Dürrenmatt had good reason to believe his message. *The Visit* was written in 1956 when memories of the Holocaust were still vivid. Since then, confidence in rational and secular values has continued to decline. In 1979, in what was almost a national paroxysm of disgust, the people of Iran rejected Western rationalism and opted for a form of government that looks very much like theocracy. The diatribes of Iran's Mullahs are hardly less passionate than the tirades of America's Moral Majority and the sermons of its radio and television evangelists. It is interesting and significant that the American Mullahs consistently identify "secular humanism" as the chief corruption of modern society. In fact, in 1979 the General Convention of the Episcopal Church, a normally moderate body, felt the pressure sufficiently to include a denunciation of "humanistic secularization" in its proceedings.

While the Schoolmasters of Western society dream of nobility, the Faithful quote the Sermon on the Mount:

> No man can serve two masters: for either he will hate the one and love the other; or else he will hold to the one, and despise the other. Ye cannot serve God and Mammon.

And:

> Take therefore no thought of the morrow, for the morrow shall take no thought for the things of itself.

And:

> Everyone that heareth these things, and doeth them not, shall be likened unto a foolish man, which built his house upon sand.

The conflict between the graven idols of secular humanism and the invisible realities known only to the saving remnant of the devout is very much alive today. If Dürrenmatt is correct, there is little to be said for humanism. It is an illusion, a fiction, a thin coating of rationalizations covering something awesome and terrifying. The Mullahs have won.

Before abandoning humanism and all its works, however, let us consider it from another angle. For the sake of speculation, let us imagine a humanism that is a way of seeing. The things it sees are human creations or things that have special human significance. This sort of humanism will be interested in the values these things express but not in any particular set of those values.

A humanism that is a way of seeing will be committed describing what it sees. It will seek to fix the condition of the human spirit at a particular place in a particular moment of time in relation to a particular experience, and it will choose its places and times and experiences because they express the condition of the human spirit with particular clarity. They are the evidence concerning the nature of the human spirit that has accumulated throughout history. In other words, they are to humanism what the raw materials of physics, biology, and chemistry are to science.

References to the human spirit sound religious. Perhaps, but not necessarily. The Old Testament may be right. The human spirit may be a remnant of the divine breath infused by God into the dust of the newly created earth. However, it may equally well be a convenient name for an entirely natural phenomenon also called consciousness and a by-product of processes that are, as Jacques Monod put it, "a huge Monte-Carlo game" played in utter indifference to the outcome. Either answer may be correct; the point is that no matter how the human spirit originated, it will not go away. Since experience is impossible without consciousness, it is the ground of human reality.

This is an explicitly anti-behaviorist position. It assumes that the human spirit is not an association machine operated by the outside world on the model proposed by B. F. Skinner but an entity through which sensations are made into coherent experience in time and space. This conclusion seems obvious on the basis of everyday life: people do not experience light waves or sound waves or vibrating water molecules, they experience the *Mona Lisa* or Beethoven's Fifth Symphony or hot water. What they experience may be hallucinations, but there is something that is doing the experiencing. As Descartes announced three hundred years ago, it is possible to doubt the reality of everything outside the self—it may all be a dream—but it is impossible to doubt the existence of the mind that dreams and doubts.

To define the humanities as evidence concerning the nature of the human spirit is not only an accurate definition but the only accurate definition possible. Its first consequence is to make the humanities far more encompassing than they are normally taken to be. Within the definition, anything can be a humanity. A mountain can be a humanity, and, since most people go to the mountains to admire them rather than to study their geological peculiarities, mountains usually *are* humanities. To respond to the beauty of a mountain is to respond to something spiritual that the viewer discovers in it. This "something" must be either an element in Nature that answers a human need or the reflection of a value that originated in the observer.

If a mountain can be a humanity, so can anything else in Nature—the sea, a tree, a bird, even a rock. William Blake found the world in a grain of sand and heaven in a wild flower, and T. S. Eliot discovered terror in a handful of dust. Contrary to popular belief, science humanizes Nature as often as art. Lucretius described atoms in his scientific epic *On the Nature of Things* as little spheres with hooks on them falling through space. John Dalton, who formulated the atomic theory, made them into miniature solar systems, each with a nucleus like the sun and a planetary system of electrons. Today (if I have it right), they are clouds of particles in constantly changing states of excitation, resolvable finally into quarks and anti-quarks, charmed quarks and gluons (which glue everything together) observing a Zen-like discipline known as the Eight-Fold Way. The poetry of atoms is austere and disciplined, but it is poetry of a very high order.

What is true of Nature is also true of man-made objects, with the difference being that man-made objects embody human intentions. They communicate as well as reflect. The root of the English *poet* is the Greek *poietes,* meaning "maker," whether of a teakettle, or a scientific gadget, or a drama, or—in Neoplatonic uses of the word—the Maker of an entire cosmos. The message communicated by a man-made object is the conscious or unconscious purpose of its maker. A Morris chair, for example, communicates something quite different from that of a post-and-dowl Shaker chair or a stainless steel and plastic chair by Norman Bel Geddes, and the message depends less on the mood of the viewer than on the design used by the craftsman. The message of the Capitol building in Washington is different from that of the United Nations building in New York. The Capitol expresses specific cultural values—the values of Greece and Rome—to which the American government traces its political system, while the United Nations Building is a universal form free of local cultural bias and hence expressive of the values that are shared by the various parochial cultures that make up world culture.

This tendency of man-made objects to communicate is so fundamental that messages are conveyed even where none is intended or imagined. Henry Ford of Detroit, for example, had two entirely practical goals in making automobiles: to put America on wheels and to make money. The mind recoils in considering the variety of messages that this simple act released into American culture. Interpreting these messages has kept historians, political scientists, sociologists, economists, and writers of fiction occupied for the last two generations, and they are not through yet. One ramification with particularly humanistic aspects is so enormous that, so far, it has not even been confronted. In creating the modern automobile, Ford and his fellow entrepreneurs unintentionally produced the dominant art form of the twentieth century, which might be labeled "thin-steel sculpture." Like the United Nations Building, this art form is functional and abstract. All efforts to associate it with forms other than itself, natural, historical, or artificial, by, for example, putting flowerpots in the passenger compartment or naked ladies on the radiator cap or rocket fins on the rear fenders, have quite properly been rejected. A well-designed automobile looks like nothing so much as a well-designed automobile.

To take one other example: when NASA decided around 1960 to send a space vehicle to the moon, the stated objectives were scientific and political in nature. Yet the chief message of the moon flight of 1969, conveyed by the image of a blue and white disk floating in the endless darkness of space, was humanistic. The image implies that the earth is tiny and fragile and that only the thinnest of curtains stands between it and the titanic forces raging around it. People knew this before the Apollo flight, but the knowledge had remained on the surface of the mind. An image, planted in the world, was needed to objectify it. Only when a camera had gone into space and brought back that image did the lesson begin to sink in.

Evidently, humanistic experience offers a sense of order, of coherence, of a relation between man's inner reality and the reality around him. From the religious point of view, this order is a part of reality. That is, it has an objective existence in Nature. It is, as it were, the intention of the Divine Maker. St. Thomas Aquinas taught that wherever we look, if we can only manage to see, we discover a radiance that shines up from the deep structure of things; and St. Bonaventure wrote in his commentary on the *Hexaemeron*: "The whole world is like a mirror, bright with the reflected light of divine wisdom; it is like a great coal radiant with light." Gerard Manley Hopkins translated the metaphor into one of his loveliest sonnets, "God's Grandeur":

> The world is charged with the grandeur of God.
> It will flame out, like shining from shook foil;
> It gathers to a greatness, like the ooze of oil
> Crushed. Why do men then now not reck his rod?

Why not, indeed? If the world is charged with a divine light, why do so few people see it? Perhaps they do see it and have difficulty only when they try to name it. Hopkins's more pessimistic answer is that they fail to see it because they are too busy to look:

> Generations have trod, have trod, have trod;
> And all is seared with trade; bleared, smeared with toil;
> And wears man's smudge and shares man's smell. . . .

If Hopkins is right—if man fails to see the beauty around him because he is too involved in economic activity—the fact has an obvious relation to the conflict between faith, which turns away from the things of the world, and secular humanism, which seeks enlightenment but ends in the worship of graven idols. For Hopkins the glory of faith is always there, and to ignore it is to ignore the deepest reality of life:

> Because the Holy Ghost over the bent
>> World broods with warm breast and with ah! bright
>>> wings.

Of course, there is an alternate point of view. While it would be absurd to deny Hopkins's own testimony that he has seen radiance in the world, that radiance may come not from God but from his own imagination. If so, it is a purely human radiance. He is not a Prometheus taking fire from a divine source but a Narcissus in love with his image in a mirror. Or, to put the idea more positively, he is responding to those human elements in his perception of reality without which perception of any kind would be impossible.

Like Hopkins, William Wordsworth believed that beauty is everywhere and that man fails to see it because he never looks:

> The world is too much with us; late and soon,
> Getting and spending, we lay waste our powers:
> Little we see in Nature that is ours;
> We have given our hearts away. . . .

It is hard to say exactly where Wordsworth stands on the subject of religion, for he took different positions at different times in his life. His solution to the indifference of which he complains is not religious in the conventional sense but is both ingenious and significant. Religion is a way of opening our minds to the spiritual quality of experience. Even a fake religion, Wordsworth announces, is better than apathy:

> . . . Great God! I'd rather be
> A Pagan suckled in a creed outworn;
> So might I, standing on this pleasant lea,
> Have glimpses that would make me less forlorn;
> Have sight of Proteus rising from the sea;
> Or hear old Triton blow his wreathèd horn.

It is an easy step from the idea that a fake religion is better than none to an entirely secular point of view. If there is no absolute truth, there are only fictions. People may not like

fictions but they cannot get along without them. Some fictions
are so general that they are called religions. Some are scientific,
and they are called hypotheses. And some are moral or political
or economic or purely personal. In any case, it is better to
choose fictions that are adapted to human needs—better, that
is, to be pagans in a creed outworn—than to gaze into the world
with Jean-Paul Sartre and see nothing. "Nothing" is not the final
truth of things; it is only another fiction.

A more refined and probably more adequate statement of
this position is that it is not possible to see nothing. The mind is
a fiction-making machine, and the only way for it to stop making
fictions is to die. In "Notes Toward a Supreme Fiction" a twentieth-
century American poet, Wallace Stevens, begins with the notion
that reality is a mirror. It is, he says,

> . . . our own.
> It is ourselves, the freshness of ourselves,
> And that necessity and that presentation
>
> Are rubbings of a glass in which we peer.

The problem for Stevens is to discover in the midst of the endless lesser fictions that the mind creates a supreme fiction, a fiction
of things as they are:

> . . . to impose is not
> To discover. To discover an order as of
> A season, to discover summer and know it.
>
> To discover winter and know it well, to find,
> Not to impose, not to have reasoned at all,
> Out of nothing to have come on major weather,
>
> It is possible, possible, possible. It must
> Be possible. It must be that in time
> The real will from its crude compoundings come.

But it is not possible short of religious conversion. Stevens ends
on a resigned and ironic note: "They will get it straight one day
at the Sorbonne."

*   *   *

Reality, then, may be a radiance from the deep structure of things or an endless series of reflections of the self; the Holy Ghost brooding over the bent world or a necessary fiction concealing what is at best a supreme fiction. Both points of view are humanistic because both insist that our most important experiences are those of the spirit. The first is religious and the second secular. They agree and, at the same time, they conflict. To recognize this is to move beyond the nature of humanism in general to the specific nature of humanism in Western culture. Consequently, it requires turning from poetry to history.

Probably the most elementary generalization possible about Western culture is that it is an amalgam of two different traditions, that of Palestine and that of Greece. Both are so deeply involved in Western man's sense of humanity that he cannot abandon them, despite their many conflicts. He is a child of history, like it or not, and they are part of the texture of his consciousness.

Hebrew culture is based on a single book, the Word of God. Greek culture, by contrast, is based on a thousand books, all of them by human authors. The god of the Hebrews sternly rejected graven idols. Consequently, the Hebrew tradition is iconoclastic —it scorns all attempts to materialize the divine. The Greek gods, conversely, admired the material world. Their admiration, as a matter of fact, often seems to have been tinged with envy, as though they considered the material world better than the celestial. They *wanted* to be materialized. They approved of statues, and the statues they inspired were so beautiful that they eventually set standards for human beauty, at which point, in a curious reversal of roles, humans began to set standards of beauty for the statues.

The Hebrews, one might say, invented the invisible world and protected it with the most severe sanctions against the visible. Even the name of their deity was forbidden because it came, in itself, suspiciously close to limiting Him in a material way.

Taking the opposite path, the Greeks invented the visible world, a world where the gods not only had shapes and names but persistently visited mankind in forms of men and animals and begot a considerable progeny of demigods on mortal women— another symptom of their desire to materialize. And having invented the visible world, the Greeks set about filling it with sculpture, temples, epics, plays, music, athletic contests, political systems, and gadgets; and explained it through philosophy, biology, geometry, medicine, physics, geography, and history. And, having filled it and explained it, they celebrated it, and there is the rub. It is hard to separate celebration of the visible world from worship of graven idols. It is not very far, really, from setting limits to divine freedom by writing books of rational theology and ethics to the mad presumption of announcing: "An honest God's the noblest work of man."

By an accident of history, Christianity inherited both worlds, and it has been uncomfortable with them ever since. St. Jerome had nightmares about being a Ciceronian rather than a Christian. St. Augustine wept over Dido in Vergil's *Aeneid* even though he knew that she was a debauched woman and had committed suicide, a particularly dire sin. He admired classical learning and understood its utility, but he felt guilty about it. In his *de Doctrina Christiana* he justified its use: it was like the gold of the Egyptians which the prudent Hebrews took with them upon their departure for the Promised Land. The analogy is based on the idea of theft, and theft is innately questionable, even when divinely inspired.

Meanwhile, a saving remnant of early Christians flatly rejected the lures of graven idols and Egyptian gods. The Desert Fathers imitated the Hebrews by flying to the wilderness where the invisible is a constant, brooding companion. St. Benedict was more practical but no less committed to invisible realities. His monastic rules provide a blueprint for the establishment of whole com- munities of Christians determined to avoid the snares of the world, the flesh and the devil. These rules were regularly revised and made more rigorous during the later history of monasticism —by the Cluniacs, the Cistercians, and the Carthusians.

Meanwhile, the laity went its own way. While the Desert Fathers proclaimed their new order and hermits slept on log pillows in the forest or immured themselves for life in tiny cells, pious Christian gentlefolk ordered sarcophagi decorated with images of Orpheus descending into hell, or of deer panting for the water font, or of the infant Hercules wrestling with the serpent, and crowned with images of souls being transported by angels looking very much like Nereids to Arcadian pastures where the lamb of God grazes. Thanks to an alliance, useful to both, between pagan magistrates and Christian propagandists, the number of martyred saints soon equaled or exceeded the number of the pagan gods they were replacing. As this happened, images of the saints began to invade previously unadorned churches. In their train came music, vestments, ceremonies, poetic liturgies, stained glass, and service books illuminated in lapis lazuli and gold.

It was beautiful. In many ways it transcended the achievement of the Greeks in making the divine visible. But as its critics have always pointed out, it was perilously close to idolatry—perhaps even to secular humanism. The Protestant reformers of the sixteenth century were not barbarians. They read their psalms in Hebrew and the Acts of the Apostles in demotic Greek, and they thought of themselves as the saving remnant destined to lead their fellow Christians away from the fleshpots of Egypt and of Rome into the deserts of the living God. The impulse that led many of them to burn illuminated manuscripts, smash stained-glass windows, and mutilate statues of the saints and of the Blessed Virgin was deeply religious. They wanted to destroy the visible world before it overwhelmed the invisible one.

Knowledge itself can be a snare of Satan. St. Francis learned more from the sun and the birds than from all the disputations of the theologians. Erasmus of Rotterdam, one of the major prophets of the humanism of the Renaissance, began *The Praise of Folly* (1509) by satirizing medieval Christianity and ended it by reiterating St. Paul's observation that the wisdom of man is the foolishness of God. Folly, in this sense, is the beginning of wisdom, a return to the innocence of childhood. For the child-like, the grandeur of God flames out "like shining from shook foil," and the Holy Ghost broods comfortingly over the bent world. Knowledge—at least secular knowledge—is a concern of the City of Man, not of the City of God. One does not need to read Aristotle to be saved, and, in fact, reading Aristotle may jeopardize salvation.

The flight from knowledge is a perennial motif in Western culture. Elements of it can be found in the philosophies of flower children and Ramakrishna disciples, in the teachings of Zen and the attacks of today's Moral Majority on secular humanism. The saving remnant sees truth face to face. The sophisticated, trapped in the vanities of the intellect, cannot even find a supreme fiction, much less a living truth, amid the graven idols that surround and baffle them. It was not a fanatical Protestant reformer but a Catholic monk, Girolamo Savonarola, who made a bonfire of the books of the humanists in the central square of Florence in 1498 and urged all the well-heeled citizens of the town to abandon the world before they were destroyed by it.

The contradictions between the invisible and the visible world, between the truths of the saving remnant and the graven idols of secular knowledge, are deeply embedded in Western culture. We have not outlived them, and it is not certain that we want to outlive them. For better or worse, they are our heritage, our sense of where we came from and where we may be able to go. Beyond that, they constitute the special insight of Western culture into the nature of the human spirit. If they are contradictory, it is because the Western heritage, perhaps more than that of other cultures, is contradictory. Western man is blessed—

or condemned—to honor two ideals; to bow down to graven idols even as he prepares to join the saving remnant in the desert.

Consider, by way of illustration, T. S. Eliot's poem "Little Gidding," written during World War II when Eliot was an air-raid warden in London. It is not a narrative but a transcript, a kind of diary, of the states of consciousness that Eliot experienced as a representative child of the twentieth century during this crisis. It speaks in images not ideas, and its dominant image is fire, which is obviously the right element for this violent country. The poet watches firebombs bursting everywhere in the ancient and lovely city. As they fall, their fire is transformed by an amazing spiritual chemistry into an image of the love by which man endures:

> Who then devised the torment? Love.
> Love is the unfamiliar Name
> Behind the hands that wove
> The intolerable shirt of flame
>   We only live, only suspire
>   Consumed by either fire or fire.

The idea that suffering and love are closely related comes from the Book of Job. But Eliot's allusion is more complicated. The "intolerable shirt of flame" to which he refers comes from Greece, not from Palestine. It once belonged to Nessus the Centaur. As Nessus was dying he gave it to Deianira, the wife of Hercules, and told her that it would restore her husband's love. When, in desperation, she persuaded Hercules to wear it, it burned into his flesh like a cancer. Finally, to end his suffering, he threw himself onto a funeral pyre on Mount Oita. The gods, admiring his nobility at that moment, raised his soul to heaven and granted him immortality.

There are themes here that are undreamed of in the Old Testament. When Job despairs of his future and asks for death, Jehovah's advice is pointedly unsentimental: "Gird up now thy loins like a man." Why does Eliot bring a pagan myth that includes lust, revenge, and suicide—a noble suicide, at that—into what would otherwise be a straightforward statement of faith? The answer is that he does not "bring it in": it is a part of the history that has shaped his consciousness, and he cannot ignore it without betraying the first imperative of art, honesty.

Consider another example. Perhaps no two activities are as antithetical as writing poetry and waging war. One is a free activity of the spirit and the other is so depressingly utilitarian that even economists sometimes doubt its value. Yet poets are drafted into armies along with carpenters and doctors, and soldiers sometimes carry copies of *Othello* and *The Canterbury Tales* with them into battle. In the final episode of Erich Maria Remarque's *All Quiet on the Western Front,* the youthful veteran who is the story's protagonist dies because he is sketching a bird singing just beyond the trenches.

The epilogue of Stevens's "Notes Toward a Supreme Fiction" begins with an image that summarizes the conflict between the spiritual and the utilitarian: "Soldier," he writes, "there is a war between the mind and the sky." It *is* a war. Perhaps it has been fought in other cultures, but history has made it a fundamental characteristic of Western culture since the early days of the Church. Stevens's conclusion, which is emblematic of the problems considered here, is that the mind and the sky cannot exist without each other—the soldier needs the poet just as much as the poet needs the soldier:

> The soldier is poor without the poet's lines—
>
> His petty syllabi, the sounds that stick,
> Inevitably modulating, in the blood.
> And war for war, each has its gallant kind.
>
> How simply the fictive hero becomes the real;
> How gladly with proper words the soldier dies,
> If he must, or lives on the bread of faithful speech.

This is a secular statement, but not entirely so. If Eliot's Christian love includes a shirt of flame borrowed from pagan mythology, Stevens's exploration of the fictions that the mind makes out of the world ends with an image of communion—"the bread of faithful speech."

If the real purpose of life is "getting and spending," time used waiting for Proteus to rise from the sea or the Holy Ghost to brood over the bent world is time wasted. But Proteus and the Holy Ghost are there. They are manifestations of a divine reality, or they are there because the mind, being a fiction-making machine, has put them there along with such other fictions as economics and music and the Eight-Fold Way of atoms and the thin-steel torso of the Ford Mustang.

3

The Open Society

In one of the familiar episodes in *Hamlet*, Ophelia is told to walk and to pretend to read a prayer book while she waits for Hamlet. When he appears, he is deeply perturbed. He feels betrayed by everyone around him—Claudius, his mother, his friends Rosencrantz and Guildenstern. All of them pretend to love him, but he suspects they are all seeking to destroy him. When he sees Ophelia, he forgets his problems for a moment: "Soft you now,/The fair Ophelia! Nymph, in thy orisons/Be all my sins remember'd."

When Ophelia offers to return the love trinkets he has given her, Hamlet is surprised but also suspicious:

> *Hamlet:* Ha, ha! are you honest?
> *Ophelia:* My Lord!
> *Hamlet:* Are you fair?
> *Ophelia:* What means your lordship?

An exchange that began with tenderness veers abruptly and sickeningly toward sarcasm: "That you be honest and fair, your honesty should admit no discourse to your beauty." From this point on in the dialogue Hamlet becomes increasingly bitter. Eventually, he stalks off stage leaving Ophelia to weep in her father's arms.

This exchange hinges on the word "honest." It has one meaning for Hamlet and an entirely different one for Ophelia. "Are you honest?" is the most searching question Hamlet can ask. It means "Are you sincere? Do you really love me? Can I trust you, or are you, too, using love to destroy me?" "I have heard of your paintings, well enough," says Hamlet, "God hath given you one face, and you make yourselves another."

For Ophelia the word "honest" has an equally personal meaning. In the English of Shakespeaere's day "honest," applied to women, could mean "chaste." Shakespeare prepared carefully for the Hamlet-Ophelia episode by including a scene in Act I during which Laertes tells Ophelia that Hamlet cannot marry her. Being a prince, he is destined for a state marriage. Therefore his intentions toward Ophelia must be dishonorable. When Hamlet asks, "Are you honest?" Ophelia interprets the question as a sexual overture, which is exactly what Laertes had warned her to expect. She is deeply hurt and recoils in confusion. Her reaction, in turn, is so far from what Hamlet expects that he is offended. He begins to mock her. The possibility of communication is lost—perhaps it was never a real possibility at all.

We are all Hamlets and Ophelias from time to time and probably much more often than we realize. We were born at a particular moment in history and in a particular society. We were shaped by these conditions as surely as a blank round of metal is shaped into a coin by the die that stamps it. When we attempt to understand other times and other societies, we are baffled by their strangeness. Even features that at first seem familiar—the shape of a loaf of bread, the numbers in a merchant's account book—begin to seem alien as they become objects of serious attention.

Medieval historians sometimes called their chronicles *specula* —mirrors. Perhaps they were more honest than modern historians. Perhaps our understanding of the past is an illusion created by our ignorance, and the best we can hope to discover in other ages and other societies is the distorted reflection of our own faces. H. P. Rickman, a modern historian, puts this idea as follows in his introduction to a 1961 collection of Wilhelm Dilthey's historical essays:

> In their views of history, individuals or whole ages have expressed their own conceptions of life. Because such conceptions govern not only what we select as relevant from a mass of facts, but also what forces we believe determine the course of events, they colour historical presentation. This presentation, in turn, is adduced to justify the original point of view. In short, our ideas of history reflect our own philosophic, religious, moral and political attitudes, and at the same time, reinforce them.

If this is true, the past is a mystery. The truths we think we discover about it are really platitudes about ourselves.

And if we were each born at a particular moment in history and in a particular society, each of us was also given a special and individual character by the circumstances that affected his life—by his personal history as well as the common history of his society. Hamlet and Ophelia are creatures of their personal histories. Hamlet brings the experience of intrigue and assassination to the meeting with Ophelia. She brings the anxieties of a sheltered and insecure virgin. Because their personal histories are different, their language is different. Their encounter, turning on the most commonplace words, is a disaster. In spite of appearance, they are from different countries. The attempt to communicate merely widens the gulf between them.

We are all locked in this way in worlds of personal circumstance. We act on the blind faith that our personal worlds are open, at least intermittently, to others, but we know from experience how often they are closed. In the twentieth century, because we have learned so much about the interior life, we are probably more aware than any previous generation that the self is an unexplored country, a region of fantasies and dreams and undisclosed motives. Freud's *Interpretation of Dreams*, which was published at the very beginning of the twentieth century, shows how remote from our comfortably reasonable ideas of consciousness we really are. In the course of a year of fifty-minute hours a trained psychoanalyst may—just may—enter the interior life of his patient. And if chances for understanding are dubious on the psychoanalyst's couch, what are they in the casual encounters of everyday life? Consider the discoveries of Professor J. Barre Toelken of the University of Oregon while teaching English composition to Navajo Indians, in *English for American Indians* (1971):

> The first-person narrative, a stock assignment in beginning writing, seemed to be the wrong exercise for Indian students. Mr. Toelken notes that many Indian tribes disapprove of first-person expression among the young. A person must reach maturity, establish his substance, before he can turn to speaking in his own person. Similarly, the eye contact which seems so necessary between teacher and student runs counter to the cultural conditioning which leads an Indian student to turn his eyes away from someone giving instruction.
>
> The common seating arrangement in rows and files does not very well suit students like the Navajos, brought up in a genuinely round world. Nor is the Navajo's sense of future and past, Professor Toelken observes, like that of his white classmates.

In addition to being an illustration, in minature, of impediments to communication between people, Professor Toelken's discoveries are relevant to the racism and class conflicts that have so divided American and European society in the twentieth century. Hamlet and Ophelia meet. They have the very best intentions. Instead of bridging the space between them, their words—and doubtless their gestures and expressions—drive them apart. Alienation occurs even though both parties want to cooperate. Those who lived through the early years of the civil rights movement will recall a similar pattern. The civil rights movement began as a coalition of blacks and white liberals. For blacks, however, the good intentions of the liberals eventually began to seem ominous, to look more like condescension than indignation. James Baldwin, Stokely Carmichael, Rap Brown, and Malcolm X made this concern explicit. The movement ended not in the homogenized society the liberals had hoped for but in riots, political assassination, black separatism, George Wallace's Legion for the Preservation of Yesterday, and Daniel Patrick Moynihan's advocacy of benign neglect.

Perhaps the idea that a coalition of right-thinking individuals from many different backgrounds can create a just society works only as long as the members of the coalition do not know each other very well. Perhaps the better they know one another the more irreconcilable their differences become. To raise this possibility is to call into question the ideal of the open society that modern democracy inherited from Athens. The alternatives to open communication are force on the one hand and alienation or surrender on the other. Does the future lie with openness or closure?

When a child is born into the world, its mind is a potential. Since the infant's mind has no shape but can take any of the thousands of shapes that historians, anthropologists, and psychologists have observed in human society, it may be called "omniform." However, to realize itself as a unique and individual consciousness it must take one shape and, in so doing, reject the others. As the scholastic maxim has it, *omnis determinatio est negatio*—every definition involves negation. A person comes to know what he is by knowing what he is not.

Call the potential that is born with each human being by its traditional name, "imagination." "The world" is the whole range of experience that presents itself to the imagination. The interpenetration of imagination and the world produces two entities —the self on the one hand and reality on the other. The word "self" means nothing more complicated than personality. "Interpenetration of imagination and the world" means only that personality is shaped by experience, especially childhood experience.

"Reality" means the world as it is perceived. We perceive less than what is available in the world; hence we select our reality. What we select is also deeply colored by personal values and associations. Reality and the self must therefore be considered reciprocal. If reality is the set of external conditions to which the self adjusts and which shape the self, reality is also, and with equal validity, the creation of the self as it projects outward into the surrounding world and selects from the endless variety of external possibilities the specific materials that it puts together to make its house. A medieval serf did not pretend the world was flat; for him it *was* flat. Its flatness was his reality. To the chairman of the board of Xerox a policeman is doubtless a reassuring symbol of law and order and the American dollar a distressing reminder of mutability; these are parts of his reality. At the same time, to a recently paroled pickpocket a policeman is a threat and a dollar the price of a doughnut and a cup of coffee. To a Navajo, reality is circular; to a European, reality is extension mapped by rectangular coordinates. All these examples show reality being shaped by the self.

It is easy to cite examples of reality shaping the self. The creation of arbitrary environments that control the individual's inner experience is commonplace. In a theater, for example, the viewer sits in a fixed location (his chair), and his impressions are ordered according to the normal experiences of space and time. Call this a natural environment. It is the form of reality created by the legitimate stage. When the same viewer goes to the movies he enters an "unnatural" environment. Through the characteristic techniques of film, he is made to move instantaneously, without effort, from one place to another—from middle foreground, to close-up, to panoramic view, to the hero's left eyeball, and then back to middle foreground. The images on the screen impose a form of reality the ground rules of which are impossibilities in everyday life. In sum, not only does each person see the world differently, but different environments create different ways of experiencing the world. The self is the center and reality the inner surface of a sphere.

Actually, the metaphor of the self and the sphere is inadequate because it does not account for growth. Reality is not a given but develops gradually. The image of a Chambered Nautilus manufacturing its own beautiful but increasingly convoluted shell is more precise. One part of the process, the imagination shaping the world, is elegantly described by Wallace Stevens in "Anecdote of the Jar":

> I placed a jar in Tennessee
> And round it was, upon a hill.
> It made the slovenly wilderness
> Surround that hill.
>
> The wilderness rose up to it,
> And sprawled around, no longer wild.
> The jar was round upon the ground
> And tall and of a port in air.
>
> It took dominion everywhere.
> The jar was gray and bare.
> It did not give of bird or bush,
> Like nothing else in Tennessee.

The second part of the process, the hardening of the shell of reality around the self, is described in Wordsworth's "Ode: Intimations of Immortality":

> Heaven lies about us in our infancy!
> Shades of the prison-house begin to close
> Upon the growing Boy.

A prison, if it is well furnished and has considerate attendants, can be a very comfortable place. We need security. That is why the Ptolemaic universe, nestled securely inside ten indestructible Freudian spheres, was so durable, and why, a century after

Copernicus, men still fought to preserve it, if not by mathematics then by the rack and thumbscrew.

Most societies before the Renaissance were insulated. They were protected from other societies by geography and from internal change by tradition and the hangman's noose. Ancient Egypt was probably the most perfectly insulated society in the history of the world. Its stability lasted four thousand years. Changes of dynasty, wars, abortive religious reformations, and occasional disasters aside, the first decisive event in Egyptian history was the coming of the Greeks. It was also the last decisive event, since it utterly destroyed traditional Egyptian society. The Aztecs, too, achieved a kind of equilibrium until the Spanish conquistadores swept them into an oblivion so deep that their writing remains almost as undecipherable as hieroglyphics before the Rosetta Stone.

In stable societies the defining as well as the confining force is tradition. It creates a situation in which the self almost perfectly complements reality. If history creates a culture with square holes, it also creates individuals who are square pegs. Eventually, however, long-preserved traditions become liabilities. The spirit is suffocated by the same conventions and rituals that once gave it life. The society becomes brittle. It will shatter like a glass vase at the first intrusion of alien values.

In *Escape from Freedom* (1941) Erich Fromm argues that societies embrace stability and resist change. As long as a prison is not too obviously a dungeon it is preferable to a raft in the middle of a hurricane. During periods of rapid change, including the period of technological change that is being experienced throughout the world today, the need for security can lead to political and personal regression—to the police state on the one hand and ineffectual dreams of Utopias and pastoral retreats on the other. The freedom that change makes possible is experienced as a threat rather than an opportunity. As Fromm explains:

> . . . modern man, freed from the bonds of pre-individualistic society, which simultaneously gave him security and limited him, has not gained freedom in the positive sense of the realization of his individual self. . . . Freedom, though it has brought him independence and rationality, has made him isolated and, thereby, anxious and powerless.

Consequently, society tries to escape from freedom. To quote poet Kenneth Patchen's epigram, "The impatient explorer invents a box wherein all journeys may be kept." In the words of Dostoevsky's Grand Inquisitor: "Dids't thou forget that man prefers peace, and even death, to freedom of choice in the knowledge of good and evil?"

These observations pose two questions. First, if we live in separate worlds, if we have all invented boxes to contain our journeys, what does openness mean? Is it a real option or simply an impossible ideal? Second, in view of its liabilities (and assuming that it is a real option) is openness really better than closure?

Take the second question first, for it can be answered directly. For better or for worse, and in spite of much backsliding, Western culture has been committed to openness since the Greeks. Its history is not one of closure but one of development through assimilation and internally generated change. The Greeks borrowed from the Phoenicians and the Egyptians. Instead of being destroyed by new ideas, the Greeks fed on them and waxed fat. The Romans borrowed from the Greeks with similar results. Greeks and Romans both eventually borrowed their religion and world history from Palestine, and modern Western science, as it gradually emerged, was borrowed in part from the Moslems, who had, in turn, already borrowed most of theirs from Greece.

Eventually, internal change became more important in Western culture than assimilation from other cultures. The forces generating change apparently reached a kind of critical mass, and their reaction became self-sustaining. At about the same time that Arab thought was being strangled by the religious fundamentalism of al-Ghazzali, European thought was becoming progressively more dynamic. In the thirteenth century at the University of Paris, Siger of Brabant was able to question the immortality of the soul. He was exiled for his boldness, probably to Italy, but he survived, and his questions—questions about the apparent incompatibility of science and divine revelation—continued to be debated. In the sixteenth century Copernicus demolished the theory of ten spheres built around the earth by God and pushed the earth from the center to the suburbs of creation. We have not yet ceased to feel the loss in this. The music of the spheres was silenced. The angelic intelligences who supervised the spheres retreated back into the invisible world, leaving only their photographs in the stained glass of cathedral windows. There was also a gain. The great machine of the solar system began to look more reasonable, hence more human.

In the seventeenth century, toleration itself began to be examined as a value. Milton argued with equal fervor for religious freedom and freedom of the press. "As good almost kill a man," he wrote in *Areopagitica*, "as kill a good book" and later, "a book is the precious lifeblood of a master spirit, embalmed and treasured up on purpose to a life beyond life." The two major revolutions of the eighteenth century—the American and the French—canonized this point of view. They made liberty— and hence the right to dissent—a cardinal political value and wrote it into their fundamental law.

These developments can only be understood as prophetic adaptations to the needs of a society that would not emerge in coherent and definable form until the twentieth century. They encourage change rather than oppose it. In so doing, they run directly counter to the innate conservatism of church and state.

Evidently the history of Western civilization, from the beginning, has been one of continuous failure to settle down to routine. Its culture heroes have not been the passive mystics and genial sages of Oriental tradition but rebels—Socrates and Christ, Augustine and Luther, Voltaire and Marx, Darwin and Freud. The only explanation for this catalogue of leaders, which is really a catalogue of outlaws and skeptics, is that Western society is committed to openness as an absolute value, a condition necessary to the discovery of the world. For this good, Western society has been willing to endure almost any degree of social turbulence.

Here we are touching on the question of what openness really is. If we cannot escape the shades of our prison-house, we can at least make the prison as large as possible. As our reality is enlarged, it intersects with other realities both natural and social. The enlargement of our sense of Nature by science since the seventeenth century is self-evident. Equally self-evident, though less often remarked, is the enlargement of our sense of the range of human culture through art. Although we can never enter fully into the world of another person or another culture, any more than Hamlet can enter fully into the world of Ophelia, we can begin to imagine what different people and cultures are like. If Hamlet had been able to look beyond his own problems, or if he had been able to imagine Ophelia's world, or if he had been less certain that his own values were universal ones, he might have prolonged his conversation sufficiently to learn that Ophelia really loved him.

During the eighteenth century the bias of Western civilization toward openness was objectified as theory in philosophy and codified into laws protecting freedom of speech, assembly, and the press. The theory turned on epistemology—on the way the mind is formed by and, in turn, shapes reality. The laws were derived from Protestant tradition—the stiff-necked insistence that each Christian is as good as any other Christian—on the one hand, and from the concept of the social contract as developed by Locke and Montesquieu on the other. The philosophical theory created a new framework within which culture could be understood, while the developments in political theory flowered in the American Constitution and Bill of Rights. However these influences differ in their implications, they agree on the validity —indeed, the crucial importance—of openness. They are unalternably opposed to all forms of closure: censorship, intimidation through public opinion, political repression, and all efforts to impose conformity on society by scientific fiat or ideological absolutism.

Early in the eighteenth century Alexander Pope explained that the poet should write "What oft was thought, but ne'er so well express'd." This is the typical attitude of a society at peace with its tradition. After Jean-Jacques Rousseau's *Confessions* (1765), the artist ceased to be regarded as a spokesman for tradition. He was asked instead to record his own experience with absolute fidelity. If each person is unique, then each work of art that deserves the label is, by definition, unique, and thus original, and thus an assault on the past. To add insult to injury, the duty of an open society is to defend the artist at the very moment he is mounting his assault.

If so, Western society has institutionalized revolution. It has institutionalized revolution in politics by the party system, in science by the assumption that hypotheses exist only to be replaced by better ones, and in the arts by the criterion of originality. It has made all established orders provisional. They exist only to be demolished. In the nineteenth century, "established order" meant the bourgeoisie—its economics, its morality, and its religion. These were successively laid in ruin by Karl Marx, Charles Baudelaire, and Charles Darwin. In the twentieth century the same imperative has led the arts to a still deeper questioning of established order involving the order of perception itself—in the art of Piet Mondrian and Jackson Pollock, for example, the music of Arnold Schoenberg and John Cage, and the writing of James Joyce, André Breton, and Wallace Stevens.

In fact, these examples understate the case. The influence of self-conscious artists has probably been slight in the twentieth century compared to the transforming influence of newspapers, movies, television, and recordings. One could dwell here on the surrealism of mass media: the montage effect of the front page of the *New York Times*, or the alternation of story and commercial in a typical hour-long television program, or the bewildering opulence—the sense of a gigantic, well-lighted junk shop— created by a great museum like the Louvre or the Prado or the Smithsonian Institution's Museum of American History. But it may be more instructive to consider two specific examples to illustrate the revolutionary impact of art on modern society. The first is entirely orthodox—a museum exhibition. By the simple act of exhibiting its collection, the Museum of African Art in Washington, D.C., contributes to the changing self-image of black Americans. It restores to them a history, and thus an identity, as dramatic and as complex as the history and the identity found by white Americans in exhibitions of classical art. In doing this, it changes the network of relations governing the way blacks and whites perceive each other. New realities and consequently new dimensions of the self are created.

This example is neither especially revolutionary nor especially controversial. The second example is perhaps more unorthodox: the skin flick. The skin flick was born from three very sound motives—greed, lust, and the impulse, both playful and truly artistic, to flaunt the taboos of the tribe. During its underground years, which extend almost from the beginning of the silents to the 1960s, the skin flick played to a constantly expanding audience. Because, as an art form, it recognized only the imperative of freedom to be itself, it explored ever more arcane, not to say bizarre, aspects of sexuality along the way. In 1970, without any special fanfare and hardly a cry of doom, it suddenly went public. At that point, the revolution it created recreated the art form. *Deep Throat* (1972), humble in execution though it may have been, was sufficiently heroic in concept to win the affection of millions. After *Deep Throat*, the big-budget, erotic spectacular was inevitable. *Last Tango in Paris*, though not a true skin flick, is a formula romance in the buff and has already managed the transition from motion-picture theater to home television screen. What began as an art form so crude that many people would prefer not to call it art at all suddenly became respectable, high-budget formula entertainment. Since *Last Tango*, nudity has become commonplace in movies and is now available as a functional and legitimate artistic strategy.

The skin flick did not create but encouraged a well-publicized revolution in American attitudes toward sexuality. It thus illustrates Carl Jung's theory that the basic function of art is to redress the imbalance of values that occurs when a society adopts one set of norms and rejects alternatives. This is another instance of definition requiring exclusion. As Jung explains:

> People and times, like individual men, have their peculiar tendencies or attitudes. The very word "attitude" betrays the necessary onesidedness that every definite tendency postulates. Where there is direction there must also be exclusion. But exclusion means that certain definite psychic elements that could participate in life are denied their right to live through incompatibility with the general attitude.

To Jung, the revolutionary bias of art—even the art of the skin flick—is a sign of its health. Its function is to restore to man "psychic elements," which the circumstances of being born at a particular time and in a particular place always deny him.

If Jung's theory is true, Erich Fromm's position in *Escape from Freedom* is also true. The liabilities of too much openness are real. Too much openness happening too rapidly creates an intolerable psychological strain, a thesis also explored in Alvin Toffler's *Future Shock*. A society experiencing too much openness can revert, as Fromm makes clear, to fascism or Philistinism. An individual can surrender to apathy, seek to drown himself in pure sensation, defect to a commune, or join a singles club, an encounter group, or the nearest chapter of the Minutemen. Perhaps the most common retreat—a retreat made irresistibly appealing by the conditions of modern society itself—is into specialization: the surgeon immerses himself in surgery, the topologist in topology, the Old English specialist in *Beowulf*, the beer chemist in the chemistry of beer. Modern society cannot function without such specialties, and the advance of knowledge is constantly creating new and more minute ones. Consequently, nothing is easier for modern man than isolating himself in a specialty. What created the specialty if not modern society itself, in which he lives as a fish in an aquarium? He adapts to the environment. He gazes intently at the splash of golden light in front of him while he ignores the blaze of colors filtering through the glass behind him.

Once the need for stability is admitted, the interesting question is whether society should encourage it—and hence give comfort by affirming the closure of life—or encourage openness and thus compel its citizens to confront the diversity of the world around and within them. Or is there some middle ground of the sort suggested by the British educator A. S. Neill in his reply to critics: *Freedom Not License!* Is there any such thing as a form of freedom that cannot be called license by those who dislike it?

The history of politics in the twentieth century suggests that no middle ground exists. If freedom is not protected even when it is called license by those whose values it threatens, it ceases to be freedom; yet protecting it requires an extraordinary act of faith. The consequences of freedom are unpredictable. Since those who advocate an open society cannot say where the openness will lead, their faith must be in the value of freedom itself, in the idea that, if given freedom, people will adapt themselves to the real conditions of their lives and that this adaptation—no matter what it is—will be superior to anything that can be predicted or legislated.

The world that has been created by open societies is unprecedented in its richness and variety. Unfortunately, there is an enormous cultural lag between this world as it is and the value systems on which individuals must depend to cope with it. Cultural lag is manifested in tensions among traditional arrangements across the whole spectrum of social relations—the family, the work force, the political process, the nurturing of the young, and the utilization of the elderly. It is also manifested in the inability of law to keep up with technology in such fields as telecommunications, finance, biology, medicine, automation, and surveillance. And it is manifested internationally in the chasm between institutions based on values associated with national sovereignty and the reality of an interdependent global community.

In many areas of the world, the tension between the past and the future has caused a breakdown in the social structure needed to meet such basic human needs as food, shelter, and protection from violence. More typically, the pace of change has produced repressive, which is to say closed, systems of government, ranging from would-be theocracies and military dictatorships to socialist governments balanced ambivalently between the autocratic tradition of Stalinism and the attractions of more liberal, hence more open, political models. In an apparently diminishing number of countries, the tradition of openness has been preserved at least as an idea, but these countries are also racked with anxieties and antagonisms. Their fear of the future contrasts oddly with their real achievements in the past.

It is easy to say that modern man has unleashed forces that he cannot fully control. It would be more accurate, however, to say that he has gained power over matters that were previously in the hands of God or Nature. His bafflement is caused by the fact that he is not sure whether or not he can meet the challenge he has posed for himself.

How can he be sure? It was never certain that *Homo sapiens* would survive at all, and it is even less certain that he can survive his own success. If certainty is impossible, what is left is faith of the kind associated with the open society.

4

Politics and Beauty

Politics and art must be considered dispassionately. Are they not on opposite sides of the fence? Politics is a way of making things happen while art is a way of making things. These things have their own mode of existence quite apart from politics even when they were inspired by overtly political motives, as, for example, is true of Vergil's *Aeneid* or Edmund Spenser's *The Faerie Queene* or Picasso's *Guernica*. It can even be argued—in fact, affirmed—that criticism of the arts should stay away from politics and be directed toward the things themselves. In the 1930s John Steinbeck was considered a propagandist, an author of novels of social protest. When the political issues of the Depression lost their immediacy, his works were largely ignored. The current revival of his reputation dates from Peter Lisca's *The Wide World of John Steinbeck* (1958), which concentrates on his achievement as an artist.

Evidently, the quality of an artwork is more important in the long run than its ideology. If so, the distinction made by Jean-Paul Sartre in *What Is Literature?* between poetry, by which Sartre means trivia, and literature, by which he means art committed to political reform, is mistaken. It is, in fact, a way of selling out to politics. Leon Trotsky proclaimed, "Art is not a mirror; it is a hammer." Trapped in a century in which everything seems to boil down to the question "Which side are you on?" the artist can only protest as did Shakespeare:

> How with this rage shall beauty hold a plea,
> Whose action is no stronger than a flower?

From the artist's point of view, the classic illustration of the chasm between politics and art is censorship. There is probably no kind of art that has not seemed threatening to the established order at some time or another. Plato wanted to ban tragedy from his Republic because he was afraid it would breed effeminacy in the armed forces. The Moslems plastered over the mosaics in liberated Christian churches because they considered religious images idolatrous. The Protestant armies of the Reformation smashed the stained-glass windows of cathedrals, mutilated statues of the Blessed Virgin, and burned whole libraries of illuminated manuscripts for equally reasonable reasons. Music, except for national anthems and protest songs, would seem to be neutral; but not so. A few years ago the *People's Daily* of China informed its readers that Beethoven's seventeenth sonata "only serves to disseminate the filthy nature of the bourgeoisie." (Now things have changed in China, and Beethoven is once more acceptable.) Poetry has always been a hot potato. Hence Osip Mandelstam's tribute to the Soviet Union: "Poetry is honored only in this country—people are killed for it." That Mandelstam died in a Soviet prison camp for having written an epigram against Stalin lends weight to his remarks.

Once the dichotomy between politics and beauty is admitted and the artist has been given his fullest dues, the issues ought to be clear; but unfortunately they are anything but clear. Politics and beauty are related in as many ways as they are separate.

First, beauty is a social phenomenon. This means that beauty generates its own politics, which is at least semi-independent of the politics of government. Take patronage as an example. Traditionally, patrons are wealthy connoisseurs like Lorenzo de' Medici or Henry Huntington or J. Paul Getty. They collect beautiful objects and endow art galleries and libraries and public gardens for reasons that seem, to them at least, entirely benevolent. What could be less political than the Pierpont Morgan Library or the gardens of Dumbarton Oaks or the Vivian Beaumont Theatre at Lincoln Center? The only obvious motive behind the creation of such institutions is a generalized patriotism, a desire to enhance the quality of American life.

But this is not the whole story. To a certain degree, such institutions prop up the established order and thus are inherently conservative. Moreover, patrons often commission works of art that convey explicit political messages. Michelangelo was not paid to decorate the Sistine Chapel with anything that came into his head but to create an overpowering blast of propaganda on behalf of Roman Catholic Christianity. The enormous murals by Diego Rivera on the walls of the Detroit Institute of Arts are a modern equivalent of the Sistine Chapel. They celebrate workers in general and industrial workers in particular. Typically, this kind of art is created by a strong, centralized, and solidly entrenched politics, an imperial politics. The message comes first, the quality second. In extreme cases, art that does not have an overt and acceptable political message is automatically labeled subversive. The imperial motto is, "He who is not for me *enthusiastically* is against me." The Soviet Union officially supports what it calls "socialist realism" and condemns abstraction and "art for art's sake." Renaissance Popes and American robber barons had equally strong views about artists. By contrast, the patrons of today's pluralistic societies tend to be nervous about messages. Diego Rivera's murals at Rockefeller Center made a statement, but it was not an acceptable one. They were painted over almost before they were dry. The politics of pluralism is sympathetic to abstract art. The works of artist like Joan Miró,

Henry Moore, and Jackson Pollock, for example, are open. Whatever the political views of their creators, the works themselves
have no overt political message. They can coexist with whatever
ideology happens to predominate. They will never have to be
painted over.

When the analysis is carried from the studio to the marketplace, politics appears in association with art in a more familiar
form. Among other things, beauty is a commodity. People speculate in art as they speculate in grain futures, and like the grain
exchange the art market is subject to manipulation. The auction
price of a single Matisse or a single first edition of *The Scarlet
Letter* affects the value of every Matisse and every Hawthorne
first edition throughout the world. When a museum pays a record
price or makes a record appraisal of a Matisse, the value of every
other Matisse increases. This fact is not lost on art dealers or on
museum boards. The academy is also involved in the politics
of art. The fact that Matisse is a standard curriculum artist and
Hawthorne a standard curriculum author helps to stabilize the
market. What might be called "curriculum status" is the foundation on which the publication of textbooks and reproductions and
editions of the classics is based. Moreover, the fact that the
academy provides modest but intensely coveted livelihoods for
scholars encourages them to become a political constituency.
They tend to resist changes in the approved list of classics
because change threatens to make their skills obsolescent. The
circle created by the patron who invests in beauty, the professor
who makes his living by explaining it, and the students who are
programmed to admire it and to buy it when they become
patrons is not perfect, but anyone who looks for it can find it.

Let us move from the politics of art to the politics of government, The dichotomy between life and art often obscures the fact
that governments devote much more energy to encouraging
beauty than to suppressing it. For every author it exterminates,
the Soviet Union supports thousands. In the United States, the
most obvious cases in point are the National Endowments for

the Arts and the Humanities. The visible operating budget of the two endowments was around $150 million apiece in 1980, not very much by the standards of the Defense Department, but sufficient to make the Endowments the largest patrons of the arts and humanities in America. In comparison, the Ford Foundation was spending around $16 million annually on the arts and humanities in the same year.

The authorizing legislation of the Endowments insulates them from obvious political arm-twisting, but the mere fact that they have to give away large amounts of money requires that decisions with political implications be made. Should they distribute their grants evenly across all fifty states, for example, or should they support the urban centers where most artistic talent is located? Should they concentrate on well-established artists and institutions or should they place their major emphasis on new talent? Should they award grants through panels, and if so, how should the panel members be chosen? Or should they rely on a small number of advisors selected for their good taste or intellectual brilliance or party standing or ethnic background? These are political questions, complicated by the inborn imperative of every bureaucracy to grow, and growth for the Endowments depends on their ability to persuade Congress and the White House that they are performing services the voters want. The way the questions are answered influences the response of the voters and, at the same time, determines who is supported for what, which is another way of saying that it helps determine the shape of beauty in America.

The Endowments are easy to discuss because they are public entities and continue to be even after the budget cuts of 1981. Actually, the most important source of government money for the arts is the Internal Revenue Code. Under section 501 (c) (3), full deduction is permitted for contributions in cash or in kind to non-profit organizations like arts groups, museums, symphony societies, and certain theater and opera guilds. Tax write-offs favor the wealthy, thereby giving the establishment special control over beauty. But such write-offs are also the bedrock on which most of the arts rest, especially the performing arts. To appreciate their importance consider the implications of one minor provision, that governing donations of personal manuscripts to libraries. Prior to 1969, authors could donate their manuscripts to libraries and deduct a fair appraisal from their taxable income. In 1969 this provision was canceled because of the publicity surrounding the enormous write-off Lyndon Johnson received when he donated his papers to the presidential library in Austin, Texas. With the notable exception of President Nixon's papers, legislation pretty much ended the abuse that the provision encouraged. It also ended the flow of official papers and literary manuscripts to American libraries. Today, authors either keep their manuscripts or sell them to private collectors. To generalize from this instance, a few changes in the Internal Revenue Code could bring the whole structure of beauty in America down in ruins within months.

Politics regulates the arts as well as supports them. Copyright law determines the rights of authors, publishers, and consumers. It is a hot political issue. It took ten years for Congress to revise the American copyright law so that it covers such developments as Xerox, tape recording, and cable television. International copyright also has important political implications. Until 1977 the Soviet Union refused to recognize international copyright. When it did agree, there was great rejoicing among American authors. At long last they could collect royalties on Russian editions of their works. At the same time, however, the Soviet Union gained the legal right to block foreign publication of Soviet authors. International copyright can thus be a tool of censorship as well as a means of protecting authors.

Other government agencies are equally influential on the arts. Through its licensing authority, the Federal Communications Commission regulates commercial radio and television. Its policies can determine whether a boxing match or a play by Shakespeare or a locally produced talk show appears on prime-time television. The U.S. Customs Service determines whether *Ulysses* or *Lady Chatterley's Lover* can be brought into the country, while the State Department can admit the Bolshoi Ballet and deny a visa to Tomas Alea, the Cuban film director, although in 1973 his *Memories of Underdevelopment* won the Rosenthal Award of the National Society of Film Critics. Postage rates spell life or death for magazines. Minimum-wage laws and airline passenger rates determine whether performing arts groups survive or go bankrupt. Meanwhile, commodity policies, many of which are regulated, affect the cost of everything used to create beauty, from the paper on which books are printed to the petrochemicals used to make phonograph records to the silver used in photographic emulsions and the propane gas used in reduction firing of pottery.

These examples could be extended indefinitely, but the point should already be obvious. Politics supports beauty directly and indirectly. It regulates beauty, and it touches, sometimes intentionally and sometimes by accident, every aspect of the lives of artists and every material from which beauty is created.

There is a second, more speculative side to the topic. If it is true that beauty cannot get along without politics, there is also a sense in which politics cannot get along without beauty.

The reference is not to government grants or tax write-offs or regulating agencies: these are arbitrary. They come and go depending on public opinion, the state of the economy, and the influence of various lobbies. The reference is, rather, to an essential relation that has endured throughout the history of politics. It is a more difficult relation to explain than to illustrate.

From the earliest periods of civilization, the state has been a patron and consumer of beauty. The world's museums are filled with statues, mosaics, paintings, furniture, and ceremonial objects commissioned by forgotten despots to celebrate their governments and their resident gods. Numerous monuments too large to be carried off to the museums remain on location in Egypt, the Near East, India, China, Mexico, and elsewhere. Many of the crowning glories of Athens were commissioned by the tyrant Pisistratus and his sons, while the Parthenon is owed to Pericles. Augustus Caesar found Rome brick and left it marble. Louis XIV devoted much of his life to the monstrous and many-faceted vulgarity of Versailles. Napoleon rebuilt Paris, and Mussolini constructed Foro Italico outside Rome because the city itself was already filled to capacity with monuments and buildings and works of art created by his pagan and Christian predecessors. In literature, Vergil's *Aeneid* was written to glorify imperial Rome and advertise the family clan of the emperor. Tasso's *Jerusalem Librated* glorified the Italian house of Este. In England, Shakespeare was able to ply his trade because his acting company was protected from the London Puritans by a succession of noble patrons culminating in King James I. Not surprisingly, Shakespeare's history plays applaud the divine-right theory of monarchy and the legitimacy of the Tudor claim to England's throne, while abounding in passages that have been used ever since they were written to screw British patriotism to the sticking-place.

Moving across the Atlantic to Washington, D.C., the Library of Congress required the services of no less than fifty artists during the ten years of its construction, while the interior dome of the Capitol is covered by a 4,664-square-foot mural by Constantino Brumidi depicting the apotheosis of George Washington, a composition that earned Brumidi the title "Michelangelo of the Capitol."

Politics has an innate hunger—even a lust—for beauty. Part of this need is the vanity of power and part is propaganda, what is called cultural imperialism. But to stop at vanity and propaganda is to miss the real point. After all, not all states are totally corrupt, and not all artists who work for them are hacks. The basic need of politics is self-respect. It needs to think of itself as a useful, even noble, activity. It symbolizes these aspirations in aesthetic terms. As has been noted earlier, in Chapter 1,

Burckhardt devoted the first chapter of *The Civilization of the Renaissance in Italy* to "the state as a work of art." This is a universal—not merely a Renaissance—idea. Politics is driven to express it physically through beautiful emblems because it cannot create beauty directly in the relations between the governing and the governed that characterize a real political system.

By way of illustration, consider two statements about the ideal state. The first is from a letter by John Adams to his wife Abigail in 1780:

> I must study politics and war, that my sons may have liberty to study mathematics and philosophy. My sons ought to study mathematics and philosophy, geography, natural history, naval architecture, and commerce, in order to give their children the right to study painting, poetry, music, architecture, statuary, tapestry, and porcelain.

This is not a statement about government grants or tax write-offs. President Adams was asserting that if the American political experiment was successful, the result would be a nation of artists dedicated not to politics but to beauty. Beauty is the visible symbol of political success.

In the *Republic*, Plato makes the relationship hinted at by President Adams explicit. Here is Socrates's explanation of how to create the perfect state:

> At present, I take it, we are fashioning the happy State, not piecemeal, or with a view of making a few happy citizens, but as a whole. . . . Suppose that we were painting a statue and someone came up to us and said, "Why do you not put the most beautiful colors on the most beautiful parts of the body. The eyes ought to be purple, but you have made them black." To him we might fairly answer: "Sir, you would not surely have us beautify the eyes to such a degree that they are no longer eyes; consider rather whether, by giving this and the other features which are their due proportion, we make the whole beautiful."

Socrates is speaking as a politician interested in establishing an ideal state, but he cannot describe the object of politics without referring to beauty. His statement is more than a metaphor. He implies that the fundamental principles of the state—wholeness, appropriateness, and coherence—are aesthetic, and the success of the state is evident through its aesthetic appeal: "we make the whole beautiful." The Platonic state is, quite literally, a work of art.

Plato's *Republic*, as everyone knows, is a dream. Judged by the record of politics in the real world, it is only slightly less preposterous than John Adams's dream that his grandchildren would all be artists. The problem is that it is a necessary dream. On the one hand, politics desperately needs to believe in itself, to have an object. Without an object it degenerates into oportunism. On the other hand, to take the object seriously—that is, to impose it by force on the governed—is to become a Don Quixote tilting at windmills or a tyrant. Medieval politics recognized this paradox and confronted it honestly. It located the ideal government in heaven. God, the archetypal ruler for the Middle Ages, is an incomprehensible Being, surrounded by a cloud of light so brilliant that to gaze on Him is to be blinded. Beneath His throne extends a euphoric bureaucracy of cherubim, seraphim, dominions, princes, and powers. These celestial bureaucrats not only grovel joyfully before those placed over them, but compose hymns of praise to their superiors. Shakespeare was recalling the medieval idea of the beautiful hierarchy when he had Ulysses remark, "Take but degree away, untune that string,/ And hark what discord follows." The metaphor is an aesthetic one. Shakespeare's state is a work of art, a musical composition played on the lute of the class structure.

According to the Christian tradition, man is a fallen creature. He can imagine the beauty of the heavenly hierarchy, he can even imitate it in art, but he knows that he cannot achieve it in a real political system. The idea of original sin kept medieval and Renaissance political theory sane while the transcendent ideal of politics allowed great artists to celebrate the state rather than attack it.

Since the Romantic period, politics has tended to move along two divergent paths, both of which have created problems for the artist. One kind of politics has insisted that the beautiful state is not a dream, that it is attainable here and now, as though the *Republic* were a textbook of poltical science. Driven by this obsession, politicians have claimed the right to impose perfection on the governed, destroying anything that clashes with their aesthetic conception as ruthlessly as a novelist revising a rough draft. The result of this approach has been a series of unmitigated political disasters, extending from the Reign of Terror through the Third Reich to Chairman Mao's Great Leap Forward. Human beings have been asked to behave as though they were (or could be) objects in a painting, and when they have failed they have been crushed. The beauty related to this kind of politics is beauty divorced from humanity. It is an advertising agency beauty: posters of Hitler youth yodeling their way through the Black Forest or ruddy-cheeked Stakhanovite workers feverishly oiling their flywheels at the Red Dawn locomotive plant. For artists it has posed brutal choices: join in the lie—and hence be false to beauty—or get out or die.

The other kind of politics that has emerged since the Romantic period has retained the idea of human imperfection and extended it to politicians. If even politicians are imperfect—if they have no mandate by birth or special relation to the gods—then it follows that they have no right to impose their dreams on others. The motto of this kind of politics is: "Government is best when it governs least." Such a politics makes no claim to imitation of the government of heaven. Its object is to keep people from bumping into each other, as much as possible, while they follow their own devious paths to salvation. If the beauty of medieval and Renaissance politics is borrowed from a celestial archetype, the beauty of democracy is immanent. It is a beauty that is realized at any given moment in the lives of real citizen. John Adams did not say what his grandchildren would be painting; he only said that if democracy were successful they would all be artists. Many of his spiritual grandchildren are practitioners of abstract expressionism and op and pop. The fact is significant even though it is probably just as well that Adams never had to confront it.

Clearly, democracy poses unique aesthetic problems. Throughout most of history, the beauty associated with politics has been an imperial beauty, beauty meant to glorify authority. The emblems of imperial beauty celebrate the gods who protect the state, the rulers who are their visible instruments, and the offices and laws and ceremonies those rulers use to impose a measure of divine harmony on human affairs. The rulers of ancient Assyria were always depicted in the company of a resplendent winged disk that represented the immortal charisma of the living king. The Doges of Venice annually married the sea in a brilliant ceremony designed to ensure good fishing and high returns on invested capital. Renaissance monarchs were crowned in cathedrals to the chanting of choirs and at death were laid to rest by columns of uniformed men marching slowly to the beat of muffled drums, while their immortal powers were transferred to their successors through the emblems and symbols of the royal office. In short, the traditions of architecture, sculpture, and ceremony that the modern world has inherited are imperial traditions. Where, in the history of beauty, is there an art to express the idea that government is best when it governs least?

Does the capital of the United States, the world's oldest democracy, provide an answer? It is obvious that a great deal of effort has been lavished on trying to make Washington beautiful, whatever its success. Yet the answers that Washington provides are ambivalent. On the one hand, the characteristic architecture of Washington identifies America's cultural debt to the political tradition extending through Europe to Greece and Rome. This architecture does not express—in fact, it seems to deny—the idea that government is best when it governs least. As noted in Chapter 1, the American sculptor Horatio Greenough depicted

George Washington as a Greek god. Thomas Jefferson stands serenely, but incongruously, under a replica of the Roman Pantheon. Abraham Lincoln, most American of Presidents, sits in a facsimile of the Parthenon. Why not a marble Oval Office or a granite log cabin? Most curious of all, congressmen descended from the dour elders of Massachusetts Bay hold their debates in a building surmounted by a replica of the Dome of St. Peter's Cathedral, which any seventeenth-century Puritan would identify as a temple of tyranny, not to mention the earthly home of the Antichrist, the seven-headed beast of Revelation, and the Whore of Babylon.

All of these monuments conflict with what might be called the democratic solution to the beautification of the capital city. The initial and authentic response of Americans to the creation of a national capital was not a great outpouring of native art but indifference. George Washington and Pierre L'Enfant labored mightily, but the major creation of the first fifty years of Washington's history was the White House, which was not even white until it was repainted after the British burned part of it in 1814. As late as 1861 Horace Greeley described Washington as "a place of high rents, bad foods, disgusting dust, deep mud, and deplorable morals." This hardly suggests a program of imperial beautification. Washington's streets were not paved until 1871, some two thousand years after Rome began letting out paving contracts. The Capitol building was not completed until 1865; the Washington Monument, 1884; the Library of Congress, 1897. Most of the characteristic beauties of Washington, in fact, have been created in the twentieth century: the reflection pool and Lincoln Memorial, 1920–22; the National Gallery of Art, 1941; the Kennedy Center for the Performing Arts, 1970. (The National Gallery and the Kennedy Center are mentioned here both for their structures and for the beauty they contain, the portable and ephemeral arts of painting, drama, and music being just as important for the life of a great capital as its buildings and monuments.)

How *does* one express artistically the idea that government is best when it governs least? One way is to suggest that politics *per se* has no beauty, that beauty becomes evident in proportion to its distance from all things political. The most authentic current in American art of the Federal period appears to have taken this direction: the genteel pastoralism that is evident in Jefferson's many references to the pleasures of agrarian life, the paintings of the Hudson River school, and the frontier novels of James Fenimore Cooper. This art does not depict man in relation to politics but in full flight from it. Its attitude is summed up in the resolve of Huck Finn to "light out for the territory" after having experienced the full array of horrors that civilization along the Mississippi River had to offer. The natural corollary to this attitude, as far as the capital is concerned, was studious neglect. The city should remain humble. Imperialistic pretensions should be suppressed.

A few characteristic beauties in Washington seem to show awareness of the need for new art forms to express the American vision. Two examples will suffice. Rock Creek Park is a tract of relatively uncontaminated woodland running through the center of Washington. It was created to permit citizens to escape from the benevolence of their government into Nature. It is a manifestation of the Hudson River aesthetic in the midst of a growing city. The second example is offered tentatively. The Washington Monument is an obelisk, the most abstract of ancient forms. In spite of the classical connotations noted in Chapter 1, its simplicity gives it an oddly contemporary flavor, a kinship with the abstract art encouraged by twentieth-century pluralism as well as with numerous other buildings in Washington that make no statement or express themselves in nearly inaudible monosyllables—the office buildings of the Department of Health and Human Services, the Pentagon, the Museum of American History. Is the Washington Monument a democratic abstraction, or is it part of Washington's classical program?

Greenough wrote, "The obelisk has to my eye a singular form

and character. . . . It says but one word. But it speaks it loud. If I understand this voice, it says 'Here'." Clearly, Greenough felt the Washington Monument is part of Washington's classical program. The strength of his case is slightly disturbing. If the Washington Monument really does say "Here," the word has ominous implications for a political system based on the idea that government is best when it governs least. It is a monosyllable, the least possible word, but it is blatant. It brings us back to the idea of a Roman milestone and the imperial classicism of Chapter 1. "Here" may therefore be the Faustian monosyllable that summons into being the vast network of roads that all lead to Washington. By contrast, several recent memorials in the capital resurrect the Hudson River aesthetic. Senator Taft is memorialized in Washington by a bell tower set in a grove of trees. President Lyndon Johnson will be remembered by a large rock set in another grove of trees. A grove of trees does not say "Here"; it says, "This is not Washington."

Whatever the problems for official art created by democracy, the relation between politics and beauty is perennial and essential. If Socrates is right in the *Republic*, politics cannot be conceived without reference to beauty. It symbolizes beauty with beautiful emblems—the monuments and buildings and arts and ceremonies that adorn its cities and celebrate its ideals. At the same time, politics is bound to fail. Most of the grandchildren of middle-class American citizens will end up GS–12 administrators not artists. But beauty sustains the hope, too important to be allowed to languish, that they will be more than hollow men. Say that President Kennedy was right: politics is the art of the possible. If so, beauty is a way of keeping the impossible sufficiently real so that politics cannot ignore it.

A final word about beauty. When politics creates beauty, it does so for a particular reason. It wants to use beauty for its own ends, as, for example, Augustus Caesar wanted Vergil to prop up his imperial machinery. Beauty, however, is protean. It has its own life, which is larger than the uses it is told to serve. Whatever the immediate purpose of the *Aeneid*, its significance today is its achievement as a work of art having nothing to do with politics.

If politics seeks to define and contain human experience, beauty, whether classical or abstract, announces that all such attempts are inadequate because they leave out more than they include. Although men cannot avoid signing a social contract, beauty reminds them how much of their humanity they surrender upon doing so. In this sense, beauty saves politics from itself. It is not only an adornment of the state and a symbol of the transcendent goal of politics, it is also an assertion that the human spirit is larger than any political system. The Greeks admired the *Republic*, but they loved the *Iliad* because they found their truest identity in Homer's portraits of Agamemnon and Odysseus and Andromache. The Roman Empire ruled the known world for four centuries, but Vergil was still alive in the fourteenth century to lead Dante through nine circles of the Inferno.

A quotation from Friedrich Schiller's *Letters on the Aesthetic Education of Man* offers a parting thought on the subject. Having lived through the euphoria of the Rights of Man and seen it degenerate into the Reign of Terror, Schiller concluded: "Man will never solve the problem of politics except through the problem of the aesthetic, for it is only through beauty that man makes his way to freedom."

IN MAZES LOST

5

Medicine and Values

The theory of history as a dialectic is immensely useful for understanding cultural change. It rejects the idea that culture seeks stability. The stability of traditional cultures is an illusion created by a pace of change so slow as to be invisible to those who experience it.

According to Hegel, the process is a spiritual one. The succession of thesis, antithesis, and synthesis extends as far into the future as the mind can reach. According to Marx, the process is a material one. It is driven by economic conditions—the "mode of production," as Marx called it—and is limited. Feudalism is succeeded by capitalism, which is succeeded by the dictatorship of the proletariat, which is succeeded by . . . Utopia. The classless society has no antithesis. It is an end, a point of final rest.

Although the conditions of nineteenth-century society appeared to justify Marx's economic bias, Hegel looks better in the closing decades of the twentieth century. Knowledge rather than economics is the driving force of contemporary history, and economics follows in its train.

Dialectic is a tragic as well as a creative process. It requires the destruction of earlier values and the production of new ones. Hegel and Marx both believed that it operated slowly, over generations, and history seemed to confirm this opinion. What they failed to understand, because they could not see the future, is that knowledge grows geometrically in a technological society. Perhaps a critical mass of knowledge and expertise was reached after World War II. At any rate, since 1950 the pace of change has accelerated. Changes that once would have taken centuries or generations occur in a decade, and destructive processes are accelerated as well as creative ones.

Consciousness, however, is a social product. It is formed by experience, and once formed it resists change. This is especially true of the central, mostly unstated values that create the sense of identity. Consequently, man is increasingly finding himself out of phase with his world. A consciousness shaped by one world struggles painfully and with only limited success to comprehend another. A vivid expression of this situation is provided by the disintegration of the human form in modern art. Botticelli has been replaced by Mondrian, Rembrandt by Kandinski, and Van Gogh by Jackson Pollock. Abstract painting exhibits consciousness as a perceptual grid devoid of historical and local content. It is a form of imitation in the precise sense of the word: it imitates a world that is no longer intelligible in historical terms.

Medicine is a unique discipline. It draws its techniques from every area of science and applies them directly to people. Even when limited to the treatment of the human body, it challenges values. When it moves from the treatment of the human body to the treatment of the mind, it not only challenges values but acts as an arbiter of value, often in situations over which the recipients of its services have no control. It thus nicely illustrates the operation of the historical dialectic in a restricted field over a short period of time.

To begin with a preliminary example, sexual identity has been a given for most of human history. Today, hormone therapy and surgery can alter sexual identity. The Johns Hopkins University Hospital, which pioneered in this field in the 1960s and early 1970s, reached an average of over one hundred sex-change operations a year until its trustees had second thoughts in 1979. Other hospitals continue to offer the operation to anyone who can afford it.

Sex-change operations are sensational, imperfect, and—in the long run—probably not very significant. They do not fascinate the public because of their benefits, which affect only a tiny minority of the population, but because they undermine the traditional concept of identity as an unalterable given. They suggest that the humanity of each individual is plastic and that the essential features of that humanity can be changed at will. The same suggestion is implicit in organ transplants, which can now successfully deal with some sixteen parts of the body.

If so, identity is not a constant but a medium to be shaped in whatever form the individual or the physician or some collectivity considers appropriate. One result is a change in the idea of what medicine is. It ceases to be an art that assists Nature and becomes a creative art, an art that reshapes Nature according to human will, a kind of sculpture.

Genetic engineering illustrates the same point. As the identification of imperfect chromosomes has become more accurate, it has become possible to predict the occurrence of such inherited defects as Down's syndrome and to abort defective fetuses if this is desired. The procedure is different in kind from the use of abortion for birth control. It is selective, and its purpose, when the health of the mother is not a factor, is to shape the humanity of the future.

An apparently contradictory sort of control is exercised by euphenics, the science of treating those genetically defective human beings who survive infancy. Euphenics can control several hereditary diseases including phenylketonuria, pyloric stenosis, galactosemia, and diabetes. It cannot cure these diseases nor can it prevent adult carriers of the defective genes from spreading them through reproduction and thus contaminating the human gene pool. If abortion for genetic hygiene is radical, euphenics must be considered conservative. The procedure that is conservative from the point of view of value can thus be considered harmful from the point of view of genetics.

Full-scale genetic engineering is only beginning, but it is developing rapidly. Selective breeding of people based on similar breeding of animals was discussed in the nineteenth century and practiced in a minor way by the Nazis. The late H. J. Muller proposed selective breeding for intelligence rather than for racial purity. As early as 1939 he suggested that sperm banks filled with semen collected from the world's most brilliant men be set up for this purpose. By 1973 Dr. Jerome Sherman reported over five hundred successful births from frozen semen, and there are now at least nine non-commercial and three commercial sperm banks in the United States, one of which offers sperm from Nobel laureates (the going rate in the seventies for non-laureate specimens was $10 to $50 per unit donation). Although "egg banks" are not yet practical, at least three live births have resulted from an ovum fertilized *in vitro* and then implanted in the mother's womb. The first such birth, that of Leslie Brown, was achieved by Drs. Patrick Steptoe and Robert Edwards at Oldham, England, in 1978. It led almost immediately to the establishment of an American program at the Eastern Virginia Medical School in Norfolk, Virginia, under the supervision of Drs. Georgeanna and Howard Jones.

A more reliable strategy for remaking humanity is promised by cloning. In cloning, the haploid nucleus of an ovum (containing one-half of the full complement of chromosomes) is replaced by the diploid nucleus (containing the full complement) of an adult body cell. The resultant creature is genetically identical to the donor of the diploid cell. The procedure has been applied successfully to frogs, amphibians, and mice, though not yet to humans. Its advantage for would-be sculptors of humanity is that it avoids the Monte Carlo gamble of normal fertilization. At a still more intimate level of intervention, gene splicing promises to transform the individual in the middle of life. Such a transformation would be as intimate as the implantation and multiplication of a cell. It would change existing humanity rather than future generations.

Not much insight is needed to predict the next step. If man can transform himself at will through surgery, counseling, and genetic manipulation, he has come close to the moment in his history when he can control his own evolution—can even create new human species for specific tasks as he now creates new varieties of *E. coli* bacteria to produce substances such as human insulin and interferon.

In 1969 the National Academy of Sciences sponsored a symposium titled *Biology and the Future of Man* which was published in 1970. The book is as close to being an official statement of biological science as is possible. Its final chapter announces the assumption by human beings of full responsibility for the future of humanity:

> *Homo sapiens* has overcome the limitation of his origin. . . . Now he can guide his own evolution. In him Nature has reached beyond the hard realities of physical phenomena. *Homo sapiens*, the creation of Nature, has transcended her. From a product of circumstances he has risen to responsibility. At last he is Man. May he behave so!

This is impressive and explicit: the gods have been overthrown, and man is the master of his own destiny. But is there not also a contradiction of values in the statement? The traditional concept of man implies, among other things, the subordination of human to divine and natural forces. If these forces have become irrelevant, the being that is so optimistically forecast may be an *Übermensch*—a superman—or something quite different, but it cannot be man in the original, normative sense of the term. "At last he is Man. May he behave so!" is therefore pious nonsense. In changing man medicine has changed the definition of humanity.

If the radical and exotic abilities of high-technology medicine point to the rapid obsolescence of deep traditional values, the same result follows more slowly from commonplace procedures. Thanks to modern life-support technology, death is increasingly a matter to be decided by committees rather than by God. Karen Ann Quinlan was kept alive in a deep coma by a respirator until her parents, in a celebrated case tried in Morristown, New Jersey in October 1975, won a court order instructing Karen's physicians to turn off the machine. Although Karen survived the turning off of the respirator, "pulling the plug" has since become a euphemism for allowing a comatose patient to die.

Many individuals, physicians included, were repelled by the court order. They felt the preservation of life to be an absolute medical imperative. Others felt that the preservation of life would become an inhuman value if it led to unbearable suffering or to the saving of a body with no consciousness. The point is that once the technology to keep Karen Ann alive was available, a decision had to be made. Responsibility had descended from God to man.

In a column in the Washington *Post* of August 18, 1979, titled "Playing God with Life," Ellen Goodman provides two exemplary illustrations of this issue. In California, thirteen-year-old Phillip Becker, a victim of Down's syndrome, was discovered to have a congenital heart defect. When Phillip's parents refused to submit him to surgery, they were taken to court. On July 19, 1979, the California Supreme Court decided in their favor. Parents have a right, the court said, to decide "life and death questions involving minors who will not lead 'a life worth living.' "

In Boston the issue was decided differently. Andrew Stinson was a premature baby, weighing one pound, twelve ounces at birth. He was kept alive for "six months of respiratory diseases, suctionings, tube insertions, blood transfusions, fractures, gangrene, abscesses . . . pain." According to Andrew's parents, his physicians made him into "a research animal." When the parents asked that Andrew be allowed to die, the physicians accused them of "wanting to play God and go back to the law of the jungle." Eventually, Andrew did die. The bill was $104,403. 20.

The case of Phillip Becker is relatively clear-cut. Since Phillip's heart defect could be cured by surgery, not to perform the operation became as much a decision as proceeding. A choice had to be made and was. The court ruled in favor of euthanasia. Euthanasia by private initiative is not uncommon and is practiced by physicians as well as laymen. A court decision, however, elevates it to the status of an official social value.

The case of Andrew Stinson is more ambivalent. It touches the popular fear that doctors become isolated from humanity in their green-and-chromium wards where unbearable pain is called "intractable" and a dying person "terminal." Once a part of this world, the patient risks becoming an object, and certain patients like Andrew may become "research animals." Andrew's parents obviously felt that in asking his physicians to give up their experiments they were asking them to allow God—or Nature—to take the normal course. On the other hand, the physicians (if quoted accurately) saw themselves on the side of God, which placed Andrew's parents on the side of Satan and "the law of the jungle."

Since God permits both death and medical procedures to forestall death, there is no clear right or wrong in this conflict, only the ambiguity of a fundamental value, caused by the success of modern medicine. "In our technology," Goodman comments, "the definition of 'life' is as unclear as our right to one." Evidently, man *has* risen "from a product of circumstances . . . to responsibility." The journey has not taught him how to exercise that responsibility, however. It has demonstrated that he does not know how to exercise it, that his traditional values are inadequate, if not irrelevant, to the choices he is being compelled to make by his own achievements.

Preventive medicine is one of the brightest chapters in the history of science. Its heroes include such attractive figures as Louis Pasteur, Charles Lister, Walter Reed, and Jonas Salk. It does not cure patients; it keeps them from becoming ill in the first place. Since the mid-nineteenth century it has eliminated or controlled many of the diseases that have decimated whole populations: cholera, typhus, scarlet fever, plague, dysentery, pellagra, polio, and many others. A measure of its contribution to public health is the estimate in *Biology and the Future of Man* that the application of DDT since 1950 has prevented over 500 million deaths. Malaria remains a serious health problem in spite of DDT, and several other widespread diseases including schistosomiasis are essentially uncontrolled. In spite of these lingering problems, preventive medicine and basic public health have transformed the lives of most of the world's inhabitants. What could be more in keeping with the traditional humane values of medicine than the prevention of suffering and death?

At the same time that it is an almost unqualified success, however, preventive medicine is a form of ecological intervention, and intervention at one point in the ecological chain produces compensating effects at others. The massive intervention of preventive medicine into biological controls on population has consequences that are, at the very least, mixed.

In 1980 world population stood at around 3.5 billion. According to the most responsible current projections, it will reach between 6 and 6.5 billion by the year 2000. Thirty cities will have populations of over five million. Mexico City may have a population of thirty million. If so, its citizens may well be battling each other for space to die. If they are not, it is hard to understand how they will achieve the minimum economic security and human dignity needed for satisfactory lives.

The possible consequences of rapid growth in world population have been widely discussed. A graph of population growth to the year 2000 prepared by the National Institute of Health in 1969 looks ominously like the mushroom cloud of an atomic explosion. Popular treatments of the subject abound. Two particularly dramatic, though perhaps exaggerated, such treatments are Paul Ehrlich's *The Population Bomb* (1968) and Donella H. Meadows's *The Limits to Growth* (1972). C. P. Snow put the concerns of such literature into layman's terms when he wrote in the *Times Literary Supplement*:

> We are walking . . . into a situation more ominous than any in recent history: different from previous dangers but quite possibly worse than any the human race has known. This is the situation in which those [young people] . . . we are now discussing will be living in early middle age.

Clearly, the success of preventive medicine in achieving what everyone agrees is a desirable and morally elevated objective is leading to results that may be far more devastating than the ills it has eliminated. This is true not only for hundreds of millions of the world's poor who may survive childhood only to starve as adults but for the prosperous as well. The notion that prosperity can create islands of security in a sea of human anguish is an illusion. The authors of *Biology and the Future of Man* announced that man has attained full responsibility for his condition. What happens to his responsibility if his most humane values turn out to be destructive? The dialectic is particularly clear in this case: the quest for life in modern medicine may be leading to death.

Death is exactly where medicine has already led many thoughtful physicians. Having been dedicated to saving life, these physicians are now providing the means to end it.

Abortion is a controversial subject. Until recently, it was illegal in the United States, and it remains illegal in most Catholic countries. Nevertheless, about one million legal abortions are performed annually in the United States, and abortion is an officially sanctioned method of population control in much of the developed world. According to an article on "World Abortion Trends" published in 1980 by the Population Crisis Committee, about 40 million abortions are performed annually, worldwide. The highest abortion rates—one for every live birth —are in Italy, Portugal, and Uruguay, where the procedure is illegal. In Japan, Austria, and the Soviet Union, where abortion is legal, the average is roughly one abortion for every two live births; in the United States the ratio is one to four.

The trial of Dr. Kenneth Edelin forced Massachusetts physicians to confront the question of when human life begins, which is perhaps as difficult as the question of when it ends. Edelin was convicted by a Boston jury in 1973 on manslaughter charges for performing an abortion. Underlying the immediate issue of the Edelin case was a deep conflict of values. The American physician who three decades ago would have been considered a criminal for performing abortions is now considered a hero by many of his or her fellow citizens. However, others still feel that abortion is criminal, and they are making their views powerfully evident at the ballot box. In 1980 the Supreme Court upheld the so-called Hyde Amendment, which makes it illegal for federal monies to be used to provide abortions. This was a victory for the "Right to Life" forces. Voicing their fears about the effect of abortion on the tradition of the sanctity of human life, George F. Will observed wryly in a 1979 editorial:

> A million abortions a year proves that the [pro-abortion] movement has achieved its primary goal, which is to transform attitudes. Obviously many people already regard abortions as the birth-control method of first resort, like taking a pill—in short, as a triviality.

This view is patently unfair to the opposition. Most physicians who accept abortion as a birth-control method do not regard it as a triviality but as a procedure that is better than its alternative: unwanted and abandoned children, hopeless poverty, the creation of a permanently dispossessed class.

Ethical considerations aside, medical research has played a central role in the development of improved abortion procedures. Until the early seventies, the standard procedure was dilation and curettage (*D* and *C*). This was risky under the best conditions and extremely risky when carried out by poorly trained personnel and/or under non-sterile conditions. The currently favored procedure uses laminaria, a Japanese seaweed, to dilate the cervix and suction rather than scraping. Being safe and comparatively simple, it has enhanced the attractiveness of abortion for middle-class women and greatly reduced the cost to the poor. It thus confronts us with an apparent inversion of a central medical value. Instead of devising ways to preserve life, in the case of abortion, medicine is doing everything possible to improve ways of ending it.

Contraception is a clean solution to the problems of surplus children. It may be considered a branch of preventive medicine in that it forestalls the ills, physical, psychological, and social, that result from more children than the woman, the family, or the economy can support. If so, Margaret Sanger is its Louis Pasteur and its Walter Reed. Mrs. Sanger considered family planning a moral imperative. When accused of undermining the biological and religious laws on which the family depends, she replied that birth control would strengthen the family, not weaken it. By the end of the 1960s Dr. Alan Guttmacher, president of the Planned Parenthood Federation, could congratulate himself that Margaret Sanger's battle had, essentially, been won. Birth control was not universal and was still opposed in some circles, especially on religious grounds, but it had become the norm rather than the exception for American women.

This victory would not have come so soon or have been so decisive without medical technology. Rhythm, douches, condoms, and diaphragms are unreliable in varying degrees and require conscious planning in the midst of an act that is supposed to be passionate and spontaneous. Oral contraception is preferable in both respects, and when it became generally available, it became the method of choice for most American women in spite of nagging questions about the side effects of long-term dosage. The success of the pill is reflected in the extraordinary drop in the American birth rate between 1950 and 1970. Today, although use of the pill has declined, the American birth rate remains extremely low, evidently as a result of alternate contraceptive technology and the habits first induced by the pill.

Because contraception is more humane and more efficient than abortion, it is favored by countries that have incorporated population control into national policy. The largest such effort was the campaign launched by Indira Gandhi and her son Sanjay to bring India's population growth under control. This campaign stressed vasectomy and IUDs rather than oral contraception because of the difficulty of teaching poorly educated rural women to follow the schedule required by the birth-control pill. It also visibly dramatized the relation between medicine and values, for it was a major factor in the political reaction that swept Mrs. Gandhi from power in March 1977. Between 1975 and 1977 there were 11 million sterilizations in India; during the Janata Party rule, which succeeded Mrs. Gandhi's, there were 400,000. The issue in India was the same one that Margaret Sanger confronted in the United States in the early years of the century; namely, the collision between the rational values of technological society and the religious values of traditional society. Until her defeat at the polls, Mrs. Gandhi considered birth control the key to progress in her country and thus to a better life for all of its citizens. To the conservative Indians who opposed her, it appeared to be an attack on the laws of God and Nature. Since her return to office, Mrs. Gandhi has preferred not to argue with them.

A more complex reaction to birth control emerged during the 1974 World Conference on Population in Bucharest. Western delegates considered the conference an opportunity to focus attention on the world population explosion. The underdeveloped nations, however—in which most of the explosion was and still is occurring—refused to accept this perspective. To them the problem was not population but inequitable distribution of the world's wealth. Several representatives argued, in fact, that proposals for population control in the underdeveloped world were disguised plots to ensure the continuing dominance of the haves over the have-nots and that they were genocidal. The political overtones are obvious. Whatever their validity, the Bucharest conference showed how deeply contemporary medicine is entangled in political as well as purely medical value conflicts.

But contraception has personal as well as social implications. What happens in those developed societies where it has become commonplace?

As has been noted, Margaret Sanger considered contraception a means of stabilizing the family. Until recently, most of her followers agreed with her. By the mid-sixties, however, certain implications of her program which she could not have anticipated were becoming evident. A so-called new-morality, in which adults were achieving active and socially acceptable sex lives outside of marriage, was beginning to emerge. In 1977 the U.S. Census Bureau estimated that over one million couples were living together out of wedlock. Moreover, children were rapidly disappearing from family life with or without marriage. A report by George and Eunice Grier of the Greater Washington Research Center gives a profile of the impact of the new life-styles in a typical urban area. Between 1970 and 1977 the number of households with children in greater Washington rose by 4500. During the same period the number of households without children rose by 149,000. By 1980 three-quarters of the urban and one-half of the suburban households in the area were childless. Complementing this situation, there were changes in the large-scale social and economic patterns of the area. Adult apartment complexes, in which children are forbidden, become common. Adult-oriented entertainment and restaurants burgeoned. Schools were closed and teaching staffs cut. Voter opposition to school taxes and other revenues intended for children and teenagers rose.

Perhaps the most dramatic effects of the lowered birth rate appear in the lives of women. The lowered birth rate has released women from the home and allowed them to enter the work force in record numbers. As the number of employed women has increased, they have insisted on equal treatment at every level of work from the production line to the boardroom. And as they have gained independence, divorce rates have increased. In 1977 the Census Bureau estimated that 40 out of 100 American marriages involving women in their twenties would end in divorce. This phenomenon is not uniquely or even primarily American. In Sweden in 1977 the rate was 60 out of 100.

In itself, a rise in the divorce rate is not ominous. There is no reason to keep married partners shackled together by law when they have become burdens to one another. In fact, a high divorce rate may express an idealism so strong that it rejects marriage that fails to measure up to its promises. On the other hand, high divorce rates and sexual activity out of wedlock have made traditional conceptions of the family as a stable unit shaped by divine sanctions obsolete. This fact, in turn, implies an adjustment in values that may be particularly complex as those values relate to children. America's birth rate is falling, but children are still being born. About one-fifth will be "one-parent children," and almost half will spend at least one year with only one parent. If a study issued in August, 1980, by the Kettering Foundation is correct, they will experience severe emotional stress and adjustment problems. In place of the family, society offers them day-care centers, nursery schools, boarding schools, orphanages, and reform schools—and the streets of the cities. Except for the streets of the cities, these institutions are better than nothing, but the children who grow up in them will be different from the children of the past.

By changing the nature of the family, medical technology has changed the conditions under which children are conceived, reared, and educated. The traditional family is obsolete, but the institutions to replace it are slow in coming. Eventually, they will come, and although Margaret Sanger would probably be unhappy with the form they are taking, they will suffice. Man—including child—is infinitely adaptable. In the meantime, however, the transitional generation is going to suffer. Sad evidence of this fact is provided by the observation of Crista Papastergio, a psychologist, that as of 1980, the attempted suicide rate at the Sprucedale Training School for Adolescents in Ontario was sixteen percent.

A standard dictionary defines the verb "to cure" as "to heal; to restore health, soundness or sanity." This definition assumes norms that characterize "health, soundness or sanity." Disease prevents the individual from functioning according to these norms. To cure a patient is to eliminate the disease and thus to restore normal function. If this is impossible, as in the case of amputation, the aim of a cure is to restore normal function as nearly as possible.

Sigmund Freud seems to have begun with this understanding. His patients behaved abnormally because of mental illness—Freud originally called it hysteria—and to cure them would be to make them normal by eliminating the illness. Freud called his method "cathartic."

In the process of searching for cures, Freud came to recognize that many kinds of behavior long considered abnormal are actually commonplace. To say that a pattern of behavior is commonplace is to raise the question of whether it is not normal rather than abnormal. In effect, in devising his cure Freud began to undermine many of the norms by which the cure was determined.

The French have a saying that "to understand everything is to pardon everything." In post-psychoanalytic society, many forms of behavior that were once considered abnormal—and were proscribed by law—have become entirely acceptable. Masturbation was a favorite target of nineteenth-century physicians and ministers. Ministers pointed out that it led down the primrose path to Hell, while physicians offered frightening case histories that showed softening of the brain and attendant mental deterioration resulting from it. Today, masturbation is considered a normal adolescent practice. At least one physician, Dr. Alex Comfort in a book titled *The Joy of Sex*, has provided easy instructions for those who have been deprived of its therapeutic value so that they can remedy the oversight.

A more important instance of cures that disintegrate the norms for judging them is provided by the recent history of homosexuality in the United States. Freud and his disciples were convinced that homosexual behavior was deviant. The seeds of a change in this opinion can be found in early psychoanalytic literature, however—at least as early as Havelock Ellis. Those seeds have now flowered. Not more than twenty years ago homosexuals were told by physicians that they were mental cripples. Various cures, ranging from the couch to the electric-shock table to behavior-modifying diets of heterosexual pornography, were urged upon them.

By 1970 homosexuals were questioning both the medical theory and the legal and social barriers against homosexuality that medicine had helped to justify. In 1975 the National Organization for Women overwhelmingly voted a resolution introduced by then-Representative Bella Abzug to make discrimination against homosexuals a federal offense, and in meetings held in 1980, delegates to planning sessions for the White House Conference on the Family voted in favor of a definition of "family" that included single-adult families and families made up of homosexual couples. Although Sergeant Leonard Matlovich lost his 1975 challenge to the United States Army for discharging him because of homosexuality, by 1979 the police department of San Francisco had initiated an Affirmative Action program to hire homosexual officers, and Gay Rights political parties were flourishing in several American cities, including the nation's capital. That same year, The Village People, an overtly homosexual rock group, became internationally prominent. During its

1980 tour, it attracted capacity audiences throughout the United States with songs like "Macho Man," "YMCA," and "In the Navy." David Hodo, a member of the group, was indignant at the suggestion that the group's songs have double meanings: " 'In the Navy' was written for the kids in our audience because we found out we have a lot of kids.'

Affirmative Action programs for gay policemen and public acceptance of overtly homosexual entertainers suggest that homosexuality has been cured. The cure has been to decide that there was no disease in the first place; or, if there was, that it existed in warped social values rather than in the homosexuals—that society was the real patient all along.

The coin has a reverse side as well. If judging the norm becomes more puzzling, judging the insane is becoming equally puzzling. In the massive revision of America's criminal statutes, *The Revised Uniform Criminal Code*, which was placed before Congress in 1979 and again in 1980, the right of defendants to plead "not guilty by reason of insanity" has been severely curtailed. Both medical and legal definitions of insanity—based largely in the 1970s on the work of Dr. William Menninger and a 1973 NIH study by Dr. Louis McGarry—lack the precision needed in trials. As. Dr. McGarry has remarked, the insanity plea "Is not a neatly assessible legal or psychiatric or even human question. It is a question of morality and social policy." The revision of the criminal code is thus another instance of the search for a cure disintegrating the norms by which the disease was identified in the first place.

If some cures define the disease out of existence, others permanently change the patient. Some of these cures, like enforced sterilization and castration for sexual offenders, the mentally retarded, and indigent women who refuse to practice birth control have been declared illegal in most states of America but have been practiced widely in the past—with the encouragement of respected physicians.

Lobotomy became fashionable in the 1950s as a treatment for

violence-prone behavior. In this procedure, neuron connections in the prefrontal lobes are surgically disrupted, leaving the patient permanently disoriented but more tractable. In the late sixties, lobotomy dropped out of favor. It has not disappeared, however. Just as diaphragms and condoms were partially replaced by the pill, lobotomy has been replaced by more refined techniques of behavior-modifying surgery. Physicians have traded their scalpels, as it were, for electric probes; but they are still at work.

For economic reasons, the most extensive use of medical procedures that change patients is found in institutions: mental hospitals, prisons, homes for the elderly, and schools. Most of these institutions operate on inadequate budgets. They must process the largest possible number of inmates or patients or students at the least possible cost. This can only be accomplished if behavior is standardized. Standardization, in turn, is greatly facilitated if those who resist standardization can be defined as mentally ill. Medicine can then be asked to devise a "cure" for the illness, and the stigma of coercion disappears. Authorities can explain that they are doing their best to restore their charges to full and active lives.

As early as 1975, testimony before Senator Birch Bayh's Subcommittee on Deliquency confirmed the extensive use of psychoactive drugs to control inmates of several types of institutions, including nursing homes for the elderly. The paradox here is striking. On the one hand, medicine does its best to prolong life. The miracles of geriatric medicine are almost as brilliant as the miracles that kept Andrew Stinson alive for six months after his premature birth. On the other hand, medicine provides drugs that reduce those whose lives it has prolonged to vegetable docility so that they can be processed at minimum cost.

If wholesale drugging of the elderly is repellent, drugging of the young is more so. Yet if Peter Schrag and Diane Divoky are correct in their work *The Myth of the Hyperactive Child* (1975), many normal but obstreperous children are being diagnosed by educators, parents, and physicians as victims of a disease called "hyperactivity" or "minimum brain dysfunction." Somewhere between 500,000 and 850,000 were under treatment in 1975. Many undoubtedly needed treatment, but clinical definitions of the illness are hazy. Schrag and Divoky maintain that diagnosis is often little more than the rationalization of a strategy to keep the children obedient:

> As a consequence, millions of children are no longer regarded as part of the ordinary spectrum of human personality and intelligence . . . but as people who are qualitatively different from the "normal" population; individuals who, as a consequence of "minimal brain dysfunction," or "hyperactivity," or "functional behavior disorders" constitute a distinct and separate group.

And again:

> All are being taught that it is normal to be tested, and treated, that deviance is a disease, and that punishment, which used to be direct and overt, is now meted out in the guise of therapy.

The Myth of the Hyperactive Child is a cry for reform and may be somewhat exaggerated. One hopes so. However, it points up a curious paradox in values that are encouraged by medicine. Apparently, while homosexuals are being returned to the social fold, children are being cast out. What was deviant in the nineteenth century has become healthy, and what would have been considered normally obstreperous behavior fifty years ago has become deviant. Woe to Huck Finn if he should decide to light out for the Territory today. He would end his days in a Missouri mental institution spaced out on Ritalin, Dexedrine, and Cylert.

Has medicine declared war on children? Homosexuals do not have children. Heterosexual adults have the pill. Meanwhile, children who are born in spite of all efforts to the contrary are on notice from the first day in this world: conform or be cured.

If this is legitimate even as a speculation, it is so far from the values consciously endorsed by individual physicians and by the human race in general that it raises the question of whether medicine is not creating a radically new value system even while it believes that it is observing its time-honored pieties. Do the values that are emerging from the practice of medicine today have any meaningful relation to the traditional values of Western society? Is there not an irresistible dialectic operating in medicine? Medicine is forced to innovate by technology, but in area after area, the application of new knowledge forces it to adapt new *de facto* values that are different from, and in many cases antithetical to, the traditional values to which the physician still offers public homage.

Medicine is an empirical rather than a theoretical discipline. There is a theory of physics and even a theory of biology, but the basic rule of medicine is "use what works." If medicine has a philosophy, it is a mixture of two seemingly analogous traditions. The first is humanitarian and religious. It stems from the rational humanism of Hippocrates on the one hand and Christian reverence for the sanctity of life on the other. The second is progressive and stems from sources like Auguste Comte's *Discours sur l'esprit positif*.

Comte's *Discours* appeared in 1844. It announced the death of superstition at the hands of science and the beginning of an era of scientific progress that would eventually solve all of man's problems. Comtean positivism appears to be humanitarian and thus to complement the humanism of Hippocrates and the compassion of Christ, but it values innovation more than continuity and it is self-consciously hostile to religion, and thus to all absolutes, including the idea of the absolute sanctity of life. In general, when medicine has had to choose between Christ and Comte, it has chosen Comte.

A deeper problem as far as its usefulness to medicine is concerned is that Comtean positivism is naïve in its understanding of the historical process. It assumes that history is linear—that man passes from one success to the next without fundamental change and without the need for constant destruction and renewal of social values. As has already been noted, Hegel is a better guide to the real process of history. The historical process is dialectical and produces destruction and suffering as well as creation. The history of medicine in the last century is anything but a history of continuous progress. Each major advance has caused problems and crises that have required the abandonment of old values and the creation of new ones; and as medicine has progressed, the process of destruction has begun to outpace the process of creation.

Does the movement lead anywhere? The question can be applied to technological society in general as well as to the branch of it labeled "medicine." Hegel believed that the larger movement was progressive in spite of the destruction it entailed; but he also believed that it was infinite, so that its end is a matter of faith rather than knowledge.

Perhaps there is only change without direction. Most scientists, including physicians, reject that possibility. They believe in truth. Underlying their pursuit of truth is a stubborn confidence, inherited from the traditions of the open society, that it can be discovered and that when it is, its values will be better than those they replace.

6

The Future of Old Age

Thanks to birth control, health care, and geriatric research, old age has a brilliant future. In 1900 there were three million Americans over age 65. In 1978 there were 24.1 million. In 2035, if the projections of the Department of Health and Human Services can be trusted, there will be 55.8 million. Most of them will be women, for women live longer than men. In 1977 there were 14 million women in America over 65 and 9.5 million men; in 2035 the numbers will be 32 and 23 million respectively.

Most of the elderly live on fixed incomes and depend heavily on government maintenance programs. Fixed incomes tend to be eroded by inflation, so the government's share in supporting the elderly will increase. Today, about a million of America's elderly are in nursing homes, which are expensive to operate if they provide reasonable care and medical services. The number will obviously increase, with a corresponding increase in the price tag.

Meanwhile, the demographic clock is ticking away. As the average age of the population moves upward, the increasing number of elderly persons assisted with public funds will be dependent on a decreasing percentage of taxpayers in their most productive years. In 1950 there were 7.5 active workers for every retiree on a pension. In 1979 the ratio was 5.4 to 1. By 2035 the ratio will be roughly 3 to 1. In certain industries liberal early-retirement policies have accelerated the natural demographic trend. In the automobile industry, for example, there were 7 workers for every retiree in 1970; there are 3 today, and by 1990, if current trends continue, there will be 2. Automation will accelerate these trends.

What about pensions? Many pension plans are unfunded or so poorly funded as to be irresponsible. Even the best ones were designed on the basis of demographic assumptions made invalid by the rapid aging of the population. In 1979 the grim facts were spelled out in two books: *Pensions for Public Employees*, published by the National Planning Association, and *Policymaking for Social Security*, published by the Brookings Institution. The first examines a total of 6700 retirement plans covering 22 million federal, state, and local government workers. The problems it reveals are illustrated by the fact that one of the funds it treats—the Federal Civil Service Retirement Fund—has an unfunded future obligation of approximately $120 billion. Social Security is an even more massive headache. It covers the majority of American workers and is at present paying benefits to some 35 million of them every month. In 1977 Congress revised the Social Security withholding schedules in order to prevent massive future deficits. The action was politically unpopular—and an effort to fund the deficits from general tax revenues was only barely forestalled—but, as the saying goes, Congress bit the bullet. Whether it bit hard enough is still unclear. Almost certainly it will have to bite again. In 1981 the Congressional Budget Office predicted that without further changes Social Security would be $63.5 billion in debt by 1986.

Behind the statistics are human problems. Increasingly large numbers of the elderly will be housed in decaying facilities, tended by poorly paid, often incompetent workers, and rendered docile by a regular diet of tranquilizers. Other groups of the elderly will struggle desperately to avoid the tender mercies of public nursing homes on incomes that drop farther and farther below the poverty line. Their plight will be especially difficult because they will have to fend for themselves. Many of them will be childless. Those with children will receive little help because their children will live in small apartments, will move frequently, and will themselves be hard-pressed by inflation. In general, the bonds between the generations have weakened, and even where they remain strong the social patterns encouraged by technological society tend to erode them except among the wealthy. At the same time, the young have their own rights and responsibilities. They have careers to follow, goals—including financial ones—to meet, and children to support and educate.

Demography and technology are thus setting the stage for a new kind of social war—that between youth and age. It is a war in which the elderly have a powerful advantage: their vote. Their numbers are growing, and they go to the polls regularly. During the 1976 election 62 percent of those over 65 cast ballots, in contrast to 49 percent of those between 18 and 34.

In 1971—little more than a decade ago although it almost seems a century—a much-heralded White House Conference was held on the subject of aging. It had been authorized by Congress in 1968, and active preparations were carried out for three years, drawing on the input of almost one million persons. The Washington meeting was held between November 28 and December 2, 1971. Four thousand people attended. They considered fourteen major topics ranging from health care and mental health to volunteer roles for the elderly. Chief Justice Earl Warren opened the conference, and President Richard Nixon closed it.

In his closing speech the President emphasized the urgency of the concerns of the conference and offered his solutions. He proposed an overhaul of welfare legislation relating to the elderly, the use of revenue-sharing to reduce property taxes on the homes of citizens over 65, a guaranteed retirement income, reform of private pension funds, expansion of Medicare, and a quadrupling of the budget for the Administration on Aging. Whether he realized it or not, Mr. Nixon's speech was an announcement of the coming war between the generations over the division of America's wealth.

Two sections of his speech are especially interesting in retrospect. First, in order to emphasize his commitment to the problems at hand, the President indulged in a little rhetoric concerning the upcoming political campaign:

> There is one provision [in the present tax reform bill] that provides between 50 and 100 million dollars to go for the purpose of paying the campaign expenses of an individual who is running as the nominee of his party for the Presidency of the United States. Now, my friends, just let me say this: It is very important that campaigns be adequately financed, but I say, rather than have the taxpayer's money used for the purpose of financing a candidate's campaign for election, that money should be used for the purpose of allowing the elected President to keep his campaign promises once he gets into office.

In view of the unique methods of financing political campaigns that the President is now known to have used, his concern for the taxpayer seems ironic at least. However, the main thrust of his argument is clear: the needs of the elderly are urgent, and if elected he will use his office to meet them.

The President returned to this point in another part of his speech. It seems that he was worried about dust in the Library of Congress: "Down in the Library of Congress," he said, "there is a whole floor with many, many stacks of volumes, volumes with the records of White House Conferences. . . . These volumes, very many of them, when I have seen them down there, just gathered dust." Presumably, the stack attendants at the Library of Congress got the message. Whether they did or no, the dust problem led to an important pledge:

> I do not want the volumes—and there will be volumes on this Congress—simply to gather dust. . . . Each one of you has made a very important pledge this morning, a specific commitment for action in the post-conference year. I am here to join you in that pledge.

After reviewing the two volumes of the Conference Report—and after washing the dust off his hands—the thoughtful reader may pause to wonder about the enormity of the effort that went into the conference and the paucity of the results. What happened during the year of action to which everybody had pledged himself? The year of action came and went. It brought an election. There was the high drama of Dr. Kissinger's attainment of peace with honor in Viet Nam. Problems were discovered in the President's campaign finances. Phase I of the White House plan to shore up the economy turned into Phase II and then disappeared into history. The dollar was devaluated, and there was a balance-of-payments crisis. And there was a major effort to cut back on the welfare spending inherited from President Johnson's Great Society by dismantling the Office of Economic Opportunity.

It was a crowded year, that year of action, but the history books fail to record decisive improvements in the status of the elderly. It is, in fact, questionable whether the elderly were substantially better off on December 2, 1972, than they had been on December 2, 1971, when the conference ended. In the ensuing decade, their welfare benefits have increased and the number of the elderly below the poverty line has decreased correspondingly. But the improvement seems now to have been temporary. Since 1978, the plight of the elderly has again worsened. Inflation, taxes, energy costs, and sheer numbers have all taken their toll. The mountains labored in 1971. Unfortunately, they brought forth a mouse.

Perhaps it was inevitable. Perhaps the real crisis was too far in the future. Perhaps, at the time, continuous adjustment of existing programs was the best that could be expected.

This is not to say that the White House Conference on Aging was an exercise in cynicism. If anything, it was just the opposite. It can best be understood as a last echo of the idealism that gathered force in America during the Kennedy years and culminated during the administration of President Johnson. This idealism was based on the assumption that in America everything is possible and the corollary assumption that government is the natural instrument for achieving it. Although President Nixon had well-publicized doubts about the value of government efforts in the areas of poverty and race, help for the elderly must have seemed as safe as motherhood. After all, who was *against* the elderly in 1971? The influence of this conviction is evident in the President's pledge to the conference; but by December 1971, the times were already out of joint. The idealism of the sixties was dying.

What happened was more serious than the mismanagement of American politics. America came to the end of a two-hundred-year period of growth. If the problems of the elderly had been America's only challenge during the years following the White House Conference, or even its most urgent challenge, they would have been met head on. But they were not.

The lesson of the seventies has been that America is entering a period of diminished expectations. Its resources are finite, and they have already been severely strained. Energy is limited, food is limited, raw materials are limited, and the capacity of the environment to absorb the punishment inflicted by efforts to increase productivity is limited. Although America remains one of a small number of affluent nations in an ocean of poverty, it cannot sustain its prosperity through its own resources. As long as it was relatively independent of the rest of the world in raw materials and as long as it possessed overwhelming technological and military superiority, America could afford to behave as though its own destiny were not linked with that of the global community. Perhaps its independence was never as complete as Americans liked to believe. At any rate, America is now competing in the world marketplace for many of the commodities it needs for survival, and the consequence is a new era of diminished expectations. As the economy struggles to adjust to these conditions, the burden falls with special weight on the elderly.

When the White House Conference was being organized, nobody thought about including youth. Late in 1971 Secretary of Health, Education and Welfare Elliot Richardson added "youth think sessions," as they are called in the report, to the agenda. About one hundred specimens of youth were hurriedly rounded up and dispatched to their think sessions. Those youths must have experienced rough going: they were lectured to by a director of the Boy Scouts, a program specialist of the Girl Scouts, a director of the Boys' Club of America, and a member of the governing board of the Red Cross. It is dubious in the extreme whether the Boy Scouts, the Girl Scouts, the Boys' Club of America, or the American Red Cross had anything of value to say to representatives of a generation that had marched in Alabama, overthrown the administrations of Berkeley and Columbia, battled the National Guard at Kent State, and helped to write *finis* to the political career of President Lyndon Johnson—even to the well-scrubbed, primly dressed, almost archeological youth specimens of that generation depicted in the official photographs of the conference.

These doubts are reinforced by the report of the Youth and Age Section, which appears fourteenth and last in the Conference Report. This section still repays reading. It correctly identifies the central issue of the conference as a conflict of social values, and it attempts to define a just society rather than proposing strategies to lever more money from government agencies.

Nine years after the conference, Bruce C. Vladeck reached much the same conclusion in a book titled *Unloving Care: The Nursing Home Tragedy* (1980). Vladeck charges that the government has never developed a coherent policy for the elderly.

Instead, it has tinkered with existing programs and added new ones piecemeal. Vladeck calls this approach "incrementalism." It is caused by the refusal of Congress and the Executive to face up to the problem identified by the Youth and Age Section of the White House Conference. It results in a patchwork quilt of programs that overlap in some areas, ignore others, and are sometimes so poorly designed as to be an invitation to graft and other kinds of abuse.

Three recommendations of the Youth and Age Section stand out. The first goes directly to the central issue:

> [We propose] a radical and immediate reordering of our national spending policies and economic priorities to place human needs before the material needs of the military and space program.

A phrase like "radical . . . reordering of . . . priorities" activates a small Pavlovian gong somewhere deep in the mind. It is familiar. It is the rhetoric of Stokely Carmichael, Rap Brown, Tom Hayden, Phil Berrigan, and all those other youths who have disappeared like the snows of yesteryear along with SNCC, SDS, and the whole alphabet soup of the radical sixties. Placing human needs before material needs is one of those ideas that appeals to everybody in the abstract and to nobody in practice. But in the case of a national policy for the elderly, it is an idea that will not go away, simply because there are more elderly every day and they vote. One solution might be to put a ceiling on the voting age—say, 55. The best way to silence a disaffected social group is to remove its vocal chords. A poorly made but intriguing movie called *Soylent Green* (1973), starring Paul Newman and Edward G. Robinson, explored a variant of this option and came up with an idea that Jonathan Swift would have appreciated: voluntary euthanasia centers for the elderly that contribute to American productivity by supplying the young with large quantities of protein-rich diet supplement at a time in history when the greenhouse effect has made normal agriculture a losing game.

There are, however, other options. The sixties and early seventies were immensely productive of experiments in alternate value systems. Perhaps the Youth and Age Section had the experiments of the sixties in mind. These included the commune, the open family, group-interaction programs like sensitivity and encounter groups, rock and drug cultures, and religious movements ranging from Zen to Charismatic Christianity to Jonestown and the Charles Manson gang. The American middle class caught the virus too, although its reaction was milder. One of the sleepers of the fifties was a potboiler called *Five Acres and Independence*; Euell Gibbons converted nostalgia for five acres into a national stampede to the forest with *Stalking the Wild Asparagus* (1962), and a generation learned how to cure pneumonia by burying old socks at the nearest crossroads from *The Foxfire Book* (1965). Those who could not go all the way with Appalachia satisfied their consciences with *Organic Gardening* and *The Whole Earth Catalogue*. Backpacking, white-water rafting, rock climbing, and camping in national parks became enormously popular. The ecology movement grew into a significant political force, and Barry Commoner announced that he was a presidential candidate. A book that arrived too late for the conference, E. F. Schumacher's *Small Is Beautiful: Economics as if People Mattered* (1975), proposed a reordering of priorities much like that proposed by the Youth and Age Section and was hailed as a major contribution to the problems of world economics.

All of those trends—the bizarre, the naïve, and the serious—revealed a dissatisfaction, varying from mild to obsessive, with the dominant values of American society. The dissatisfaction was not new; it can be found in Thoreau. But its pervasiveness *was* new. It was the equivalent in society of the rebellion that occurred during the 1960s in the academy. It questioned both the pyschology and the physical and social forms imposed on modern society by technology, including the habit of equating success with material possessions, the dehumanization of personal relations by large-scale organization and compartmentalization of work, and the destruction of the natural world in the name of progress. In place of these tendencies the reformers proposed that something like Edenic harmony be achieved through small communities living close to nature. They did not deal explicitly with the problem of the elderly because the solution to this problem was implicit in their larger aim: a society shaped by human ties which include the ties of kinship and mutual respect and compassion for the weak. In this kind of a society the elderly would not be a problem because provision for their needs would be part of its structure.

Unfortunately, most of the experiments of the sixties were failures. The flower children of Haight-Ashbury were not decimated by their vices as their critics predicted, but they did leave San Francisco. A fair number migrated to Mendocino County and other rural areas of northern California and Oregon where they reclaimed whole counties from depression by raising sinsemilla pot. They became capitalists, pillars of the community with an annual gross estimated in 1980 by the FDEA at around $3 billion, complete with police protection, harvest festivals, and experimental stations evaluating growing techniques and hybrid products. Others joined the establishment. The communes were mostly abandoned, and the apostles of radical change settled down to rountine jobs. Some of the religious groups lasted, but at a price. Their dogma hardened, and they developed organizational structures that are mirror images of established churches. The Charistmatics, who began in a common search for the guidance of the Holy Spirit, now sponsor radio and television ministries, buy real estate, budget for annual donations, and practice hard-sell evangelism with a fundamentalist flavor. The success of their experiment thus looks to an outsider very much like incipient failure.

If recent history is a guide, nothing like the "radical reordering of priorities" called for by the Youth and Age Section of the White House Conference is possible. This does not mean the Youth and Age Section was wrong: it was undoubtedly right. It established a principle by which the varying degrees of failure, which are the best achievements politics has to offer, can be measured. Short of "radical reordering," it should be possible for Congress—even a Reagan Congress—to move beyond Bruce Vladeck's "incrementalism" to a rational policy regarding the elderly. The policy will be inadequate, but if it takes the recommendation of the Youth and Age Section into account, it has a chance of pointing in the right direction.

A second recommendation of the Youth and Age Section stems from changes in the American family:

> [We propose] that we must bridge the gap between young and old by encouraging alternate forms of social organization to supplement family structures from which young and old are often withdrawn.

This recommendation identifies one of the basic social dislocations caused by technological society. Technological society places a high premium on workers who contribute to the productivity of society as a whole. It has not adequately confronted the biological versus the economic facts of life; namely, that human beings in modern society are generally non-productive until they reach age 17 and generally non-productive again after they retire. It regards the young and old as encumbrances rather than as assets. One consequence of this attitude has been the universal tendency in developed societies to value women more as wage earners than as mothers and to push them into the labor force where they are productive in economic terms. That this undercuts a previously useful method of decentralized child-rearing is seldom confronted honestly. It is currently an article of faith that the state has created or will create institutions that provide the equivalent of family child-rearing at a net increase in productivity and without loss in the quality of nurture provided for the children.

Because children eventually become workers, technological society has a considerable stake in how they are reared and educated. If current institutions are unsatisfactory, society will eventually be forced to develop new ones. The elderly, on the other hand, have made their contribution to society. Unless they speak loudly in the voting booth, their problems will have low priority, and planning for their welfare will continue to concentrate on biological and economic needs while ignoring equally urgent psychological needs. Such planning is dominated by a charity syndrome. It does not begin by recognizing that the elderly are adult citizens with a full relationship to society that involves giving as well as taking, but with the assumption that they are collectively passive, that they take without giving, and that the primary duty of society is to feed and house them, preferably in isolation from the active community, until they die.

In pointing out that "young and old are often withdrawn" from the contemporary family, the Youth and Age Section of the White House Conference was calling attention to the disappearance of an institution that once provided the elderly with a continuing tie to the society around them. The extended family of the nineteenth century was a tiny community. It consisted of wage earners and ancillaries, the ancillaries being in-laws, children, servants, and the elderly. Because it was held together by ties of kinship strengthened by long-term personal relations, it prevented the elderly from becoming isolated. And because the family was a working unit, it required the elderly to contribute to the common effort. The need to give provided the elderly with a strong sense of function and prevented them from declining into the kind of passivity that is commonplace in nursing homes.

It is almost impossible to discuss the extended family without sentimentalizing it. It was probably much less common than is normally assumed, and contemporary images of it are undoubtedly distorted by nostalgia. It could be cruel and repressive as well as gentle, and it was better adapted to a rural society than to an urban one. At any rate, it was unable to survive the upheavals of the last fifty years. Modern society is urban rather than rural; its living units are built for single people, couples, and families with children, not for extended families; and it is fluid rather than stable: middle-class adults move constantly because of job requirements, shifting job markets, and the simple desire for change. There is no place in this kind of society for elderly ancillaries except among the very wealthy. Nor have any adequate "alternative forms of social organization" of the sort called for by the Youth and Age Section emerged. Those forms that do exist are adaptations of past forms, and they are woefully inadequate: retirement communities, subsidized "senior citizen apartments," and nursing homes. All of them isolate the elderly in geriatric ghettos where they are deprived of functional relations with society as a whole.

It is this isolation, this stripping away of function, that is the most depressing aspect of aging in America. Yet very little beyond "phone buddies" and Meals On Wheels has been proposed to improve the situation. Implementing alternative social forms is extremely difficult for government because truly alternative forms would require changes that go against the grain of technological society. Government does what is easy and natural. It does not change, it invents new agencies. It has created the Age of the Agency, beginning with the nursery school and ending with the nursing home.

Given this fact, it should be admitted that the government has done what it can to help the elderly. In 1977 approximately $12.6 billion was spent on nursing-home care. The figure is generous and also ominous in view of the future demands on the national economy that will occur as the American population continues to age. But the expenditure has to be measured against the results obtained, and here the picture is mixed. While many nursing homes are well run by the standards of the profession, many others are "scandalous," to use Bruce Vladeck's phrase. The root problem is not abuse of responsibility (although Vladeck shows that abuse is common) but the institution itself. It is a typical creation of the agency mentality, an artificial environment divorced from the common life of society, designed to make the best of a bad situation. The most efficient and thoughtful of such institutions are dehumanizing; the worst are inhuman.

The paradox of the well-run nursing home that turns out to be a prison is a special case of the problem of bureaucracy identified by the reformers of the sixties. It is a reminder that the sixties protests were justified, that the best plans go sour if they are imposed on instead of created by the people directly affected. Government cannot solve the problems of the elderly, and yet it cannot ignore them either—such is the confusion of politics. Here it is useful to recall the old democratic theory: "That government is best that governs least." To the degree that the theory is still valid, it suggests that government should cooperate with the affected individuals in setting its goals. This, however, is precisely what modern government seems unable to do effectively. It can cooperate with other governments, with political parties, with private corporations, with agencies and bureaus and officials, but it cannot cooperate with individuals.

There is a consensus among students of aging that the elderly are better off in their communities than in special facilities. Considerable efforts have been made to devise ways of keeping the elderly from being isolated, but Bruce Vladeck considers them only a beginning. Again, the problem of the agency mentality intrudes itself. According to Senator David Pryor of the Senate Select Committee on Aging, for every $1 billion spent on health and social services to maintain the elderly in their communities in 1979, about $30 billion was paid to agencies, i.e., nursing homes and medical-care facilities. It is easy to see that the priorities are wrong and that the consequence is the perpetuation of a bad system, but money talks. Meanwhile, the geriatric ghettos grow larger, the elderly continue to suffer, and the bill to the taxpayer gets bigger.

The Youth and Age Section agreed that the elderly need to be integrated into society rather than separated from it. They expressed special interest in the contribution the nation's educational system might be able to make toward reaching this goal:

> [We propose] that society should adopt a policy of education for life such as preparation for job, family, retirement and use of leisure time.

This proposal confronts the paradox of a work-oriented society in which large numbers of people no longer have useful work. Perhaps a society that had developed true alternative social forms would not have to confront this problem because it would have useful work for everyone. But American society in the twentieth century is still emerging from a love-hate relationship with work that makes leisure the reward for labor: weekends for the week and retirement for a lifetime. As has already been noted, the reward is ambiguous. Many who receive it discover that it is an intolerable burden, and one of the continuing problems of nursing homes is creating enough artificial activity to disguise the essential emptiness of the schedule.

The Youth and Age Section assumed that certain activities are genuinely rewarding even though they may be useless to society as a whole and are performed in leisure time. It considered education especially rewarding and therefore proposed that schools become "life-long learning centers." As such, they would serve two functions: to train working adults for second careers and to provide intellectual stimulation for the elderly.

The first suggestion has already been accepted by the schools. Community colleges have led the way toward "life-long learning" programs, and four-year colleges and universities have now joined them. Since 1977 the National Registry for Continuing Education has maintained a centralized, computer-based storage system for information for schools about "non-credit" and "continuing education" courses throughout the country. It offers half-day conferences on the subject (thirteen in 1979) and for a fee will provide mailing labels for all students listed in its annual roster. Another program, sponsored by the Management Center of the Edwin Cox School of Business of Southern Methodist University, advertises two-day conferences with the headline: "How Your University Can Capitalize on the 30 Billion Dollar Continuing Education Market."

Eleanor Greenberg is a spokesman for continuing education. In an article titled "The Opportunity of a Lifetime," published in the spring 1970 *Report* of the Association of Governing Boards, she states that 1233 of America's 3000 colleges and universities now have continuing-education programs and that the number of students in the programs is increasing every year.

Most of the programs described by Ms. Greenberg are for career development of adults in the work force and women returning to the job market. What about leisure-time activities for the elderly? Ms. Greenberg writes: "As the youth population shrinks and our older population grows, as more people change jobs, as more education breeds desire for education, as leisure time and income rise, and as the quality of work and of life become increasingly more important issues, the need, demand and market for learning throughout adult life will increase." The emphasis here is on education for self-cultivation rather than for jobs and on retirement and leisure rather than work. Ms. Greenberg adds that continuing education in the humanities "can add a dimension of quality to people's lives, increasingly difficult to find elsewhere."

What are "leisure-time activities"? Many of them are exquisitely boring—loafing, endless gossip, and waiting in lines at various government agencies. Judging from the lives of successful retirees, the best leisure-time activities are remarkably like the Saturday and Sunday activities of the gainfully employed: bridge, golf, gardening, boating, hobbies, reading, television. The Edwin Cox School's Management Center explicitly promises to tell participants in its two-day conference how to set up courses in "cooking, photography, tennis and more."

There is, of course, no doubt that retirees enjoy "cooking, photography, tennis and more" as much as their fellow citizens.

But Ms. Greenberg and the Youth and Age Section of the White House Conference think that they may have deeper interests. Having lived most of their lives in a struggle for survival and success, they may be tempted to look back, to try to see the struggle in perspective. If so, they may be as interested in Plato and Shakespeare and Cézanne as in cooking, photography, and tennis. While Plato and Shakespeare and Cézanne are not likely to provide access to a $30-billion-a-year market, they may be genuinely useful to the elderly. There is considerable evidence from "life-long learning" programs for the elderly and from the sale to the elderly of reduced-price tickets for plays and concerts that this is, in fact, the case. An important experiment in education for the elderly called Elderhostel was begun in 1975 by Martin Knowlton on five New Hampshire campuses. By 1979 it enrolled some 12,000 participants on 235 campuses and is still growing today.

In an ideal world, and even in an imperfect one, the provision of cultural opportunities for the elderly, including education and access to the performing arts, is humane and beneficial. It emphasizes their continuing involvement in the general social enterprise and thus reduces their isolation. It is not a solution to the problems of the elderly, but it should probably be part of any proposed solution. Obviously, it can only be considered if the educational system and the performing arts remain strong in society as a whole, and the current outlook for them is distinctly mixed. Yet artificial humanities and performing-arts programs created exclusively for the elderly will increase their isolation not reduce it.

Technological society has contributed both to the growing size of the elderly population and to the attitudes that make the elderly difficult to assimilate. The situation is typical of the modern dialectic. The tensions that it is creating are acute and rapidly becoming more so. Before they are resolved there will have to be more demolition as well as creation. The Youth and

Age Section of the White House Conference realized this fact and stated it clearly in its call for a "radical . . . reordering of . . . priorities" and for "alternate forms of social organization."

The elderly will speak for themselves at the ballot box. They will undoubtedly echo Sir John Falstaff, who put the non-negotiable demands of the elderly into four words: "Us youth must live!"

7

Education and Technique

The idea of humanity is not so much an idea as an article of faith that history goes somewhere. History may be a cycle or a spiral or a momentary tremor in eternity or a line toward eternity called progress. In any event, it has a form. The modern world favors progress: political progress, biological progress, economic progress, spiritual progress, continuous progress, dialectical progress. Jacques Monod, a biologist, concludes from his research that existence is a matter of chance, but underneath Monod's professional endorsement of randomness the passionate faith in progress of a disciple of Auguste Comte can be detected. The mind is a machine for creating order, whether or not order actually exists. It can cope with anything but randomness. Poets, including poets of biology like Monod, remain the unacknowledged legislators of mankind.

The fundamental ideas of humanity are embodied in the lives of gods or are delivered by the gods to mortals in groves or on mountaintops or are incarnated in the lives of demigods. They are also expressed in grammars of languages, sounds of words, shapes of pottery, transactions between children and parents, and calendars and liturgies. When abstracted from their mythic soil, they become art and theology and law, and they are called truths. "We hold these truths to be self-evident, that all men are created equal, that they are endowed by their Creator with certain unalienable rights, that among these are life, liberty, and the pursuit of happiness." As myth becomes truth, reason takes its place beside experience in the idea of humanity. The contribution of the mind to reality is recognized, and the gods are understood to be projections of the mind into the world.

In its traditional role education is the custodian of society's idea of humanity. During the Middle Ages, education was organized around scripture. Religious texts formed the center of the curriculum, and professors made scripture the object of their methodologies and the subject of their disputations, commentaries, learned treatises, and poetical speculations. The humanists who succeeded the schoolmen in the fourteenth and fifteenth centuries thought they had formulated a more comprehensive idea of humanity. Although they were not indifferent to religion, they shifted the emphasis of their curriculum from scripture to the secular classics of Greece and Rome and from contemplation of perfect truth to action in an imperfect world. At the same time, they changed their method from logic, which is a form of analysis, to rhetoric, which is a form of communication.

The scholastics and the humanists agreed on one important point: society is made up of leaders and followers. If the leaders are educated properly, they will create a just society conforming to a proper idea of humanity. Followers do not need to be educated because they realize their humanity through obedience. The Reformers of the sixteenth century introduced a new concept into the theory of education. The doctrine of justification by faith makes each Christian personally responsible for salvation. To say "I followed blindly" or "I obeyed" or "I was betrayed" at the bar of judgment is insufficient. Society must therefore provide each Christian with sufficient education to understand scripture and to choose responsibly on the basis of that understanding.

At its best, state-supported universal education unites the commitment of Renaissance humanists to a broadly formulated idea of humanity with the commitment of the Reformers to preparing citizens for lives of responsible choice. It is based on secular rather than religious texts. The purpose of reading the texts is not to acquire information but to develop the ability to make responsible choices within the limits of society's idea of humanity.

At the early levels of education the idea of the useful is identical with the idea of humanity. Literacy is both a useful skill and the precondition for reading significant texts. At more advanced levels, a divergence occurs. One area of the curriculum is devoted to the reading and interpretation of culture texts, and its subjects are called humanities. Other areas are devoted to useful information and skills, and their subjects are called sciences and social sciences and professions; they can be summarized under the general label "technique." As technique becomes more complex, it becomes more demanding. The natural divergence in education between technique and the idea of humanity is thus intensified until it becomes a radical separation. The humanities cease to be the foundation of the curriculum and become one of its parts.

At this point the humanities experience a crisis of identity. The system within which they exist is dominated by the idea of the useful, but they cannot demonstrate their utility. From society's point of view, they begin to look like vestigial survivors of pre-technological culture. They are supported because they retain a faded prestige, but they are understood to be luxuries not necessities. Like all activities considered luxuries, they exist by sufferance, and the price of this sufferance is their continuing good behavior in respect to the dominant interests of society.

During the 1960s in the United States there was a breakdown in the relation between the idea of humanity and the idea of the useful. It was not caused by lack of financial support for humanities programs. The American economy was strong and education shared the general prosperity. There was money for everything including the humanities.

The reason for the breakdown was a failure of good behavior that amounted to a revolution against the dominant values of American society. Since the rebels fought under the banner of the idea of humanity, they were *de facto* humanists. They accused American society of waging an inhuman war in Viet Nam, of disenfranchising and brutalizing its minorities at home, of creating an economic system that catered to wealth and poured resources into weapons while ignoring the poor, of destroying natural resources and polluting the earth, of using education for brainwashing, and of dehumanizing labor. The list goes on. It is a very American list because at every point the rebels appealed to the American idea of humanity to justify their critique. For every injustice the same remedy was offered: give the idea of humanity as expressed in the Constitution and the Bill of Rights priority over the idea of the useful as expressed in the commitment of American society to technique.

The rebels of the 1960s lost the sympathy of American society because the values they were attacking had long since become the values of most American citizens. The more vehement the rebels became, the more support they lost. When the American economy began to contract in the 1970s, the loss of support was made explicit by the mass movement of college and university students out of the humanities and into programs that offered useful knowledge and skills. As the students left, the precarious balance that had existed before the 1960s tipped heavily, perhaps irreversibly in view of the political tendencies of the eighties, toward the idea of the useful.

In 1964, during the flush years of the American humanities, the American Council of Learned Societies co-sponsored a report that recommended the creation of a National Endowment for the Humanities. The Endowment would make grants for projects like editions of literary classics, reference works, scholarly studies, symposia, model curricula, and institutes for teachers. The list was a mirror image of the humanities at the time the report was issued. It was focused almost entirely on the humanities in the academy, and it assumed that the way to strengthen the humanities is to subsidize scholarship and teaching, which is to say that it showed no sensitivity whatsoever to the issues that were already being raised by the sixties rebels.

In spite of its narrow focus, the report makes an honest effort to define the humanities in terms of their social function: "The method of education [in the humanities] centers on concern for the human individual: for his emotional development, for his moral, religious, and aesthetic ideas, and for his goals—including in particular his growth as a rational being and a responsible member of his community." The report argues that federal support is proper because massive government subsidy of the social and physical sciences is destabilizing the curriculum:

> The laudable practice of the federal government of making large sums of money available for scientific research has brought great benefits, but it has also brought about an imbalance within academic institutions by the very fact of abundance in one field of study and dearth in another. . . . Students . . . can quickly observe where money is being made available and draw the logical conclusion as to which activities their society considers important.

The National Endowment for the Humanities was established by Congress in 1965 to redress the balance. Its creation occurred at almost the same time that the revolution of the 1960s was beginning to attract national attention. Surprisingly, the Endowment was not hurt by this revolution. During fifteen years of academic turbulence and under four administrations its budget grew from an initial $2.5 million to over $150 million. The most rapid growth occurred during the administration of President Nixon when the revolution had reached its climax. The Endowment grew during these years because it avoided the revolution.

It supported traditional academic scholarship and safe innovations and stayed away from the barricades.

Even while it supported academic projects, however, the Endowment began looking for a broader, more effective base of support. Although its academic projects were respectable, they lacked public appeal. As the Endowment's budget grew, it was able to afford programs that reached beyond the academy. Some of them were oriented toward what were called "culturally disadvantaged" groups—ethnic minorities, inner-city residents, and residents of rural communities. Other, more ambitious, programs attempted to reach the middle-class public through television mini-series like *War and Peace* and *The Scarlet Letter*, high-profile exhibitions like *The Treasures of Tutankhamun*, and "courses by newspaper." Still others grew out of the need to create a national constituency to ensure the continuing favor of Congress. The most significant initiative taken in this direction was the creation of a network of state-based "councils on the humanities," which are still active today. The councils are supported by grants from both the Endowment and the state legislatures. In addition to supporting local humanities projects, they lobby for the Endowment during its annual budget hearings.

In spite of these populist gestures, during the 1976 presidential election, the Endowment was charged with "elitism"—with placing too much emphasis on academic scholarship while ignoring the public that ultimately paid its bills. The charge reflected the feeling, widespread by 1976, that the humanities in the academy were irrelevant to the larger interests of society. Paradoxically, it also revealed a hunger on the part of society for what the humanities have to offer. It was—and is—a difficult charge to answer. The National Science Foundation, which is also supported by tax money, funds academic research but can defend its policies by invoking the idea of the useful. The most esoteric scientific project may eventually produce great social benefits. It is hard to argue, however, that academic research in the humanities produces significant benefits for the average citizen.

Being unable to invoke the idea of the useful, the Endowment must justify itself through the idea of humanity. This is surprisingly difficult. Although the idea of humanity is apparently a public idea, the humanities in the academy seem to be as specialized, as remote from the interests of the public, and as opaque as the sciences. What do they have to offer society in general? Is it possible that the professors have sold out the humanities and have converted a public mission into a series of private hobbies? Does the future of the humanities lie outside the academy rather than in it?

Because those questions are hard to answer, the Endowment has increasingly stressed the public, versus the academic, aspect of the humanities in its policy statements. In 1979 the chairman of the Endowment, Joseph Duffey, remarked in testimony before Congress:

> Increasingly our literary and cultural criticism has come to be a product of college teachers. . . . And yet, ironically, enthusiasm for the humanities today is probably stronger *outside* the academy than in it. . . . We are witnessing, I believe, the end of the period in which the humanities have been dominated by research-oriented graduate schools.

Perhaps Mr. Duffey is right. Perhaps the academic version of the idea of humanity is elitist, and professional humanists have painted themselves into a corner. Before proceeding to a verdict, however, it is useful to turn from the politics of the National Endowment to the theory of the humanities; that is, to the explanations of what the humanists are doing that they themselves have offered.

Explanations of the humanities fall into three distinct categories: practical, ethical, and aesthetic. These are logical categories, and most discussions of the humanities draw materials from all of them. The first two were already linked in the ancient Greek theory of education. The first relates the humanities to the idea of the useful and the second to the idea of humanity understood as a specific, self-conscious ideology. The third also relates the humanities to the idea of humanity, but it assumes that the idea of humanity can never be fully articulated and must be discovered progressively through experience.

The practical theory of the humanities is the easiest of the three to summarize. The Greeks—and the Romans after them—had a utilitarian view of education. As was noted in Chapter 1, its function was to train the administrative class—the lawyers, magistrates, politicians, bureaucrats, and upper-level administrators on whom the stability of ancient society depended. The most successful students would, in the words of the great Roman educator Quintilian, "direct the counsels of the senate and guide the people from the paths of error into better ways."

Ancient educators believed that leadership requires a sound character, a broad knowledge of human affairs, and a well-developed ability to communicate. Their curriculum was organized around grammar, rhetoric, and logic, and rhetoric was the most important of the three disciplines. The typical classical rhetoric text began with an analysis of ways to discover and enlarge a thesis. It continued with methods of organization and devices of style and ended with comment on ways to make the delivery of a speech effective and to remember it without notes.

In addition to teaching theory, the ancient rhetoric course included readings in poetry, drama, history, and moral philosophy. The readings were chosen for their literary excellence and the soundness of their values. They provided models to be imitated in original compositions, and, at the same time, provided moral instruction and a considerable body of general information about politics, religion, geography, military tactics, law, ethics, and the like. By the first century A.D., the readings had hardened into a list of standard authors. Although this list changed over the centuries with the addition of ever-more recent "classics," many of the authors included by the Romans would be part of any modern list of "great books"—Homer, Plato, Sophocles, Demosthenes, Cicero, and Vergil, among others.

The idea that a general education based on "great books" is better equipment for leadership than a specialized education was the first line of defense, until quite recently, of the curricula of America's liberal arts colleges and private universities. General education was said to produce such qualities as flexibility, openness to ideas, understanding of human nature, and "ability to learn." By contrast, specialists were considered to be immobilized in their specialties and unable to think beyond narrow limits. Speaking at Davidson, a small liberal arts college in North Carolina, Morris B. Abram put the theory in a most attractive form:

> At the outbreak of World War II, Oliver Franks, later Ambassador to the United States, was a tutor of moral philosophy at Queens College, Oxford. He was called from that post to become permanent Secretary of the Ministry of Supply. What qualified him for the position was not any special training; it was, rather, having the mind and character, and ability to learn.

Presumably, if Oliver Franks had been an expert in inventory control, he might have worked for the Ministry of Supply, but he would not have become its permanent secretary.

That fact that technological society is constantly changing and that specialized knowledge frequently becomes obsolete gives rise to a variation on Abram's argument, although if taken literally this variation would seem to imply that no one should specialize. In 1978 Ward Hellstrom, chairman of the Department of English at the University of Florida, argued,

> None of us can know very clearly what even the next decade will require in the way of job preparation. How can we train students for specific jobs that may no longer exist by the time the students get to them? It is increasingly

apparent to me that the liberal education which produces a flexible and adaptable student is the best preparation for future jobs.

To turn from the practical to the ethical theory of the humanities is to turn from jobs and leadership to moral improvement. In its simplest form, ethical humanism regards the humanities as devices for teaching morality. As has been noted, the standard authors of the classical curriculum were chosen for the soundness of their values as well as their literary merit. The most detailed apology for ethical humanism in antiquity is Plato's *Republic*. The *Republic* sets out to describe an ideal state. Since the state *is* ideal, its values are beyond debate. There is no need to encourage students to discover new values. The task of educators is to indoctrinate the young in the established values and to reject from the curriculum any materials or activities that might create doubts about those values. The *Republic* is justly famous for its noble vision of humanity. However, it is equally famous for its rigidity, which is owed in part to Plato's interest in Sparta, and which has caused unsympathetic critics to call it an anticipation of the modern fascist state. Homer is banned from the *Republic* because he tells unflattering stories about the gods, and the Greek tragedians are excluded because they show heroes, who ought to be models for the young, surrendering to unmanly emotions. Since Plato, a fondness for censorship has frequently accompanied attempts to use the humanities to teach morality and political orthodoxy.

A nagging problem in all ethical humanism is that one man's morality is another man's depravity. Religious systems of morality can be taught in parochial schools, but they differ so widely among themselves that they are forbidden, under the doctrine of separation of church and state, in public classrooms. In the public schools, ethical humanism has to be satisfied with non-sectarian values and sometimes substitutes for religious fervor an equally fervid emphasis on "Americanism," which leads to scrutiny of textbooks and courses to make sure they contain nothing that is "un-American" or "obscene" or "immoral." This is very much in the tradition of Plato's Republic, unpleasant though the fact may be.

A more sophisticated version of ethical humanism, suitable for higher education, was formulated in the early twentieth century by Irving Babbitt, a professor of literature at Harvard University. Babbit was learned, eloquent, and politically conservative. He was convinced that the Romantic movement, beginning with his arch-enemy Jean-Jacques Rousseau, had unleashed anarchic forces that were on the point of destroying Western civilization. He invented a "new humanism," as he called it, to combat the Romantic heresies. The vehicle for the new humanism was to be the humanities curriculum, and the center of that curriculum was to be a group of classics which expressed, at least in Babbitt's interpretation of them, properly conservative values. Babbitt called the idea of humanity expressed by these classics "the humane standard." He believed that all true classics, Oriental as well as Western, exemplified the humane standard. And he believed it would be attained,

> by a few through philosophical insight, but in most cases it will be attained . . . by a knowledge of good literature— by a familiarity with that golden chain of masterpieces which links together in a single tradition the more permanent experience of the race; books which so agree in essentials that they seem, as Emerson puts it, to be the work of one all-seeing, all-hearing gentleman.

Of course, Babbitt's arguments are double-edged. If it is possible to select a list of standard authors to teach a politically conservative idea of humanity, it is equally possible to vary the selection so that the curriculum teaches a Romantic or egalitarian idea of humanity. At about the same time that Babbitt's followers were promoting the new humanism, in fact, the Marxist journal *New Masses* was promoting the classics of socialist realism and demonstrating that if properly read, the golden chain of these classics sounds as though it were the work of one all-seeing, all-hearing *apparatchik*.

It is important to admit the problems inherent in ethical humanism because in spite of them, ethical humanism contains a stubborn truth. Every great civilization defines itself through a shared set of values. Collectively, these values are its identity, its idea of humanity. Because they exist as internalized motives that appear differently in different circumstances, they resist abstraction. To retain the Protean complexity that makes them living values, they must be allowed to emerge from specific texts, images, and historical moments. They should not be taught so much as discovered.

The texts, images, and historical moments that are particularly expressive of a society's identity can be collected in a list of standard authors, or, to use a more precise phrase, a canon of classics. As has already been noted, one function of such a canon is practical, for it is used to teach skills like literacy and communication; but if skills were the only object of education, almost any collection of materials would suffice. The primary function of a canon of classics is to express society's idea of humanity to those who are exposed to it. It communicates this idea on the level of style, on the level of emotion, and on the level of knowledge. As it is assimilated it provides a center around which new experience can be organized by the individual in ways that harmonize with the larger experience of society.

The Old Testament is the prime example of a canon of classics in antiquity. It is a collection of texts that expresses the identity and central historical experience of the Hebrew people. The Old Testament is a particularly clear instance of a canon of classics because it claims divine authority. In its own terms, that is, it expresses a true idea of humanity rather than an approximate or arbitrary one. Its cultural value is evident: it has fixed the identity of the Hebrew people for hundreds of generations in spite of migrations, persecutions, and the allures of alien cultures.

The canon of modern Western classics is much more inclusive

than the Old Testament. It includes texts, images, and historical moments from pagan antiquity and medieval and modern culture, in addition to both the Old and the New Testaments. At best, it is understood as an approximate expression of the idea of humanity rather than divinely revealed truth. It also varies somewhat from one national culture to the next within the geographical area—principally Western Europe and North, Central, and South America—where it is accepted. As was suggested in Chapter 1, it has created something like a European idea of humanity among cultures that differ widely in language, religion, government, and economy. Addressing the Jubilee Congress of the Modern Humanities Research Association in 1964, William Riley Parker explained that it provides

> a common shared experience of a limited canon of significant works, belletristic and other. . . . Standard works which . . . best define the duties of a moral person and an active, responsible citizen—of a free man guiding the destinies of his society.

The linking of "common shared experience" and "a limited canon" is significant in this comment. The only way the humanites can provide "common experience" is by limiting the materials admitted to the canon. The limitation of the canon is, in other words, a part of its function. If the canon is not limited, it will not express a coherent idea of humanity. To quote a motto cited earlier, all definition requires exclusion.

The limitation of the canon explains much about academic scholarship in the humanities that is confusing to the public. Such scholarship is not a general criticism of culture but a specialized study of works that comprise the canon. It draws on traditions of prior criticism that extend back for centuries in some cases, so that being a scholar requires familiarity with the history of scholarship as well as with the works themselves. The corpus of academic scholarship in the humanities is thus something very like the Talmud, which is essentially a select library of ancient Hebrew scholarship on the Old Testament, with the reservation, already noted, that the canon of classics of Western culture is much larger and much more diffuse than the Old Testament. Like the commentary preserved in the Talmud, academic scholarship tends to be restricted in focus, highly conscious of its own tradition, and technical. Its typical products are reference works, bibliographies, textual studies, and seemingly repetitious series of monographs and articles on specific themes and works. These are both its strength and its weakness: its strength because they reflect the scrupulous fidelity of humanistic scholarship to its tradition; its weakness because they are often incomprehensible—and hence seem ridiculous or tedious or "elitist"—to the general public.

Because the canon is limited to a few among the almost infinite number of works that might have been included in it, efforts have frequently been made either to broaden it or to scrap the idea of a canon entirely. Ian Watt, an English teacher, opposes those efforts. They are, he writes, "intellectually muddled and politically short-sighted." "Muddled" because

> "We must exclude someone from our gathering, or we shall be left with nothing"; short-sighted because concessions to the complacent egocentrism of our culture, which has turned the university catalogue into a supermarket for impulse buyers, can only exacerbate the disease.

In addition to creating a problem of definition, the *ad hoc* expansion of the canon undercuts its ability to provide a "common shared experience" for those exposed to it. The result is a loss of sense of purpose on the part of both teachers and students. William Schaefer, a former executive director of the Modern Language Association of America, blames the problem on the academic humanists:

> We [have] failed to understand the students themselves. Although these young people were fragmented in their

experiences—their lives and their learning—and desperately in pursuit of meaning, we not only enabled but actually encouraged them to major in higher fragmentation. They wanted direction, some kind of unifying theme or purpose; we gave them free electives.

If Watt and Schaefer are right, the function of the humanities in the academy is different from their function in society at large. The responsibility of the academy is to offer a coherent experience, a canon. Inevitably, the canon seems conservative and narrow in comparison to the rich diversity of humanistic experience available beyond the classroom. This is a cross academic humanists have to bear if they wish to accomplish what the ethical theory of the humanities says they should accomplish—that is, if they wish to teach a coherent idea of humanity consistent with the traditions of Western society. Meanwhile, society will continue to offer a dazzling variety of ideas of humanity. Many will be orthodox ideas expressed in established classics like the plays of Shakespeare. Many will be new, and of these, some will be trivial, some perverse, and some powerful and important enough to be incorporated eventually into the canon.

The academy is not society. It may no longer be our custodian of the idea of humanity, but if it is, it is responsible for nurturing that idea. To abandon the canon is to ignore the most compelling reason for having a humanities curriculum in the first place.

Aesthetic humanism does not need to be concerned with a canon of classics. It is based on a philosophy of becoming rather than being. Its starting point is the fact that every human perception, from the trivial to the momentous, has human significance and consequently may be considered a unique value. Having accepted this, aesthetic humanism attempts to understand the significance of each experience directly and without prior assumptions, which include unconscious ones that are the result of associations and conditioning as well as conscious ones like moral codes, political ideologies, artistic conventions, and scientific theories. From the aesthetic point of view, a rose should be a rose before it is a botanical specimen or a symbol of passion or a plant to be watered. Likewise, an historical event should be appreciated for its otherness before it is made into an object lesson for contemporary politics; and a poem should be read for what it says before it is attacked for being in free verse rather than meter or used to illustrate a theory about the history of ideas or a point in Freudian psychology; and a person should be understood as an individual before being classified by race or sex or social class.

The following comments—again made by Ian Watt—describe an experience in Paris just after World War II:

> In the talk I heard then, four new words struck me. I soon got tired of the first three: *Engagé. Authentique. Absurde*; but the fourth—*Les Choses*—seemed somewhat less fly-blown. I started reading Francis Ponge's prose poems about "things" with enormous interest. I remember particularly a newspaper article about a talk Ponge had given called *Tentative Oracle*. His "attempt at a speech" circled amiably around his dislike of the common hyperboles about literature, his sense of being sickened at general theoretical and public propositions, and how in his own writing, finding it impossible to put the great literary subjects into words, he had determined, like a man at the edge of a precipice, to fix his gaze on the immediate object—a tree, the balustrade, the next step—and try to put that into words instead. It was a charming anti-talk, especially its ending. "So we haven't had a lecture?" he commented. "Perhaps not. Why did you ask me?" Then he concluded: "Dear table, Goodbye!" At this Ponge leaned over and embraced the table; then he explained: "You see, if I love it, it's because there's absolutely nothing in it which allows one to believe that it takes itself for a piano."
>
> I would like my own activities as a student and teacher of English to be as simple and yet comprehensive as that act. It should contain the same four necessary constituents: an intellectual recognition of just what I am modestly but directly attending to; an aesthetic appreciation of the object of my attention for what it exactly is; a direct commit-

ment of my feelings to that object; and lastly, perhaps
incidentally, an attempt to express all of the first three
things in words.

The tendency to treat tables as though they are pianos—and
experiences as though they exist to illustrate prior assumptions—
is common, but it is also the source of a great deal of trouble. In
the modern world there are more than enough ideologues telling
people what to believe. Somewhere in their lives people need
moments when they can abandon theories about the world and
open themselves to the world as it is.

This exercise can even have political uses. In a talk in 1978
about David G. McCullough's *The Path Between the Seas*
(1977), Senator Daniel Moynihan observed that McCullough's
book made a significant contribution to the confirmation of the
Panama Canal Treaty by the United States Senate. Not because
it took sides, but because it refused to take sides; because it
presented the real complexity of the history of the Canal. When
senators read the book, Moynihan said, it seemed to "shake us
out of ideological simplicity." History in this sense should not
grind axes; it should liberate. It can be argued further that
liberation is healthy and leads to a progressive broadening of
understanding, which is at least one of the legitimate objects of
the humanities, even though it does not offer an idea of humanity
so much as the motive to search for one.

Like practical and ethical humanism, though, aesthetic
humanism also has liabilities. Martin Heidegger made one of its
liabilities the object of an extensive analysis. He demonstrated
that the idea of an immediate response to experience—a response
free of prior assumptions—is contradictory. Consciousness is a
network of unconscious and conscious prior assumptions. It cannot exist without them, and therefore the effort to peel them
away from a response is a little like peeling an onion. Under
each layer there is another layer until, under the final layer,
there is nothing at all. Aesthetic humanism is thus based on an
impossible ideal. It has to be satisfied with degrees of failure

rather than successes. Once this has been admitted, aesthetic humanism remains an extremely useful corrective to the temptation to treat tables as though they were pianos, a temptation that is especially strong in the academy.

A second liability of aesthetic humanism is that it is an attitude toward experience rather than a content. For excellent reasons already summarized, the humanities curriculum has traditionally been organized around a canon of classics. Aesthetic humanism is not attached to a canon. It is useful in approaching classics, but it is equally useful in approaching anything else—an automobile, a kitchen table, three stones in an alley, a hockey game. In certain of its moods, the aesthetic approach can, in fact, be suspicious of the idea of classics, because this idea includes the prior assumption that one group of artworks or experiences, or one attitude or style, is significant while all others are insignificant. Minor artworks and works of popular culture have their own rewards, and the history of art shows that experiences considered beneath serious interest in one period can be the central experiences of the next. Wordsworth and the painters of the Hudson River school made Nature into a humanity. Modern photography has performed the same service for doorknobs and brick walls and other minutiae of everyday life. Marcel Duchamp taught modern man to see the bicycle wheel, Hart Crane focused on the Brooklyn Bridge, Brancusi on the airplane propeller and the turbine blade. The list can be extended indefinitely because every aspect of reality can be significant for those willing to take the time to see and listen.

This is a supremely important public truth. It is also a truth that can be acknowledged in the academy, but it is not one on which a curriculum can be based. To criticize the academy because it is concerned with a particular idea of humanity rather than a variable feast of significant experiences is to confuse an institutional function with the responsibility of each individual for his own spiritual life.

❖   ❖   ❖

Nineteenth-century science promised a great deal. Publicly, it promised to redeem man without changing human nature. Privately, it promised to assume responsibilities that had once belonged to the gods; eventually, to deify humanity. As Nietzsche's theory of the *Übermensch* shows, the decisive evolutionary leap already appeared to be in sight, while to nineteenth-century apostles of Comte it appeared that idea of the useful would lead inevitably to a superior idea of humanity. After this had occurred, nothing would exist that was not completely assimilated by humanity.

Because nineteenth-century science could not deliver on its promises, the leap did not occur and the gods were safe. In fact, they proved surprisingly durable. Nietzsche could imagine his promised land, but like Moses he died on the far shore. A century after his death, Nietzsche would have found the prevailing idea of humanity depressingly like the one whose obituary he wrote.

Contemporary science now promises to complete the work of the nineteenth century. Perhaps it can. Social and genetic engineering, psychoactive drugs, the creation of new forms of life, the enlargement of the mind by computers, the unification of humanity through telecommunications—all these are heady stuff. Surely they are pushing man toward some kind of threshhold.

None of them, however, has been able to formulate a new idea of humanity. Science fiction is fascinating in this respect because its prime objective is to see humanity from the other side of the threshold. At its best, in a work like Philip Dick's *Valis*, for example, it is a Kafka-like exploration of the impact of overwhelming strangeness on the human mind, hence a symbolic statement about the present. More typically, it projects a rather standardized version of the present into the future. Its characters are born, encounter obstacles, and die. Their lives are stretched, like the lives of contemporary men and women, on the rack of the three cardinal virtues and the seven deadly sins. The robots are friendly or threatening, depending on their masters. They do not have wills of their own. Even the aliens have recognizable motives.

How could it be otherwise? If a truly new idea of humanity were formulated, it would be unintelligible. The beings created in its image would seem monstrous or divine. People would gaze at them like goldfish from the underside of the water, seeing them as strange, wavering, unknowable shapes.

This does not mean that the threshold is a fantasy; only that until it is passed, the consequences of passing cannot be known. To examine contemporary culture is, among other things, to search for clues to an emerging idea of humanity. The search is fascinating, but it cannot succeed fully because the idea it attempts to understand has not been revealed. When this idea is revealed, if it is revealed, it will change the past (which is our present) as much as the future.

Meanwhile, the traditional idea of humanity is not so insignificant that it can be abandoned. It continues to provide a measure of common identity and purpose to a society sorely in need of both. To ignore the idea of humanity is to risk an increasingly fragmented and increasingly violent present. The canon of classics therefore remains a vital element in education. It balances—or should balance—the idea of the useful. It may be a fiction, but that remains to be seen.

8

From Knowledge to Information

To a child a library is a house of books. The books are on shelves, and they are cared for by a housekeeper called a librarian. People go to libraries to read books or take them out. The books look tidy on the shelves. It is nice to know they are dusted regularly. There are a lot of books, books about everything. Each book has a special place. If it is taken out, it has to be put back in its special place when it is returned.

A child reads books one by one. To a bright child each book is an adventure to be savored, a window on a new part of the world. The child is unable to conceive of skimming large numbers of books to recover information.

The difference between savoring books one by one and skimming them for information points up two different concepts of a library. According to the first concept, a library is a place for culture and informal education. The public-library movement of the nineteenth century was based on the ideal of making culture and informal education available to all citizens, poor as well as rich. According to the second concept, a library is a storehouse for the massive quantities of data that are the lifeblood of technological society. Although the idea of a library as a cultural resource persists, libraries are increasingly regarded by their proprietors and their most demanding users as storehouses of data.

Although the arrangement of books on the shelves is a convenience, it has a deeper significance. Lewis C. Richards, who invented the cataloguing system for the library at Princeton University, remarked in *Classification: Theoretical and Practical,* "A properly classified library is perhaps the nearest thing there is to a microcosm. A human mind which knew all things might be more perfect in this regard, but in reality no one can or does keep the whole of things in mind as a library does." W.C.B. Sayers draws the same conclusion in *An Introduction to Classification:* "The general philosophical classification seeks to arrange all things in such order that their relationship, the interdependence of the various parts of knowledge, may be understood."

Sayers carries this line of thought further. Rightly observing that philosophers are interested in the structure of knowledge along with librarians, he suggests that the two disciplines are complementary: "The philosophers from Plato to Karl Pearson . . . have tried to make classifications of the whole of human knowledge. . . . They have their counterpart in library classifications . . . that attempt to classify all knowledge—all things—as it appears, or is likely to appear, in books." H. E. Bliss adds in *The Structure of Knowledge in Libraries:* "A bibliographical classification is virtually a classification of knowledge and thought, and conversely, a classification of knowledge is available for bibliographic classification."

Three related concepts are implicit in the philosophical theory of classification. The first is data, which has its physical counterpart in individual books and documents. The second is structure, which has its counterpart in arrangements of books and documents on shelves. The third is knowledge, which can be defined in present terms as data imbedded in a conceptual system. Facts, isolated propositions, and the like are inert. They have to be related according to a theory, a model, a myth, or some other system before they have meaning. In systems of classification, it is the structuring of information that creates knowledge, and the structure of classification is an assertion about the structure of knowledge.

The earliest-known library classification system is the one used at the royal library of Assurbanipal, king of Assyria, in the seventh century B.C. The catalogue consists of twenty-five tablets. Fourteen tablets list works on knowledge of the earth, and eleven works on knowledge of the sky, i.e., the heavens and the gods. While this system may not be very sophisticated, it is unquestionably a statement about the structure of knowledge. Bliss would like every system to be "well constructed," which means, in part, that it should approximate truth or the best current version of truth. Assurbanipal's librarian probably attempted to do just that. From the distance of nearly three millennia, it appears that he derived his structure from myth rather than science.

The statements of modern libraries are considerably more elaborate. Even small libraries normally use modified versions of systems devised for large collections. When millions of books and documents are arranged in a library according to their classification symbols, they are, in effect, an enormous sculpture in paper of the structure of knowledge, a sculpture that is constantly changing because the parts grow at different rates.

The analogy does not go far enough. Sculpture is passive, while a cataloguing system is active. If the user is its master, he is also its slave. By giving knowledge a specific structure, the catalogue creates (or asserts) relationships among its parts. These extend from general relationships among categories like *Philosophy*, *Science*, and *Fine Arts* to microscopic relationships among the parts of specialties like hematology and X-ray diffraction photography. The user of a library is influenced in several ways by the relationships so established. At the very least, when browsing along a shelf of books or through a drawer in a card catalogue, a user encounters certain books and does not encounter others because the system has separated them. *Electricity*, for example, may be part of *Physics* and close to *Chemistry*, but *Electrical Engineering* may be 10,000 or 100,000 books away as part of *Useful Arts* along with *Navigation* and *Mechanical Engineering*. Or conversely, *Electricity* may be close to *Electrical Engineering* but separated by 10,000 books from *Chemistry*. Since research is often influenced by chance discovery (or serendipity), a classification influences the shape of research by making some discoveries probable and others all but impossible.

Moreover, constant exposure to the structure of knowledge expressed by arrangements of books reinforces assumptions about that structure encouraged by agencies outside the library, including the structure of courses in official curricula and the structure of academic departments and government agencies. If no assumptions exist regarding an area of thought, the library tends to create them by imposing patterns of association on the user's mind. A classification system thus encourages the compartmentalization of thought within the standard classifications. It makes orthodoxy easy and thought outside of the compartments extremely difficult. The same tool that creates knowledge may inhibit those unorthodox patterns of thought that enlarge knowledge.

The first Greek librarian whose name has survived is Callimachus, who lived in the third century B.C. The *pinakes*, the catalogue, that he devised for the Ptolemaic library in Alexandria, divides knowledge into six parts:

1. Poets
2. Lawmakers
3. Philosophers

4. Historians
5. Rhetoricians (i.e., orators)
6. Miscellaneous writers

The classification doubtless covers the major areas of the Alexandrian collection. It also reflects the major areas of the ancient educational curriculum, as can be seen by comparing it with the list of standard curriculum authors in Quintilian's *Institute of Oratory*.

The order of the list appears to move from the earliest to the most recent disciplines and from the most noble to the most utilitarian.

The Greeks considered poetry the most ancient of the arts. Because poetry is a vehicle for revelations in the form of stories (or myths) of the gods and prophetic visions, it is also the most noble of the arts. Being a poet himself as well as a librarian, Callimachus doubtless agreed. Orpheus, the earliest of the poets, received his lyre from Apollo. He composed the Orphic hymns, and his songs could move stones and animals and even the stony heart of Hades itself. Though he lived after Orpheus, Homer was also one of the revered early poets, and his two epics had an influence on classical cultures comparable in some ways to the influence of the Old Testament on Hebrew culture.

Lawmakers comes next on the list, perhaps because of the legendary activities of the Spartan lawmaker Lycurgus, said to have lived between the tenth and eighth centuries B.C., and the more historical exploits of Solon, who gave Athens her laws in the sixth century B.C. Category three, *Philosophers*, would probably have included natural philosophers (scientists) and moral philosophers. It would have begun with pre-Socratic philosophers like Pythagoras and Empedocles and Thales. The historians and rhetoricians appeared at roughly the same period in Greek history as the philosophers, but may be placed after them because their arts are less excellent. Finally, *Miscellaneous Writers* appears to be a general category. It must include technical arts and crafts like architecture, agriculture, surveying, mechanics, leaving, and carpentry. These were not considered "liberal" in antiquity and were ignored in the general-education curriculum. Grouping them in the sixth category emphasizes their low standing.

If this analysis is more or less accurate, the classification system of Callimachus is somewhat more "philosophical" than it appears to be on first glance. The categories are arranged in historical order and in descending order of excellence, and they are complementary to the subjects that formed the basis of Greek and Roman education.

A quite different and considerably more subtle theory of the structure of knowledge is outlined at the beginning of Aristotle's *Metaphysics*. Aristotle's version is incomplete, but it was extended by commentators on his work like Alexander of Aphrodisias and Simplicius. It was then absorbed into Arabic philosophy and transmitted via the Arabs to the Latin West at the beginning of the scholastic period. The theory has two aspects. From one point of view, it is a theory about the relations among the main departments of knowledge. From another, it is a practical classification of books—specifically, of the books written by Aristotle.

A central characteristic of the scheme is its division of knowledge into two levels which are not related by genus or species. The first level consists of the works included in the *Organon* (the Greek word for "instrument"). These works deal with method and have no specific content. They are arranged in order of decreasing certainty, of conclusions, beginning with *Categories*, *Peri Hermenias*, *Prior Analytics*, and *Posterior Analytics* which introduce the subject and explain the modes of reasoning that are "demonstrative," i.e., that produce true demonstrations. The *Topics* comes next, which deals with probable truth, and whose "instrument" is the syllogism whose premises are empirical or probable rather than categorical. Next comes *Sophistic*, which treats deceptive syllogisms. To these six authentic "parts" the commentators added *Rhetoric* and *Poetics*. *Rhetoric* is based on the enthymeme, or incomplete syllogism, and seeks to persuade rather than to convince by logical proof. *Poetics* is the most ignoble of the instrumental arts in this scheme, whether or not it is Aristotle's rather than his commentators'. *Poetics* creates illusions through "imaginative representation." Its instrument is metaphor and its purpose enjoyment.

The sciences proper are arranged below the instrumental arts. They are branches of knowledge with specific content. Aristotle mentions only two—theoretical and practical—but the commentators added a third class labeled "productive."

In the chapter titled "The Classification of the Sciences," in his classic study of Aristotle, A. E. Taylor lists metaphysics ("first philosophy, or theology"), mathematics, and physics (natural science) in the "theoretical" category. All three disciplines seek "truths and relations independent of human volition." These sciences depend on demonstrative logic as explained in the *Prior* and *Posterior Analytics.* Although all three sciences are demonstrative in this sense, Taylor suggests that the truth-value of conclusions decreases from theology to physics.

The "practical" category includes sciences that are based on probability. It therefore uses the strategies of probable reasoning explained in the *Topics.* These sciences are called practical because they involve action (*praxis*) determined by moral choice. From most general to most specific, they are politics, "domestic economy," and ethics. Other disciplines including medicine and, on occasion, poetry were assigned by various theorists to the practical category. As for the productive category, although it is not authorized by Aristotle, it is implicit in his thinking. It includes all arts that require "making" and are based on technique rather than theoretical knowledge. The Greek root of the word "poetry," *poien,* means "to make," and poetry was therefore sometimes called a "productive art," a second instance of ambivalence regarding poetry, a kind that librarians call "cross division" or "cross classification."

All systems of classification draw on the logic of classification.

In the late nineteenth century, principles of classification were based on logical traditions going back to the Middle Ages. The *bases* of classification were Aristotle's categories or, more frequently, his five predicables: genus, species, difference, property, accident. W.C.B. Sayers illustrates the application of predicables to cataloguing by a scholastic device known as the "Tree of Ptolemy":

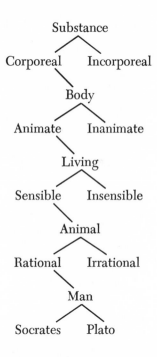

Substance is the primary genus in this scheme and stands at the top of the tree. Each of the terms in the central column is a species of *Substance* but is a genus in relation to the terms below it. In each case, the species is separated out of the genus by the addition of a defining factor: a *difference*.

The Tree of Ptolemy could be used with only a few modifications to provide an evolutionary outline of the structure of knowledge sufficient for a library catalogue. E. C. Richardson once proposed a system based on just such principles:

> Hylology (substance)
> Biology (life)
> Anthropology (man)
> Theology (God)

James Duff Brown, whose system is still found in many British libraries, had a similar idea, as the following proposal for a cataloguing system shows:

> Matter and Force
> Life
> Mind
> Record (i.e., history)

It is equally clear that the Tree of Ptolemy is a useful method for classifying within specialized categories. In fact, instances of it can be found in any large table of cataloguing schedules, as, for example:

Biology

> Zoology
> > Vertebrates
> > Invertebrates
>
> Botany
> > Cellular
> > Vascular

In spite of its neatness, the method of division illustrated by the Tree of Ptolemy creates problems. Normally, a subject is identified by several qualifying aspects. A poem, for example, may be defined in terms of form (sonnet), period (sixteenth century), and language (English), as well as by author and book title. Yet the Tree of Ptolemy allows only one system of classification to be used at a time. If, for example, a division of literature is based on period, literary genre can only be introduced as a subordinate element of each period; whereas if the division is by literary genres, the periods can only be introduced as subordinate parts of the genres. Both systems have positions for *Sixteenth-century Sonnet*, but the first lacks a category for *The Sonnet, 1500–1900*, and the second, for *English Poetry in the Sixteenth Century*. In the first system, knowledge looks historical, in the second it is organized by logical categories, i.e., genres. In the first, it is segmented horizontally, in the second, vertically. What is natural in one is awkward in the other. A decision to use one rather than the other classification scheme will therefore introduce a bias into the possibilities for mental development of those who use the scheme.

S. R. Ranganathan, a twentieth-century theorist, has studied this problem exhaustively. He has formalized what was informal and only partially understood by previous writers. In his theory, each subject is understood to have an array of "facets." A "facet" is an aspect of the specific subject at hand in which users of the system are likely to be interested. In literature, genre is a facet; in education, age; in architecture and chemistry, materials used; and so forth. Each subject has many facets, and Ranganathan arranged the facets themselves under five master headings: personality, matter, energy, space, time.

Ranganathan's analysis clears up many problems of classification at the expense of raising serious questions about the structure of knowledge. Does the catalogue offer an authoritative analysis of the structure of knowledge or at least an approximate one; or are all structures myths? These are weighty questions. Yet in spite of the doubts facet classification raises, it offers considerable benefits. It is flexable, oriented toward the needs of the user, and complementary to modern strategies for information retrieval.

There are similarities between Ranganathan's system and the use of facets of decreasing certainty in the Aristotelian system. There is also an important difference: Ranganathan's system is arbitrary. It is based on the specific item at hand rather than on an organized universal system of knowledge. The more facets that are introduced, the more knowledge is fragmented into individual, isolated boxes. The Aristotelian system, by contrast, is the product of an analysis of the characteristics of knowledge; and in theory, at least, its categories are not arbitrary but innate to the material. The classification that results is therefore not a myth from Aristotle's point of view but objective truth.

The undisputed hero of modern classification is Melvil Dewey, who died in 1931. Dewey's system of decimal classification has some of the same Yankee ingenuity that can be found in the invention of the light bulb and the tin lizzie. Like the tin lizzie, the system could be cloned indefinitely until it covered a good part of the earth. It also underwent mutations. The Library of Congress classification is largely a compromise between Dewey's number code and Charles Ammi Cutter's letter code.

Dewey invented his system when he was an undergraduate at Amherst College. Its first edition, published in 1876, was forty-two pages, twelve of which were subject tables. The sixteenth edition in 1958 was in two volumes with a total of 2,439 pages.

Like Henry Ford, Dewey was a pragmatist. He wanted a system that was simple, so that it could be applied easily; that was expandable, so that "each [could] stand on the shoulders of his successors"; and that had "practical utility and economy." In the interests of these principles, he was willing to forgo rigor. As he wrote, "No theoretical refinement has been allowed to modify the scheme if it would detract from the usefulness or add to the cost."

It is almost required in comments on Dewey that a bow be made to his alleged debt, perhaps via Thomas Jefferson, to Francis Bacon's *The Advancement of Learning* (1605). Bacon had announced his intention to replace Aristotle through the title of his major work, the *Novum Organum* (1620). He was deeply interested in the structure of knowledge, and he found its basis in the structure of the mind rather than in methodology. His three master categories are drawn from Renaissance faculty psychology: memory, imagination, and reason. *Memory* is the source of both civil and natural history, which includes disciplines like geology and geography. *Imagination,* for which Bacon had a healthy contempt, produces narrative and dramatic poetry and fables and allegories. *Reason* produces theology, physics, mechanics, mathematics, politics, medicine, the "voluptuary arts" of music and painting, logic, ethics, commerce, politics, and law. The hidden agenda of Bacon's scheme was to reduce the prestige of memory and imagination and focus attention on reason. In spite of his minor standing as a practicing scientists, his hidden agenda was remarkably successful, and he would doubtless be heartened by the heavy utilitarian bias of twentieth-century classification schemes, including Dewey's.

Dewey's system exhibits "inverted Baconianism," meaning that it lists the arts of reason first and those of memory last. Although Dewey may have derived it ultimately from Bacon, it bears a striking resemblance to a system published by William T. Harris in 1870, as well as a modest kinship to the division of curriculum subjects at Amherst College during Dewey's undergraduate years. There are ten numbered categories:

0	General works	
1	Philosophy	[Works of Reason]
2	Religion	
3	Sociology	
4	Philology	
5	Science	
6	Useful Arts	
7	Fine and Recreative Arts	[Works of Imagination]
8	Literature	
9	History	[Works of Memory]

Whatever this list owes to Bacon or Harris, it is, if anything, anti-philosophical. As Dewey regularly stated in introductions to new editions of his system, he was interested in practicality rather than "theoretical refinement."

His first category is entirely pragmatic: it is intended for whatever will not fit elsewhere. It includes subjects like librarianship, general encyclopedias, general periodicals, and newspapers. It comes first because it is general; but it might just as well have come last, like the *Miscellaneous* category of Callimachus. Categories one through nine divide knowledge along generally curricular lines, but there is no rationale for the order of the major subjects or their associations. If Dewey's organization has a philosophical basis, it is hard to understand why *Philosophy* precedes *Religion* rather than following it; why *Philology* is separated by two categories from *Literature*; and why *Religion*, *Sociology*, and *Philology* are in sequence.

The larger structure of Dewey's system is so practical as to be almost arbitrary. In fact, no matter how much he owed to Bacon, Dewey seems to have leaned toward the notion that it is more important to have a convenient system than a philosophically sophisticated one. The famous decimal notation extends this pragmatic attitude from categories to shelf placement. Having established his ten general categories, Dewey broke each one into ten subcategories, then divided each subcategory into ten, and so on. This resulted in 10,000 possible digits for the basic system. Further subdivisions are created by additional digits. The notation must have seemed more than ample in 1876, but by the turn of the century a process of revision had begun and is continuing at present.

The decimal system has resulted in a gross imbalance among the categories. Even if each of the ten basic categories contained roughly equal numbers of entries in 1876, which is doubtful, they have become distorted almost beyond recognition in the years following for the simple reason that they contain things not then invented. Automobiles, radioactivity, telephones, nuclear energy, television, aircraft, polymers, and hundreds of other branches of knowledge that have emerged since 1876 were omitted from Dewey's schedules. As they appeared, the categories to which they were assigned began to resemble bodies covered with huge benign tumors. Even when space was assigned to a discipline in the original scheme, that discipline often grew far beyond the limits originally anticipated. And as the specialties and sub-specialties grew, the identifying numbers became longer.

Since there are twenty-six letters in the alphabet, a system based on letters rather than numbers has more than twice the number of basic categories found in Dewey. A mixed system, basically a wedding of Dewey and C. A. Cutter, prophet of alphabetical systems, was adopted by the Library of Congress shortly after the turn of the century and is still in use.

The Library of Congress system, however, has needed as much revision and upgrading as Dewey's. Today all major cataloguing systems undergo constant internal revision, although the exo-skeletons of knowledge proclaimed by these systems are supposed to remain constant. The consequence for systems based on printed rules and schedules has increasingly been that they are obsolete before they are reprinted; and in the libraries that use them, the notations on the books are constantly in need of change.

One further observation may be made about the Dewey decimal system. It was the first system flexible enough to gain wide international acceptance. Because its flaws were recognized almost as soon as its strengths, a modified Dewey system was proposed by Paul Otlet and Henri La Fontaine in 1892, which later became the basis of the system of the *Federation Inter-nationale de Documentation.* This international thrust marks the beginning of library networks in the modern sense of the term. It was not stimulated by the philosophical aspects of Dewey decimal, but by its utility and its reliance on numerical notation. At the same time, the spread of a simple classification of the branches of knowledge helped to create an invisible community of librarians and readers who shared the same concept—or the same myth. The Dewey system came much closer to creating a true international community than Esperanto, its contemporary (1887), for the simple reason that it was functional. People did not choose it; they were forced to use it because its advantages made it impossible to resist. The same point can be made for other widely adopted systems such as Brown and Library of Congress. But Dewey is the Homer of international classification. He changed the dream of an international structure of knowledge into an agenda.

The movement from the *pinakes* of Callimachus to the system of the sciences of Aristotle to the Dewey decimal system reveals two tendencies: the classifications become more universal, and they become less philosophical. Their scope increases, but their claim to being anything more than a convenient way of arranging information diminishes. Dewey was willing to sacrifice any "theoretical refinement" for utility, and S. R. Ranganathan (1957) generalized this pragmatism into what amounts to a sophisticated system of *ad hoc* classification. Its only claim is that it maximizes the chance that a reader will be able to locate what interests him.

The arrival of the computer has completed this movement from theory to utility. To understand how this has happened, it is helpful to make a distinction between two types of cataloguing.

If a book arrives at a Dewey decimal library, it is analyzed according to Dewey's schedules and then placed in the system according to its relationship to them. This is called post-coordinate cataloguing, i.e., the coordinates exist before the book is processed. The book is put in a pre-existing cubbyhole. Post-coordinate cataloguing is inevitable in a library with a printed catalogue because the catalogue embodies the coordinates and new catalogue cards have to be filed in the appropriate drawers. The coordinates are useful to the readers in such a library because if the catalogue were not organized in some manner, each reader would have to scan all the cards to be sure of having found all the documents relevant to his interests. Each reader accepts, if only provisionally, the system of knowledge embodied in the catalogue.

If the catalogue is stored on magnetic disks, the need for system disappears, and full pre-coordinate cataloguing is possible. A search of the entire catalogue can be made for every query.

Documents can be arranged in any order at all or no order, so long as each document has a location. In pre-coordinate cataloguing a book or article is analyzed in itself, without reference to standard schedules. It is assigned certain "descriptors" which characterize its content and which are entered in a thesaurus of descriptors available to users. It can also be assigned key terms derived from its title or even its contents, whether or not they are in the thesaurus. A reader who is interested in commas in the first quarto of *Hamlet* can request a sort based on the descriptor "Hamlet" and the key term "commas." The computer will search the entire catalogue collecting two sets of documents, one for *Hamlet* and the other for commas. It will then eliminate items that contain only one of the two elements and present the titles of the remaining items to the user on a video screen or printout. The system is highly efficient, though not, of course, infallible, and it works with any order of book and entry arrangement, including order of accession. Being user-oriented, it does not imply a general structure of knowledge, only the transient micro-order that satisfies the query. It thus answers perfectly the call made by Jesse H. Shera and Margaret E. Egan in 1956 in *The Classified Catalog* for

> a pragmatic and empirical system in which the constituent elements are related with reference to a single isolated trait, property or use without respect to other character-istics. Referential classification admits the possibility of regrouping the same universe of things according to a different trait, property, or use. Such a classification is predicated upon the obvious truth that any single unit may be meaningful in any number of different relationships, depending upon the immediate purpose. In referential classification it is the external relations, the environment, rather than the "essence" of concepts, that are all impor-tant to the act of classifying.

There are now many programs that provide highly flexible "referential" output. By 1980 several had proved adequate to needs of large information-storage systems, and networks based on computer catalogues using these programs had been established in all of the developed countries. In the United States the most important initial source of a general database was the MARC program of the Library of Congress. The MARC program is complemented by numerous regional and specialized programs, RLIN, OCLC, ONLICAT, and MEDLAR, among others. In England an experimental telephone-access system for general information, PRESTEL, is already in operation. Although it is not a catalogue system and concentrates on explicit information such as railway schedules and sports results, it foreshadows direct home access to full information programs.

History is often surprising, and there are both individuals and libraries that remain committed to the idea that a library is a house of books whose central concern is knowledge rather than information. Daniel Boorstin, librarian of the Library of Congress, remarked at the White House Conference on Library and Information Services in 1979:

> I suggest . . . that what we need—what any free country needs—is a *knowledgeable* citizenry. Information, like entertainment, is something someone else provides. . . . *But we cannot be Knowledged:* We must all acquire knowledge for ourselves. Knowledge comes from the free mind foraging in the rich pastures of the whole everywhere-past. It comes from finding order and meaning in the whole human experience. The autonomous reader, amusing and knowledging himself, is the be-all and end-all of our libraries.

As attractive as this concept is, however, the dominant trend seems to be in the opposite direction. The traditional library looks increasingly like a relic of pre-technological culture. The emerging library is a database that makes no statement about the structure of knowledge. If the cataloguing system of the traditional library created a *de facto* community among its users, the emerging library seems to link an enormous number of users without making them into a community. As information networks expand and as satellites extend their range internationally, the number of users who are linked together by them will grow. Because they provide information rather than knowledge, their users will be a confederation without a common myth—a community of atoms perhaps, or a pre-coordinate community.

"A good book," wrote Milton in *Areopagitica*, "is the precious lifeblood of a master spirit, embalmed and treasured up on purpose to a life beyond life." He was thinking of books in the old, pre-technological sense of a canon of classics, of books savored one by one, and of concepts to be meditated rather than data to be used. Is *Chemical Abstracts* the precious lifeblood of a master spirit? Or *Poore's Industrial Index?* Or a catalogue of roller bearings or the tide tables for Norfolk, Virginia, in 1974? Reference works, articles, and ephemera rather than the *Iliad* or *Areopagitica* are the precious life-blood of technological society. Its appetite for them is insatiable, and it indulges that appetite by supporting special libraries and specialized information systems and by changing the orientation of existing libraries.

The movement of classification systems from Aristotle to Bacon to Dewey to the MARC tapes of the Library of Congress is a continuous movement away from theories about the structure of knowledge and toward devices to provide flexible access to masses of data—that is, from post-coordinate to pre-coordinate systems and from formal descriptions to facets, key terms, and descriptors.

Computer terminals are now commonplace in the children's sections of large libraries. The children are delighted. Somehow in their dreaming souls they have already adapted to the future. This future looks at present like a world with extension but no form, a world populated by citizens who create their own individual worlds from chaos every time they type *bgns* on the computer keyboard.

MIRRORS ON THE WALL

9

Words and Images

In the United States and Europe the Age of Movies is drawing to a close. The palaces of film that began with Mark Mitchell's Strand, which was built in 1914 and seated 2000, and culminated in theaters like the Roxy, which seated 6000, are empty. Most of them have been pulled down. Others dot the urban jungle, abandoned and boarded up, like the temples of a vanished race. A few, including New York's Radio City Music Hall, have come to be regarded as valuable antiques and are being preserved by restoration societies and the National Trust for Historic Preservation. Big-budget films of the kind that used to fill movie houses night after night are still being made and still make money, in some cases more money than ever, but movies are no longer a dominant cultural form. They have been pushed aside by television, which will soon be fighting for its own survival against cable TV, videocassettes, and vision discs. Already movies have some of the charm of the obsolete associated with things like handmade pottery and lute music.

Film was the first art form created by modern technology to have an impact comparable to that of printing in the fifteenth century. The comparison is apt because printing and film share the aspiration to be universal forms—to expand beyond community and region until they are national, ultimately global in scope. Film, of course, has the advantage because it is more dependent on visual images, which tend to be universal, and less on natural languages, which are geographically limited. During the fifty or so years that comprise the Age of Movies, film was the chief art form of the developed world and had a profound, sometimes wrenching, effect on the underdeveloped world.

Like all other art forms, film is a mirror. It reflects the values and attitudes of those who create it and, because of the pressure to do well at the box office, those who experience it. It is more seductive, more brilliant, and more various, perhaps, than any art form that has preceded it. By the same token, like all art, it distorts the images it reflects according to the cultural and individual biases of its creators and the special imperatives of its medium. It thus changes—has changed—society's image of itself, and, by a kind of feedback loop, the changing self-image of society changes the image in the mirror. The influences are continuous and reciprocal.

Like printing, film has thus created attitudes and modes of self-awareness at the same time that it has expressed them. These attitudes and modes of self-awareness are now part of the structure of modern consciousness just as, by the seventeenth century, the modes of awareness implicit in the medium of print had become part of European consciousness. Since the process by which this happened is as significant as the result, it will be useful here to introduce two terms from what might be called the sociology of innovation: "classic" and "expressive." They refer to what happens in a culture when a radically new technology is introduced. The classic impulse is to do better what the culture did before the new technology appeared. It is a powerful impulse, and since the motive for invention often is to improve existing techniques, it is often both the motive that creates the new technology and the dominant motive for its use once it has arrived. The motive that led to the invention of printing, for example, was the desire to do better and more efficiently what had previously been done in the *scriptoria*, where manuscripts were copied in the Middle Ages. Early printers used it for just that purpose—to create beautiful and expensive editions, that looked like manuscripts, of the same works that were being copied in the *scriptoria*. The earliest printers, in fact, tended to suppress rather than emphasize those characteristics of printing that made their books different from manuscripts.

In addition to being conservative, a new technology is dynamic. It creates opportunities for new kinds of activity and new products, as, for example, printing eventually created a class of men called authors who earned part or all of their living from royalties on the sale of their books, and whole classes of books, ranging from fiction to religious tracts to self-help manuals to political gossip, that were sold cheaply and widely and reflected that fact in their physical appearance. This is the expressive impulse. To the degree that a new technology is expressive, it seeks both to realize its own inner potential and to rearrange the surrounding culture to accommodate it.

Although the distinction between the classic and expressive impulses is theoretically clear, the operation of these impulses is complex. First, they do not normally succeed one another in a neat sequence from classic to expressive as seems to have been the case with printing. They can occur simultaneously or the expressive phase may precede the classic, which happens frequently in current technology, where the initial applications are often esoteric and applications in the area of traditional social needs come later. This is the sequence followed by movies. The earliest movies were avant garde by today's standards. They stressed visual images almost exclusively, and they used advanced techniques of photography and editing to create exotic effects. Movies that tell stories came later, and only when they had arrived did film begin to exhibit a strong classical thrust.

Second, although the classic phase looks conservative, it contains latent expressive elements. If a technology is truly new, it changes the past in the process of assimilation. Thus, a book is not a manuscript even though it is printed in Gothic type and has hand-illuminated capitals. It is more regular than a manuscript, its text and woodcuts are relatively invariant from one copy to the next, and it is adapted to mass production, which makes it cheaper. By the same token, although a movie of a literary classic may seem to the casual observer to be equivalent to its source, it is not. Simply because it is a movie, it must accede to the internal imperatives of the film medium. The classic impulse is thus ambivalent; even though it seems to be conservative, it revises the past in ways that are compatible with the present.

In a widely discussed chapter of *Feeling and Form* (1953) Suzanne Langer argues that cinema is a new artistic genre that has no deep relation to the genres that preceded it. If she is right, it would seem that the analysis of movies should be based on new, almost *ad hoc* critical principles. Most film criticism is less radical. It begins with the assumption that movies developed from pre-existing artistic traditions. The two traditions most frequently cited are visual art and literature. According to the first, movies are essentially moving pictures. According to the second, film is a twentieth-century equivalent of narrative fiction, drama, and journalism; that is, it is based on words rather than images.

The distinguished art historian Erwin Panofsky provides an exemplary statement of the case for visual images in an essay titled "Style and Medium in Motion Pictures":

> Contrary to naïve expectation, the invention of the sound track in 1928 has been unable to change the basic fact that a moving picture, even when it has learned to talk, remains a picture that moves and does not convert itself into a piece of writing that is enacted. Its substance remains a series

of visual sequences held together by an uninterrupted flow
of movements in space.

This position is attractive and historically persuasive and has
been adopted by a great many film professionals. However, it
leaves out the aspect of film that lures most people into the
theater; namely, the story. It is obvious that moving images are
essential to film and are the most fascinating characteristic of the
medium, but it is also true that a collection of pictures without
a story has very limited audience appeal. A film art that depended entirely on pictures might have created a modest place
for itself a little to the left of still photographs among the visual
arts, but it would never have become a major industry.

The alternative to film as visual images is film as literature.
The best evidence for this theory is the heavy reliance of film
throughout its history on novels and plays and the tendency of
original filmscripts to be created on the analogy of playscripts.
Since the novels and plays that are used and that provide models
for original filmscripts exist prior to the films that draw on them
—in fact, their popularity as literature is often the motive for
making them into films—the literary approach to film is closely
associated with film's classic impulse. After William Caxton set
up his printing press in England in 1476, he issued a five-foot
shelf of ancient and modern classics that included Vergil's
Aeneid, Boethius's *Consolation of Philosophy,* and Chaucer's
Canterbury Tales. A similar pattern is evident in the history of
film. The practice of converting literary masterpieces into films
began before World War I and was further encouraged by the
arrival of sound films in 1928. A.G.S. Enser's *Filmed Books and
Plays, 1928–74* is a convenient guide to the great and not-so-great
literary works that have received this treatment. The point of
view that the literary approach encourages is reflected in George
Bluestone's *Novels into Film* (1966), with chapters on *Pride and
Prejudice, Wuthering Heights,* and *The Ox-Bow Incident,* and
Jack J. Jorgens's *Shakespeare on Film* (1977).

Unfortunately, the literary approach also has limitations. It cannot deal effectively with avant garde and experimental films, and it simply ignores a great deal of the specialized technique that goes into the making of any film, whether literary or experimental. Because it tends to assume that classicism is possible—that past can be re-created without being revised—it is preoccupied with the fidelity (and infidelity) of film to source, to the neglect of more interesting questions about film as film.

As Erwin Panofsky correctly observes, during its infancy film was a novelty. The fascination of moving images was enough for the public and gave filmmakers a remarkable opportunity to explore the potentialities of their medium. The earliest films were brief sequences shown to one viewer at a time in peepshows and Kinetoscopes. They showed motion for its own sake: people running, horses galloping, machines moving. As the attraction of pure images wore off, short sequences were produced of sporting events and vaudeville and magic shows. Some of this work used trick photography that looks extraordinarily sophisticated even today. The films of George Méliès are noteworthy examples. However, vaudeville and magic shows had limited commercial potential, no matter how intriguing they were. As Panofsky himself confesses, "the craving for a narrative could be satisfied only by borrowing from the older arts."

The first film to satisfy this craving was *The Great Train Robbery* made by Edwin Porter in 1903. Porter's film was not an intriguing curiosity. It was a sustained narrative modeled on narrative fiction and told through pictures. Its commercial success demonstrated that the future of movies lay in storytelling, which is to say that the key element in the transformation of movies from a minor amusement to a dominant cultural form was a literary element, a plot.

A plot is neither imagery or words, it is a structure. The most useful discussion of plot is still Aristotle's *Poetics*. Aristotle begins by defining all art as imitation. Art is a mirror of reality, but of the inner nature of reality rather than its appearances. Artists differ, says Aristotle, according to the objects they imitate, the means they use, and the manner (or point of view) they choose. The object of narrative artists is action, and the action is objectified in plot. A proper action has a beginning, middle, and end, and the parts should be related by probability or necessity understood as internal conditions of the work rather than as natural cause and effect, since the action may involve magicians and deities as well as normal people. Plot is the first and most basic element of the six that comprise a drama. It is, says Aristotle, the "soul" of drama. Character comes next, followed by thought, language, song, and spectacle.

Turning from objects to medium of imitation, Aristotle observes that some artists use visual images (painters), some rhythm (dancers), some rhythm and melody (musicians), some words and rhythm (writers of epic), and some a combination of words, rhythm, and melody (dramatists). Where film might be fitted into Aristotle's system is relatively easy to guess. Film is a narrative art using the medium of visual images rather than language. It is a narrative art in terms of its object, action, and it is a visual art in terms of its primary medium, visual images. Since the plot is the defining characteristic—the soul—of the work in which it appears, the most basic affinities of film, at least in Aristotle's system, are with epic, but its secondary affinities are with painting.

If this line of analysis is acceptable, it explains why film inevitably transforms the past while assimilating it. In their classical phase, movies are drawn to a past that is entirely literary. Yet they are expressed through images rather than words. The glory of images is that they speak with great precision and dominate the imagination. The glory of words is that, being more suggestive, they stimulate the imagination rather than dominate it. A novel, for example, is imaginatively open. To read *Tom Jones* or *A Tale of Two Cities* or *The Big Sleep* requires an imaginative creation of characters, costumes, groupings, and settings that the words only suggest. While the reader's eyes see words on a page, his imagination sees eighteenth-century London or revolutionary Paris or twentieth-century Los Angeles. With each reading, the world that takes shape in the imagination changes because each reading requires a fresh act of creation. Pictures are less open probably because they say so much so eloquently. Much of the creation has already been done by the painter. In a movie, the creation is done by the director, the actors, the designers, and the photographers. No reader knows what Philip Marlowe, the detective in *The Big Sleep*, looks like. There are probably as many versions of Marlowe as there are readers of the book. Everyone who goes to the film, however, knows exactly what Marlowe looks like: he looks like Humphrey Bogart. This closure, or focusing does not occur because film is hostile to imagination. It occurs because film is visual. A film must decide what people look like, what clothes they wear, whether they right- or left-handed, whether their shoes are polished or dirty. This decision making takes place throughout the process of filmmaking down to the humble prop assistant who must spatter blood on the wall of the murder room or have it drip down the wall or leave it in a pool on the carpet. The imagination of a reader can compose innumerable variations or ignore the detail entirely. In a finished film, however, there can be one—and only one—bloodstain. This is a general imperative of the film medium, which applies whether the film is relatively straightforward or highly experimental in its technique. It does not make film worse or better than literature, only different.

In spite of film's use of narrative, and in spite of Aristotle, the lure of the "words versus images" dichotomy remains strong. Perhaps this is because discussions of literature have, since the Romantic period, tended to assume that the lyric poem rather than the novel or play is the definitive form of literary art. Since most lyric poems do not have plots in the normal sense of the term, language is emphasized almost to the exclusion of other elements. It is thus understandable why a filmmaker should think of literature as words: he is merely repeating what literary critics have told him. But when filmmakers manage to get away from self-conscious theorizing and into comments about the practical business of making films, they sometimes sound remarkably Aristotelian. A comment by the Russian filmmaker V. I. Pudovkin illustrates the point:

> If we consider the work of the film director, then it appears that the active raw material [of film] is no other than those *pieces of celluloid* on which, from various viewpoints, the separate movements of the action have been shot. From nothing but these pieces is created those appearances upon the screen that form the filmic representation of the action shot. And thus the material of the film director consists not of real happenings in real space and real time, but of those pieces of celluloid on which these processes have been recorded. This celluloid is entirely subject to the will of the director who edits it.

There is some reminiscence of Bergsonian flux here, not to mention a strong hint of the director as God, but the essentials are clear: a film is a representation of an action. It is created by assembling the pieces of celluloid in which "the separate movements of the action" have been fixed. The creation of a film consists of the manipulation of these pieces of celluloid, and the result depends not on reality but on the will of the director.

There is nothing in this concept that Aristotle would reject. Pudovkin's director is not a writer of words but a maker of images, a cousin to Aristotle's poet who creates plots by arranging episodes in an articulated sequence. As such he is also cousin to the modern novelist or playwright.

This, however, is not the whole truth, although it is an aspect that is often ignored. The other side of the argument is presented by one of the great artists of contemporary film, Ingmar Bergman:

> . . . the script is a very imperfect *technical* basis for a film. And there is another important point in this connection that I should like to mention. Film has nothing to do with literature; the character and substance of the two forms

are usually in conflict. This probably has something to do with the receptive process of the mind. The written work is read and assimilated by a conscious act of the will in allegiance with the intellect; little by little it affects the imagination and the emotions. The process is different with a motion picture. When we experience a film, we consciously prime ourselves for illusion. Putting aside will and intellect, we make way for it in our imagination. The sequence of pictures plays directly on our feelings.

This passage illustrates the bias toward the interpretation of literature as language noted earlier. To Bergman, literature is automatically "the written work" and film is "the sequence of pictures." Reading requires a "conscious act of the will"; film is immediate and (presumably) effortless.

Bergman may be right on both scores. It may be that in the post-McLuhan era reading demands "a conscious act of the will in allegiance with the intellect." However, literary historians can still recall a distant era when the young eagerly absorbed multivolume novels by authors like Bulwer-Lytton, James Fenimore Cooper, and John Galsworthy without feeling that the task placed a severe strain on their wills or intellects, and many of those now living can remember slipping away from homework or chores to sample the forbidden delights of Hemingway's *The Sun Also Rises* or Faulkner's *The Hamlet* or even Tolkein's trilogy of the ring. Moreover, Bergman's hint that literature makes no direct appeal to the imagination would have saddened the heart of Samuel Taylor Coleridge, who devoted most of his major work of criticism, the *Biographia Literaria*, to the thesis that imagination is the central element of both the creation and the appreciation of literary art.

Of course, to suggest that Bergman's understanding of literary experience is questionable does not in any way detract from the authority of his comments on film. Bergman is not talking about making a film but about experiencing it. The two are different, and it is possible that if he were discussing the way films are created, he would pretty much agree with Pudovkin's idea of the director as maker.

Moreover, he is saying that movie audiences are passive. Instead of participating in the creation of the artwork, as happens during the reading of a novel and in a different way during a live stage performance, the imagination of the movie audience is like a wind harp being played by the images on the screen. It is dominated by the images. This is probably one of the reasons why movies are frequently called "escapist entertainment."

Bergman has identified a genuinely non-Aristotelian element in movies. Aristotle remembered the ancient connection between drama and religion. Originally, the Greek audience was not a passive group of spectators but a kind of congregation that actively participated in the completion of a sacred rite. Today no less than in Aristotle's Greece, live drama depends on the participation of the audience as well as on the performance of the actors. Each stage performance is a communal creation of actors and audience. A film, on the other hand, is fixed. Its images have been established once and for all by the director, the photographer, and the film editor. Once the movie begins, those images will go on whether there is an audience or not, and every screening will be exactly the same, unless the power fails or the film breaks and has to be spliced.

The audience at a film has no influence whatever on how that film develops from beginning to middle to end, and the composition of the images tends to determine even how they are seen. Once the possibility of creative involvement is eliminated, the way is open to the kind of passivity that Bergman considers typical of film audiences: "When we experience a film we consciously prime ourselves for illusion. Putting aside will and intellect, we make way for it in our imagination." The audience floats, as it were, on the sea of images.

The desire to forget the burdens of will and intellect and to shed the oppressive sense of being trapped in a specific identity —local habitation, a name, a social security number, duties, enemies, personal fears and ambitions, frustrations, deadlines— is at times overwhelming. It is abetted in the movies not only by the impersonality of the images (we know they are patterns of light and shadow, and we feel none of the responsibility toward them that we might toward flesh-and-blood actors), but also by the darkness of the theater and the musical continuo that spans pauses in speech. Everything conspires to lull the film audience into reverie.

Popular cinema cooperates with desire for reverie rather than opposing it. This is why mass-audience movies are so conscious of genre formulas. A formula—the formula for romance, for example, or thrillers or westerns—is something predictable. If it is made sufficiently obvious through advance advertising and the use of identifying motifs in the introductory scenes of the movie itself, the audience can settle immediately into its reverie, secure in the knowledge that there will be no surprises. Nothing will happen that will require conscious mental effort. The art film, it should be admitted, attempts to move in just the opposite direction—to awaken and shock and engage the audience. But even today, when television is competing with movies as a source of predictable formula entertainment, formula movies remain staples of the box office, as witness the James Bond series or Clint Eastwood's spaghetti westerns or Walt Disney's family comedies or *Love Story* or *Alien* or *Star Wars*.

To carry this line of thought a step farther, if one impulse in movies is to have nothing unexpected happen, the logical extension of that impulse is to have nothing at all happen. This is clearly un-Aristotelian. A movie in which nothing happens would be an imitation of a non-action. It would be pure imagery whether or not it moved. Peep-show movies were imitations of non-actions. Andy Warhol apparently yielded to a minimalist impulse with his film *Empire*, which is a three-hour shot of the side of a skyscraper and moves, but only barely. Warhol's film was a *tour de force* and was not intended to set box-office records. It is of interest chiefly as an experiment in creating a movie without a plot. To the degree that it succeeded, it illustrated Bergman's point that the pure flow of images has a hypnotic attraction that is satisfying all by itself.

Aristotle wanted a plot to have a beginning and a middle and an end, and he wanted the parts to be connected to each other by probability or necessity. These are modest requirements, and by and large, people who create movies observe them. But people who consume movies are different. They are often just as pleased by seeing a movie from middle to end to beginning as by seeing a movie from middle to end to beginning as by seeing it in the normal order. No matter how the movie was made, seeing it this way is a step in an un-Aristotelian direction, a step, one might say, toward Andy Warhol.

It is thus fair to say that while film has literary elements in the Aristotelian sense it also has tendencies undreamed of in the *Poetics* that stem from the way images are experienced by the typical moviegoer. These tendencies are suppressed by art movies and art-movie houses, which make audiences self-conscious. On the other hand, they are encouraged in films that take advantage of the hypnotic, almost hallucinatory, quality of moving images. This category includes films like *Wild Strawberries* or *Juliet of the Spirits* (even though these are clearly in the "art-movie" category) and also, more typically, popular films that depend on spectacular visual effects rather than logical plots.

Most movies are somewhere between the extremes of the well-made play and Warhol's *Empire*. Action movies like the James Bond series, which emphasizes brilliant photography, lush imagery, constant surprise, and half-ironic formula situations that make it unnecessary to worry about the priorities of plot, are probably closer to the Warhol extreme but not so close to shock the audience into self-consciousness.

William Faulkner understood the non-Aristotelian aspect of film very well. Unlike such disgruntled Hollywood writers as Nathanael West, F. Scott Fitzgerald, and Budd Schulberg, he was quite philosophical about the difference between writing and making movies. He worked in Hollywood, off and on, for some eighteen years. During this time he contributed to such forgettable masterpieces as *Louisiana Lou, Banjo on My Knee*, and *The Land of the Pharaohs* (which includes perhaps the finest trick pyramid ever filmed) as well as to a few minor classics like *The Big Sleep* and *To Have and Have Not.* During the same period he wrote some of his greatest novels—*Light in August, Absalom, Absalom!,* and *The Hamlet.* His mature attitude toward film, like that of his friend Howard Hawks, is indulgent acceptance of its non-literary element. It is summarized in the following story from Joseph Blotner's "Faulkner in Hollywood," which first appeared in the symposium volume *Man and the Movies* (1967):

> The Chandler novel [*The Big Sleep*] was a complicated one, and whatever architectonic skills Faulkner and his collaborators were able to bring to bear were not enough to keep some reviewers from having—like Bosley Crowther —"only the foggiest notion of who does what to whom." The confusion was little dispelled by the pell-mell pace— the writers had "kept it moving"—and by the six murders dominating the action. One patron asked Hawks who had committed one of them. Hawks replied "I don't know. I'll ask Faulkner." When he did, Faulkner confessed that he didn't know either. Hawks then sent the question to Chandler, who answered that the butler had done it. Hawks telegraphed in reply, "Like hell he did. He was down at the beach house."

So much for the imitation of an action with a beginning, middle, and end, whose episodes are related by probability or necessity. To the consternation of all Aristotelian literateurs, *The Big Sleep* has been an enduring box-office success. Its emphasis on pace and tone at the expense of coherence was a foreshadowing not only of films like the James Bond movies but also of fast-paced television series like *The Man from U.N.C.L.E., Mission: Impossible,* and *The Dukes of Hazzard.*

In spite of important, even central, qualifications, literature is not words and film is not images. Both are imitations of an action, and the imitation is "made" by the arrangement of episodes, whether they are objectified in words or in Pudovkin's bits of celluloid. In spite of Bergman's very suggestive comments, film *is* related to literature, and it may be that in all but a few exceptional cases, whoever conceives of the action of a movie—the screenwriter, the director, or the editor surrounded by spools of film in the cutting room—is its essential maker. When a novel or a play is the source of a film, the person who adapts it as a screenplay is the maker in the same way that Shakespeare was the maker of *Othello*, even though Shakespeare derived *Othello* from a short story by Giraldi Cinthio and it was first staged— doubtless with cuts and improvisations—by Richard Burbage and the players of an acting company known as the King's Men.

Greek and modern European drama grew out of liturgy. Movies did not. They evolved in well-known steps from the sequential photographes used in nineteenth-century peep shows. They became brilliantly articulate before they could talk. They are dominated by a tradition, the one that best expresses their nature, that actions should be expressed visually rather than verbally. If this is true, images have the same relation to film that words do to novels and plays. Aristotle put images, which he called *spectacle*, fifth or next to last in his list of the elements of drama. Clearly, this will not do for film. What is unique in film is not its object but its means of imitation, which is moving images. Thus film is both the same and different from literature, and it inevitably changes literary works when, in its classic phase, it seeks to reproduce them. The fact that its plot is objectified in images makes the typical film both more imaginatively closed and more phantasmagoric, less dependent on causality, than the typical novel or play. Howard Hawks was a movie director when he made *The Big Sleep*. But he behaved like a literary critic when he sent his telegram to Raymond Chandler about the butler's having committed the crime: "Like hell he did. He was down at the beach house."

10

Filming Shakespeare

To such terms as "post-modern" and "post-industrial" should a term like "post-literate"? be added, as Marshall McLuhan's theories appear to require?

The term is probably needed. The global village has two communications systems. The first serves refined communication among the proprietors. Perhaps as computers learn to talk to each other more intelligently, the proprietors can stop talking to one another. Evolution will produce a race of single-fingered proprietors who push buttons. Eventually, the buttons will be mechanized. . . .

That is a long way into the future. For now, the proprietors need to communicate. They do so in various specialized languages, which have to be learned in schools as laboriously as was Latin by the clerics of the Middle Ages. The languages are called mathematics and chemistry and accounting and FORTRAN IV.

The second communications system of the global village consists of films, television, records, photographs, automobiles, furniture, and clothing. These are the outward and visible expressions of the invisible reality of world culture. None of them requires the ability to read, as is inevitable and proper. Natural languages —English, Hindi, Japanese, and the like—have divided people throughout history, have chained masses of people to particular regions, to local historical traditions, to millennia of cultural paranoia. In the nineteenth century the Polish physician Ludwig Zamenhof invented Esperanto, the language of hope, for the explicit purpose of globalizing consciousness. Esperanto turned out to be only another language, but Zamenhof's heart was in the right place.

Technology has solved the problem by making language unnecessary. The world media depend on images and music, not language. Consequently, the inhabitants of the global village have recovered either the Edenic simplicity of man before he learned to talk or the Utopia of a society purged of the need for schools and classrooms, depending on how one looks at it.

Because true technological cultures first emerged in Europe and the United States, there was a period of three or four decades beginning at the end of the nineteenth century when they were identified with Western imperialism. There were even fears that the entire planet was being Americanized. Nothing could be farther from the truth. It was not American culture but world culture that was transforming humanity. All local and parochial cultures, including American, were equally obsolete. Not surprisingly, cultures resist their extinction, some by censorship and by paroxysms of political and religious reaction. The effort is futile. When world culture is kept out of the front door it leaks into the basement, pours through the windows, and is blown down the chimney by every passing breeze.

World culture is happening in the most public manner possible, but it is almost totally ignored. It is replacing everything that men have traditionally cherished: the local gods of threshold and hearth, hallowed life-styles, the special feel of landscapes, time-honored forms of architecture and cooking and dress, and the names of heroes and sacred places. It is a revolution without wars or charismatic leaders, a revolution of world consciousness. The people who comment on it most loudly are the people who are getting hurt; namely, the people with a vested interest in the things that are disappearing. Their laments and prophecies of doom are audible enough, but nobody is listening. In the age of automobiles, who wants to hear a long-winded defense of the horse?

A great deal can be said for world culture. The unity of the human spirit is not such an ignoble ideal. According to Teilhard de Chardin, it is the supreme object, the Omega Point, to which evolution has been tending since the first proton captured the first electron shortly after the big bang that created the universe. Teilhard's name for the spiritual unity of man was the Noosphere, the sphere of intellect, which rises on the double foundation of the biosphere and the geosphere.

This is a lofty ideal. In his book *The Phenomenon of Man*, Teilhard seems to equate the Omega Point not only with the unity of man but with the union of man and God. It is as though in becoming conscious, Creation becomes the material image of the divine force that gave it existence in the first place.

Something like a world culture now exists, although it is still imperfect. Its instruments of communication are clumsy, even though they are miracles by the standards of the nineteenth century. And the culture itself is still fragmented. It retains many of the hostilities of the era of tribal and national cultures, and there are pockets of cultural lag everywhere. A few areas of the world are still almost untouched by it, and everywhere in the modern world the forces of unity are opposed by parochial habits of thought.

In spite of these imperfections, world culture is a reality. But when compared to the lofty ideal of the Omega Point, it is a gigantic disappointment. It is a culture of fads and gadgets and pop entertainment; of Clint Eastwood westerns and Bruce Lee epics of Kung Fu; of *Mork & Mindy* and the Beatles; of counterfeit Levis and Adidas T-shirts; of Hilton hotels and Disney theme parks and Honda CVCCs and Volkswagen Rabbits. It is also a culture of almost anarchic diversity produced by the confluence in the marketplace of the products and traditions of every local culture in the world community. If it is a culture filled with promise, it is simultaneously a terrifying culture, filled with changes that outpace the ability of governments and individuals to adapt. It seems to threaten identity itself. For many, it seems to be a culture on the edge of insanity.

Of course, things are not as bad as they seem. They never are. If there is an obvious disparity between the promise of world culture and what it has so far delivered, it is because world culture in the true sense is less than a century old, perhaps less than half a century old. It has no central content, no established canon of classics.

Here, an analogy from history will be useful. Roman civilization was immensely successful in the political, military, and administrative areas. Culturally, however, it was impoverished when compared to Greek civilization. The Romans solved this problem by importing the high culture of Greece wholesale. They copied Greek architecture, Greek sculpture, Greek religion, Greek science, Greek philosophy, Greek music, and Greek literature. The process had what is called in Chapter 9 a classic and an expressive phase. The two phases appeared in different ways in different areas of culture. They were not necessarily sequential, and frequently, imported Greek traditions were modified as they merged with native Roman elements. The Romans read Greek classics, for example, in the original, used Greek slaves to teach them to their children, and frequently translated them into Latin for those who did not read Greek—all classic impulses. The aesthetic attitudes that were formed by this reading experience shaped original works by Roman authors. In fact, the practice of using a classic model for a "new" literary work was so common that it was formalized in rhetoric as the theory of imitation and was taught in the schools along with the

classics to be imitated. From Homer the Romans produced
Vergil, from Euripides they produced Seneca, from Menander
they produced Plautus, from Herodotus they produced Livy,
from Demosthenes they produced Cicero. In each case, the imitation was both like the original and different from it because of
the new medium and context.

At the same time, Romans were producing works that expressed Roman traditions and for which no obvious Greek models
existed: the *Annals* of Ennius, the lyric poems of Catullus, the
odes and epistles of Horace, *The Lives of the Emperors* of
Suetonius and the *Germania* of Tacitus. The list could easily be
expanded. The point is that the expressive works were not independent of Greek culture. Even as they asserted their originality,
they were deeply influenced by Greek literary traditions in their
style and their aesthetic effects.

As long as Latin was the universal language of the educated,
that was enough. The Christian Middle Ages inherited the
Graeco-Roman tradition via the Latin language. To this tradition
they added the Bible and a succession of Christian works. Again
the pattern of classic imitation and expressive innovation is evident. During the early Middle Ages imitation predominated. By
the Carolingian period, however, uniquely Christian genres, like
the hymn in a unique, non-classical form using accentual prosody
and rhyme, had established themselves. When Latin gave way
to the vernaculars in the later Middle Ages, the pattern recurred.
Translations, imitations, and expressive works influenced by the
earlier cultural forms appeared in Italian, French, Spanish,
German, and English in the fourteenth and fifteenth centuries. In
the fifteenth and sixteenth centuries, with the triumph of
humanism, the effort to upgrade vernacular cultures by domesti-
cating the culture of antiquity became a self-conscious reform
movement. The tension between the classic and expressive
phases of this movement is evident not only in the works produced under the influence of Renaissance humanism but in the

battle, which became intense in the seventeenth century, between the self-styled "ancients" and the "moderns."

Is not the same pattern evident in today's emerging world culture? It is a culture that lacks a well-established content of its own. Consequently, at the same time that it is producing unique forms of expression, it looks to the past for guidance. Photography allows cheap reproductions of the masterpieces of world art to circulate in such immense volume that it creates what André Malraux has called "a museum without walls." The same recording companies that flood the world market with jazz, rock, and disco sell recordings of the whole range of "classical" music from Gregorian chant to Gustav Mahler. Movie producers whose staples are thrillers and westerns and romances also release film versions of *War and Peace, Don Quixote, Tom Jones,* and *Moby Dick.* By all odds the most ambitious example of the classic impulse in media art is the plan announced by the British Broadcasting Corporation in 1978 to produce all thirty-seven of Shakespeare's plays in color versions for television. Here is classicism in its purest form. The world's supreme dramatist is being disseminated through one of the most advanced technological media to a world audience. The German word for television is *Fernsehen,* "seeing at a distance." By satellite, television can cover the entire planet. Imagine the whole world watching Touchstone cavort with Audrey, or Othello, dying with a kiss, on Desdemona's bed. It is a miracle that comes close to the Omega Point. Can Cedric Messina, "onlie begetter" of the series, be the Messiah obscurely foreshadowed by Teilhard's cries in the wilderness?

Dante remarked that all translators are traitors: *Traduttori, traditori.* Marshall McLuhan refined Dante's idea into the observation that the medium is the message. The corollary of the McLuhan thesis is that if the medium is changed, the message changes along with it.

What happens when Shakespeare is translated from the stage to the movie house or the television screen? Is it possible to conserve the essential qualities of his art, or does something happen to the work along the way, much as Homer's *Odyssey* was transformed when "imitated" by Vergil and as Plutarch's life of Marc Antony was transformed when Shakespeare made it into *Antony and Cleopatra*?

If the question is approached head-on it is impossible to answer. Every stage production of a play is different from every other. The variables include the design of the theater, the actors, the director, the costumes, lighting, and sets, and the audience. Every movie of a Shakespeare play is different from every other for the same reasons. There is not one Shakespeare; there are innumerable Shakespeares. To speak of the essential qualities of Shakespeare's art is misleading because the qualities that are stressed are different in each production whether on the stage or in the moviehouse.

But this is not exactly the question posed by either Dante or Marshall McLuhan. The question they raise is whether, when a play is transposed from stage to film or videotape, there is an *essential* change in its form and message, a change that is inevitable and independent of the incidental qualities of the direction and the performance. This question is valid and important and touches on the deep structure of media culture. Rephrased, it asks whether a new culture can ever assimilate an older culture without changing it: *Traduttori, traditori.*

Shakespeare is an ideal subject for an inquiry along these lines. Since the eighteenth century, his works have been a living influence on German and Russian culture. In the twentieth they have become widely known beyond the normal range of Western literature both as literary texts and in performances in countries as diverse as Kenya, India, Thailand, China, Korea, and Japan. Inevitably, they were among the first classics to be filmed, and since the advent of sound and color, movies of Shakespeare plays have been made in England, America, Germany, Italy, Mexico,

Czechoslovakia, Denmark, and Japan—some sixty full-length features according to the *Folger Shakespeare Filmography* compiled in 1979 by Barry Parker. The list includes adaptations such as Akira Kurosawa's *Throne of Blood* (*Macbeth*) and Nicholas Nayfack's *Forbidden Planet* (*The Tempest*) as well as direct transcriptions, but it omits the considerable number of musical, operatic, and dance films based on Shakespeare (e.g., *The Boys from Syracuse,* based on *The Comedy of Errors,* and *Catch My Soul,* a rock *Othello*), not to mention innumerable educational films containing excerpts from the plays. Since many Shakespeare films have circulated—in fact, are still circulating—to a world audience in theaters and on television, it is probably fair to say that Shakespeare is the first classic author to be assimilated into world culture. There are not only "translations" of his works in abundance but the translations are significant. They meet the needs of world culture more fully than the other classics of narrative fiction and drama that were adopted once or twice by the media and then forgotten.

Two Shakespeare films are of special interest as translations: Laurence Olivier's *Henry V* (1944) and Franco Zeffirelli's *Romeo and Juliet* (1968). Both are color productions, and both were immensely successful. Using these films for reference, one can ask three questions: first, what are the differences between theater and film as artistic media? Second, how are these differences likely to affect any drama—Shakespeare included—that is made into a movie? And third, how do these differences show up in *Henry V* and *Romeo and Juliet*?

The first two questions have to do with the poetics of film. The third can only be answered in terms of the first two. In the answering, points should emerge that reflect back on and qualify the theory.

Here, then, are three postulates on the differences between stage drama and film.

The first is that there is a difference in the kinds of appeal made by stage drama and film. To put it as plainly as possible, stage drama is inherently a social medium whereas film is a private and personal one.

The social appeal of stage drama can be illustrated in several ways. For example, people typically go to the theater in groups. A play is an occasion. A flyer from a local theater club (notice the word "club") offers group subscriptions with adjoining seats and adds that "gold card" subscriptions are available to admit the purchaser not only to the play but to a gala buffet-reception afterward, during which he can mingle with actors, directors, and designers, and other gold-card subscribers. The emphasis of the flyer is explicitly on drama as a social event. Now carry the analysis from the flyer to the event itself. When people go to a play they usually dress up. Black tie and cumberbund or long dress and the family jewels are common on an opening night. Dressing up is a social act in itself, an act of display. During the play at least one intermission is mandatory. It is a chance to show off the black tie and cumberbund or long dress and family jewels, to discuss the play, and to eavesdrop on what everyone else is saying. All of this is not incidental; it is part of the life of the theater. Evidently, stage drama heightens awareness of community in the audience rather than depressing it. Even while a play is being performed, if it is a good drama, that awareness is retained.

The social bond is not something that exists only for the audience. It is also—and most importantly—a bond between the audience and the actors. Obviously, great theater demands great acting. The actor's version of this truism is that great theater demands great audiences. If the audience depends on the actors for stimulus, the actors are equally dependent on the audience for response, and the response becomes a stimulus that influences the acting. The finest actor can be made to feel incompetent by an audience that is apathetic or hostile. Certain annual dramatic festivals like the Shakespeare festivals at Stratford, Ontario, and Ashland, Oregon, have achieved remarkable artistic standards. Their successes are partly due to their audiences, which have remained relatively stable over the years. The audiences have been trained by the performers, and the performers have learned from the audiences. The social loop is better defined and more powerful at these festivals than at theaters where the audiences and the performers are constantly changing.

Anyone who attends the theater regularly knows the excitement of a production that works. A fine tension develops between the audience and the actors that is like the combination of aggression and cooperation during a game between two evenly matched tennis players. When this happens, everyone knows it is happening, and the feedback intensifies the effect. In a few productions a moment is reached when the rapport is so perfect that no *action* of the actors can be wrong, and no *reaction* by the audience can be inappropriate. The result is a communal experience shared by everyone present.

This kind of experience revives momentarily the religious experience communicated in the rituals and liturgies out of which drama grew in every culture where it is a significant artistic form. It may be added that the social dimension of stage drama is clearly recognized by theater architects, playwrights, actors, and directors: by architects in lobbies designed as promenades, in runways, thrust stages, theaters-in-the-round, and theaters with entrances that bring actors through the audience to reach the stage; by playwrights in asides, soliloquies, anachronisms, and topical allusions; by actors in everything they do that appeals directly to the audience; and by directors in strategies that gloss the action of the play in order to make it fully accessible to the audience, as, for example, by using fascist uniforms to costume a production of *Julius Caesar*. Occasionally, dramas are written that appeal directly to the communal and religious roots of the art: *Our Town, Dionysus 69, Hair, Godspell, Jesus Christ Superstar.*

What is true of theater in general is particularly applicable to

Shakespearean drama. The Globe Theatre formed a circle enclosing both audience and actors. Most of the audience stood in a dense crowd around a stage thrust forward to the center of the circle, ensuring close contact between the audience and the performers. As Shakespeare's frequent use of asides and soliloquies shows, this intimacy was used functionally by dramatists, even though it conflicted with the interior realism of the dramatic action. Since the players offered their dramas in repertory and the audience was relatively constant, the intimacy of the stage must have been reinforced by an almost personal familiarity among all concerned. The sense of community established during a performance at the Globe must therefore have been at least as intense as anything with which twentieth-century audiences are familiar.

If drama is inherently social, what about movies? In the first place, a movie theater is a dark room, almost a womb. People do not typically go to the movies in large groups, and if two people go to the movies for other than erotic reasons, they usually forget about each other the minute the lights go off. Walker Percy, in his novel *The Moviegoer*, accurately characterized the film audience as a collection of loners. (The fact that some couples go to the movies to neck reinforces the point. Movie theaters are as attractive to lovers as parked cars because they offer the same benefit—privacy. In the back row of a theater lovers are alone. Conversely, who ever took a girl to the first night of *King Lear* to pet in the balcony?)

Except for pretentious films like *Gone with the Wind* and *Lawrence of Arabia*, movies have no intermission. Practice at the end of a film varies widely. Originally, the house lights went up and there was a ten-minute break between the end of one showing and the beginning of the next. This was done for commercial reasons—to clear the theater—and on the assumption that movie audiences, like theater audiences, would prefer to come in at the beginning and leave at the end. Most theaters still follow this practice. Many, however, offer "continuous runs." The continuous run is a response to a curious fact: many people do not care whether or not they see a film from the beginning. They prefer to be able to drift in at any time. They may see a film straight through, but they are equally satisfied to see the middle and the end, to enjoy the previews and the cartoon, and then to see the beginning, and even—if they like the movie— to repeat the whole cycle. Movies are made with beginnings and middles and ends. What the continuous-run phenomenon shows is that many people are indifferent to this. They do not want Aristotelian definition but experience—raw experience, surrender to the flux, escape from definition in the way described by Ingmar Bergman in the preceding chapter, a kind of mechanically induced daydreaming.

Finally, there is the element of feedback. In a play, as has been noted, a psychological loop is established between performers and audience. Nothing like this can occur in a movie theater. The images on the screen are patterns of light, not living actors. They are not affected by applause or hissing. They will be the same in a packed house or an empty one. And they will be the same every time the movie is shown. This affects the audience. Occasionally, movie audiences applaud or hiss or walk out, but for the most part they are passive. No social bond between the audience and the actors can exist. Why should the audience join to respond to a film when response is useless?

It should be emphasized here that there is nothing wrong with the appeal that movies make. It is neither superior nor inferior to the appeal of stage drama, it is merely different. To repeat the original postulate: stage drama is inherently social, movies are personal. Stage drama speaks for and celebrates a community; movies are for individuals. Perhaps it is inevitable that an art form that aspires to world status should appeal to individuals. A community has a history and an identity that differentiates it from all other communities. A world art form has to appeal at a level that is universal rather than parochial; to individuals in their separateness rather than to individuals as members of national or linguistic or class or ethnic groups. There is a parallel here to the movement from knowledge to information examined in Chapter 8.

Second postulate: stage drama is organic, movies are inorganic. To put the idea in different terms, stage drama is an act of what critics of the Romantic period called imagination; movies are acts of what the Romantics called fancy.

Here the basic fact about stage drama is that it is written by an author. It begins with the author's intuition of a possible drama—what Henry James called the "germ" of the finished work. Whatever his ultimate success, in writing the drama the playwright seeks to make everything in it an expression of the original intuition. Ideally, the intuition is fully expressed in the completed drama, and nothing is included that does not express it. This is what is meant by organic unity. Organic unity is most natural in a literate society where each artwork is created by a single artist. Its relevance to pre-literate societies that produce folk and communal art is less clear. A similar problem is created by post-literate art forms. Media art is seldom produced by one artist. The requirements of its technologies make it communal, and in a communal situation the authorial control needed to achieve fully organic form is seldom possible.

If a play is truly or approximately organic in its script form, it tends to retain that form when produced. The objective of the director is to discover the organic center of the play and to make sure that the added expressiveness of voice, costume, gesture, and scene makes the unity even more apparent to the audience than it is on the printed page. A good performance of a drama is like a symphony being played by a group whose members work to the same purpose. Moreover, any stage performance—good or bad—is continuous. The play must be created anew each night. When the first scene begins, there is no turning back. The performance moves forward inexorably in good Aristotelian fashion from beginning to middle to end and then stops. In practice the script may be a disaster, the direction inept, and the acting abominable, but the aim is always to make the play work, which means that it should unfold as a continuous, harmonious process.

Again, Shakespearean drama is, if anything, better adapted to these conditions than modern drama. The scripts are fluid and continuous because Shakespeare's theater lacked a curtain and the plays were performed without pauses between scenes and without intermissions. The shift in the English theater of the late seventeenth century from thrust to proscenium stages and the use of increasingly elaborate scenery was detrimental to Shakespearean drama and has frequently been abandoned since World War II in favor of open stages and unit sets. This change has not only restored the original fluidity to the plays, but has forced the audience to cooperate once again with the actors in creating the imaginary world in which the action is set.

By contrast, the essential fact about the way films are made is that the process is fragmented. The original text may be the work of a novelist, playwright, or screenwriter. However, the text is almost always transformed by committee before it becomes a shooting script. In other words, it becomes a mosaic of contributions from several individuals who enter the creative process at different times and may not even know each other. This is why novelists, who are used to control of the creative act, have often been frustrated by their Hollywood experiences.

After the shooting script comes the filming. Movie making does not aim at achieving a single, continuous performance that is filmed. Instead, it requires a large number of "takes" which are seldom more than two or three minutes long. The shooting script for Tennessee Williams's *A Streetcar Named Desire*, for example, requires 128 separate takes, which means that the average take is somewhere between 60 and 120 seconds. It would seem logical to film the takes in sequence as they occur in the script. But the order of the takes is usually determined by the sets called for in the script. All of the takes that will require a given set or location are shot at the same time, and a given take may be shot half a dozen times before the director is satisfied. Thus, the sequence of the takes has nothing to do with the sequence of events in the script. To complicate things further, some takes are discarded during editing, and others may be transposed from their original positions in the script. The extent of creation done after the takes is suggested by the fact that for the 8000 feet of film in a typical 90-minute movie the film editor may have 200,000 feet from which to choose.

It follows that during the filming of a movie the actors can never respond to a given scene in terms of the whole drama. They are forced to act minute, disconnected fragments, often several times over, and their only source of understanding of how those fragments eventually fit together is from their prior reading of the script. In fact, the editing process makes it all but certain that during filming, nobody knows exactly what the finished product will be. Even after basic editing, the director may change things further, as illustrated by the well-publicized revisions by Francis Ford Coppola of *Apocalypse Now*. Needless to say, the sense of fragmentation created by working in small, disconnected units is intensified for the film actors by the fact that during takes they face technicians and other members of the film crew rather than an audience.

In all these senses, a film is inorganic in comparison to a play. A film is a work of fancy, to borrow a term from Samuel Taylor Coleridge, a work of aggregation and association, an assembly of fixities and definites. This said, it should immediately be added that the completed film can, and usually does, give the impression of being a continuous whole. In this respect it resembles the communal art of pre-literate societies. Ballads and folk epics and cathedrals are normally the work of innumerable anonymous hands; yet they seem unified to the modern reader or viewer.

Third postulate: stage drama is realistic, film surrealistic. "Realistic" means that stage drama shows the audience the world that is in front of it rather than the inner world of the psyche. This sounds complicated but is actually quite simple.

A drama is seen from a fixed point, a seat. The characters are fixed and discrete, and they have a continuous life; that is, they do not abruptly appear and disappear. Psychologically, the viewer is above them in the sense that he knows everything about them that there is to know (i.e., what is in the dialogue and on the stage). He observes them as he might observe his neighbors cooking a steak in the backyard, and he can turn his attention from one to another at will. Occasionally, the playwright calls for expressionistic or fantastic devices, but these are exceptional rather than normal; and in the case of expressionism, the distortions are not to disorient the viewer but to tell him more than can be told by non-expressionistic techniques. Transitions in stage drama are reminders of the realism of the form. No matter how fast the director tries to make them, they take time. The lights go off. Stage hands scuffle, machinery clanks, and the costumes of the actors rustle. Fifteen seconds of darkness intervene. Shakespeare's transitions are much more fluid. In theory they can be almost instantaneous, but in practice attention is called to them. The characters recite couplets or form a tableau before leaving. A new scene usually begins with someone calling out the watch or describing the moonlight. There is a formal ritual of transition. Only after the ritual is completed does the action of the new scene begin.

All this changes in the movie theater. Consider the viewer: what he can look at is controlled by the camera, and his angle of vision is constantly moving. In terms of the illusion created, the viewer is constantly being whisked from middle distance to the air over the action to a position two inches from the heroine's right eyeball and back to middle distance. This movement is instantaneous. It defies normal experience of space and time. It is wholly unnatural; hence it can be called surrealistic. Erwin Panofsky identifies the effect in his essay "Style and Medium in Motion Pictures":

> The spectator occupies a fixed seat, but only physically, not as the subject of an aesthetic experience. Aesthetically, he is in permanent motion as his eye identifies itself with

the lens of the camera, which permanently shifts in distance and direction. And as moveable as the spectator is, as moveable is, for the same reason, the space presented to him. Not only bodies move in space, but space itself does, approaching, receding, turning, dissolving, and recrystallizing as it appears through the controlled locomotion and focusing of the camera and through the cutting and editing of various shots.

The apparent movements of the film viewer are so commonplace that they are taken for granted. They seem natural rather than surrealistic. In a sense they *are* natural, for they are part of the grammar of filmmaking. They are by-products of the technique of making film by takes and then linking the takes together by cut, fade, and dissolve. In a two-minute sequence in a western, for example, the camera may shift from the sheriff with his hands on his hips to the outlaw drawing his gun to the sheriff drawing *his* gun to the outlaw, struck by a bullet, collapsing in the street. When the outlaw appears in the second take, the sheriff miraculously disappears and vice versa. In the first take the viewer may be fifty feet away from the sheriff; in the last he may have moved effortlessly to the sheriff's side; he may even be looking at the dying outlaw's wound through the sheriff's eyes. None of this could happen in a stage drama. Even to approximate it would turn a play into a sensational exercise in the tricks of stagecraft. Yet it is part of the elementary grammar of film. It seems to audiences to be simple, straightforward narration.

The indirect implications of cut, fade, and dissolve are as significant as their direct ones. For example, a scene that is intensely serious on the stage from fifth-row center can become black comedy when the faces of the actors are presented in extreme close-up—when the pores on the heroine's cheeks look like fish ponds and the creases in her forehead when she frowns like the Great Smoky Mountains. A case in point is Tennessee Williams's *A Streetcar Named Desire*. When the play was made into a movie, the close-ups undercut emotions that had seemed passionately sincere in the theater. The result was a brilliant work of film art, but it was closer to black comedy than tragedy.

All this happens without anyone really trying. It is innate to the film medium. Films cannot be made without it. Often directors consciously exploit the surrealistic potential of film. As early as the peep shows, short films were made using the medium to create magical or comic effects impossible on the stage. In 1927 Abel Gance experimented in *Napoleon* with subliminal editing, peripheral vision, three-dimensional effects, superimposition, split screen, and mirror photography. The Keystone Cops were filmed in fast forward and reverse motion to great effect. Not much has been learned since the silents about trick film effects, but modern directors have often used such effects continuously to express intense psychic experience: slow motion and distorting lenses and exotic perspectives (*Wild Strawberries*); complexly involuted time (*Petulia*); simultaneous actions (*8½*); the continuous use of the monstrous and the dream sequence (*The Cabinet of Dr. Caligari, Fellini Satyricon*).

The distinction between the realism of stage drama and the surrealism of film is significant. By happy coincidence it is similar to the distinction made by Coleridge between Wordsworth's realistic art and his own surrealistic style. Wordsworth's art, wrote Coleridge, strives "to give charm to the novelty of things of the present day . . . by awakening the mind's attention from the lethargy of custom and directing it to the loveliness and wonders of the world before it; an inexhaustible treasure, but for which, in consequence of the film of familiarity and selfish solicitude, we have eyes that see not; ears that hear not; and hearts that neither feel nor understand." His own art, says Coleridge, is "directed to persons and characters supernatural or at least romantic; yet so as to transfer from our inward nature a human interest and a semblance of truth sufficient to produce for these shadows the willing suspension of disbelief that constitutes poetic faith."

Coleridge's remarks are valid and hard to improve on. If stage drama is interested in a broader spectrum of experience than is suggested by his phrase "loveliness and wonder," it is certainly true that stage drama asks us to look at life directly and without the "film of familiarity and selfish solicitude" that usually prevents us from seeing it. By the same token, film is nothing if not a succession of "shadows" that create a "semblance of truth." Like the spinning lights of the hypnotist, they shape and direct the "inward nature" of the viewer, who gives them life from his own spirit because they have no life of their own.

If the preceding observations have merit, there is a corollary: to speak of transferring Shakespeare to film, as a crate of oranges might be transferred from California to Wisconsin, is nonsense. A change must occur during the transfer, and because Shakespeare's works are plays, not film scripts, they resist the change. A Shakespeare movie may be half play and half film, a moving experience or a disaster, but it is not—and cannot be— Shakespeare as presented on the stage. At the same time that Shakespeare is being "imitated" he is being changed.

It is tempting to assume that there are two extremes in the making of Shakespeare movies. At one extreme is the stage play photographed. At the other extreme is the film that uses a Shakespearean plot and passages of Shakespeare's dialogue.

A few Shakespeare plays have, in fact, been photographed on stage, while others have been moved with only minimum changes in text and performance styles from the stage to the studio. Richard Burton's *Hamlet* is in the first category. It was photographed on stage between regular performances in New York in 1964. Olivier's *Othello* is in the second. It was photographed with almost no changes from the 1964 National Theatre production in London. Even in these films, however, cinematic techniques are used. Camera angles change, sequences of action break down into "takes," and instead of having the whole stage constantly in view, the movie audience frequently sees a pair of characters or a single character in close-up.

The results in both the Burton *Hamlet* and the Olivier *Othello* were mixed. The stage productions were good, the films mediocre. This fact recalls Dante's complaint: *Traduttori, traditori.* If the motive for translating Shakespeare from stage to screen is to enrich the cultural content of the film medium and to disseminate classic values to a mass audience, is not a crippled translation worse treason than no translation at all? Everything was included in film versions of the Burton *Hamlet* and the Olivier *Othello*, one might say, except the qualities that made them capable of appealing easily and powerfully to audiences as stage plays. To appeal to movie audiences, Shakespeare has to fit as naturally into the film medium as he does on the stage.

Olivier's *Henry V* is much less a stage play photographed than his *Othello*. Perhaps because it is adjusted so nicely to the capacities of film, it has seemed to many viewers a definitive example of the fact that Shakespeare can be transferred to film without being changed. In fact, a close examination of the shooting script and the film itself leads to exactly the opposite conclusion.

The film begins with a playbill floating through the air. According to the shooting script, "It hits the camera and reads: The Chronicle History of Henry V with his battle fought at Agincourt, by Will Shakespeare." This shot dissolves to "Long Shot: Aerial view of London in 1600. Camera tracks back to reveal the City in extreme Long Shot, then tracks in to centre, first the Bear Playhouse, and then the Globe Playhouse." The view of London is drawn from Visscher's famous engraving of the city published in 1616. The mode of presentation is familiar. It is a standard technique for beginning a movie. Its key feature is the pan shot. The pan shot has nothing to do with the methods or even the possibilities of the legitimate stage, much less the Globe Theatre. Notice, too, that the audience is already floating around in space. Call this style A: cinematic style.

Next there is a cut to a reconstruction of the Globe incorporating most of the architectural theories—now mostly abandoned—

evident in John Crawford Adams's famous model of the Globe in Washington, D.C. Cut to groundlings entering and orange girls hawking wares. Cut to boy hanging sign giving the title of the play.

At this point the performers enter. They are not performers in the play called *Henry V*. They are performers in a drama about a group of Renaissance actors performing *Henry V*. Olivier is careful to demonstrate that he is Richard Burbage playing Henry, not Henry himself.

Great efforts ensue to achieve performances so awful that the movie audience will recognize them as *bad* acting. In case someone misses the point, the Bishop of Ely begins to fling armfuls of documents right and left around the stage. Audience (that is, Globe audience) guffaws. Canterbury flubs lines. More hilarity. The scene ends as the Chorus draws a curtain that probably never existed in the Globe across an equally imaginary inner stage. It starts to rain. The script reads: "Noise of rain and audience grumbling." The point is that the Globe was an open-air theater and that the English climate was just as deplorable in 1600 as it is today. This is the only point. It has nothing to do with Shakespeare's play. It is a distraction from Shakespeare's play. Its sole purpose is to teach generations yet unborn about the stage in the sixteenth century. Call this style B: Introduction to English Lit.

Now dissolve to Southampton. This is a major transition. The script reads: "Chorus walks back and indicates the curtain. He goes out of picture left. Camera tracks up to the curtain, and we dissolve to Medium Long Shot of Southampton, exactly as depicted on the curtain. Camera tracks on. Then pans left to reveal in Long Shot the stern of a ship, and Southampton quay."

In other words, the audience is suddenly watching a conventional movie. Fleet preparations. Real boat. Olivier has started to play Henry V rather than Burbage, and the acting no longer calls attention to itself. This is style C: standard movie realism. It continues in the next scene, the death of Falstaff.

Now cut to the French palace. It is not a real palace. It is a fairytale palace by Walt Disney out of the Duc de Berry's Book of Hours. Courtiers are strewn around the throne room like the Seven Dwarfs. King Charles is lounging on the floor. The Duke of Burgundy is reading at a lectern. Other courtiers are propped up against various pillars.

This is style D: Nature imitating art. Instead of a real court of the fifteenth century, Olivier has given his audience a fairy kingdom, a medieval court seen through the wrong end of a telescope and authenticated by its reminiscence of medieval miniatures.

Cut to Harfleur. Real cannon. Echoes of the battle of Atlanta in *Gone with the Wind*. Olivier is back to style C: movie realism.

And so on through the film.

Judging by the response of critics and audiences around the world, Olivier produced a genuine masterpiece. In fact, thirty years after its premiere the film remains as enthralling as it was when it was released.

The point is that *Henry V* is a film that has the reputation of being both successful and faithful to Shakespeare. Successful it is. Faithful to Shakespeare it is not. A relatively straightforward, highly unified play has been converted into a mosaic of different styles presented in a surrealistic framework of space and time. Within eight scenes, four entirely different styles are employed in ways that are frequently not only unrelated to the play but actually detract from it, as in the episode of the Bishop of Ely and his scattered papers. On the stage a comparable violation of the integrity of Shakespeare's play would be a debacle. In the film it is part of the flux.

Olivier alternates his styles for a purpose. Movie audiences have no trouble with remote times and strange settings. They are a part of the romance of movies. Such audiences do, however, have trouble with long speeches. They also have trouble with the kind of sustained, uncompromising confrontation with life that Shakespeare asks of them. Consequently, Olivier uses alternating styles to interiorize the action of the play, to convert it from a realistic action to an action of the mind. Style A establishes the context: it says, "I am a movie; react to me as a movie, not a play." Style B introduces the world of stage drama, pokes fun at it, and announces in no uncertain terms: "Stage plays are (were) like this; this movie is going to stay away from them." Styles C and D then introduce the wholly disarmed viewer to the glories of idiomatic film making. Style C (realism) says: "I am important. Pay attention to me." Style D says: "I am charming and lovely and associated with French politics (silly) and French love (wonderful). I am not as central to this film as style C." Style C, of course, is the style of the two great scenes in the film—the night visit of Henry to his troops and the battle of Agincourt on the following morning. Because of the mixing of styles, these scenes were triumphantly successful, and the same mixing made the wooing of Katherine in the fairytale court (style D) both moving and delightful. In keeping with the nature of the film medium, Olivier changed Shakespeare's play from a history play—something that aspires to objectivity—to a kind of musical alternation of themes and variations.

In Shakespeare films that are more explicitly cinematic—i.e., less imitations of stage plays—than Olivier's *Henry V*, the central problem is what to do about Shakespeare's poetry. Much of this poetry was originally created to offset the lack of scenery on the Elizabethan stage. Movies, conversely, have had an embarrassment of riches in the scenery department from the earliest days of the silents and got along excellently with no words at all.

There seems to be a specific conflict between Shakespearean drama, which wants to talk, and movies, which want to project images. Apparently, the more a Shakespearean film yields to the film medium, the less of Shakespeare's dialogue there is going to be. The Max Reinhardt and William Dieterle film of *A Midsummer Night's Dream* (1935), for example, discards large chunks of Shakespeare's dialogue not only to squeeze the play into a 132-minute format, but also to make room, within that format, for a lengthy ballet using Mendelssohn's music and featuring large numbers of extras in diaphanous gowns and without brassieres. Although this dance was derived from Reinhardt's earlier stage production, it fit the movie perfectly. As for the missing dialogue, it is mostly superfluous to the movie since the things it describes are obvious from the sets. Or is it? To say that Shakespearean movies can do without Shakespearean dialogue may be an easy way out. At least one producer, Joseph Papp, demonstrated in his television version of *Much Ado About Nothing* that by becoming more rather than less cinematic through the use of close-ups during description, the director can preserve a surprisingly large percentage of Shakespeare's lines.

Franco Zeffirelli is a filmmaker rather than an actor-director from the legitimate stage like Olivier. Consequently, his Shakespeare films are cinematic from the beginning. They are not compromises with stage drama or mosaics of different styles that allude to the uneasy tension between stage and screen, but movies pure and simple. Zeffirelli's *Taming of the Shrew* has many delightful features, but it is crippled by a problem that is characteristic of the film medium. Its two stars, Richard Burton and Elizabeth Taylor, were having a much-publicized love affair at the time that they played Petruchio and Katherine. This was not fatal to Shakespeare's text. It did, however, shift attention from the text to the stars, and from first-rate acting to the delight of seeing two notorious lovers playing out their roles in Renaissance costume. Whether for this reason or for its Max Sennett zaniness, the most delightful episode in the film is Burton's long chase of Taylor over a tile roof, which ends when both tumble through a hole onto a haystack. This has no more to do with Shakespeare than Reinhardt's diaphanous ballet, but it is irresistibly funny. Another feature of the film that is attractive but non-Shakespearean is its evocation of Renaissance genre painting. On the other hand, *The Taming of the Shrew* is one of Shakespeare's talkiest plays, and the talk is obviously functional. Zeffirelli did not think so. He cut the dialogue heavily in order to speed up the action. Where the dialogue is retained, it is mostly mumbled. No matter. The attraction of the film is its stars and its sight gags rather than Shakespeare's language.

In *Romeo and Juliet* Zeffirelli reversed his field. Instead of choosing two well-known stars as his leads, he chose two unknowns: Leonard Whiting and Olivia Hussey. The strong plot and the clearly drawn characters of the original play were retained, and all of the essential—that is, the familiar—dialogue was kept, although there was extensive cutting which was increased when the film's original running time of 152 minutes was reduced for the English language version to 139 minutes. Even after this cutting, some of the dialogue seemed digressive. Mercutio's Queen Mab speech and Friar Lawrence's speech on the magical properties of herbs are examples. Zeffirelli emphasized action, and in the context he established, the speeches often impeded the action. His film is probably best understood in relation to the action-thriller genre familiar in both movies and television.

The most brilliant scenes in the film were those which caught the excitement of Zeffirelli's approach—the brawl between the servants of the Capulets and the Montagues, the ball scene, the nude love scene, and the brilliantly photographed duel between Romeo and Tybalt. All of these evolved from Shakespeare's text but took on a life of their own in the film. Action, however, needs to be paced, and Zeffirelli's solution to this problem was highly effective. It has nothing to do with Shakespeare and everything to do with film. Time and again in his movie, the camera pauses to study scenes and faces. As in *Henry V*, the technique is authenticated by the allusions of the images to Renaissance genre paintings and portraits. In general, Zeffirelli's film is more consistent than Olivier's. It is entirely in Olivier's style C—movie realism. Since Renaissance paintings are themselves realistic, Zeffirelli's allusions to them reinforce his effects instead of providing counterpoint, as in Olivier's allusions to the miniatures in the Duc de Berry's Book of Hours. The images flow as smoothly as they do in formula action movies like *A Fistful of Dollars* or *Moonraker*. The viewer's psyche is caught up in the flux, hypnotized, enchanted. The film is not Shakespeare at all. It is a curiously hard-edged costume thriller to which each viewer contributes the delights and anguish of buried experiences.

As the classics are translated and assimilated, they are changed. Certain kinds of experience that they express cannot be expressed in the new language, while others that were impossible in the old language become not only possible but natural.

Even though Shakespeare's plots are retained, when translated into film they become visual rather than verbal. The sense of community that is the foundation of living theater is replaced by the pleasure of directed reverie, which is a solitary occupation. An art that held a mirror up to nature is replaced by an art that is phantasmagoric, fragmented, surreal. It may be a mirror, but the images that it produces are different. Logic in the form of necessary or probable relations between events counts less than rhythm and tone. Psychological analysis gives way to psychic stimulation. Love is not a matter of words but of naked bodies, and conflict is expressed by charging masses of horses and flashing swords rather than by the point-counterpoint of debates and challenges. The plot is a constant, but the method of objectifying its underlying significance changes from speeches by living actors playing to a living audience to images that resonate only because they summon responses deep in the psyche.

A parallel was suggested early in this chapter between the post-literate culture of technology and the pre-literate culture of the Middle Ages. This parallel can now be extended. The mass medium of the Middle Ages was liturgy, which communicated to the illiterate masses through music, vestments, ceremony, and ritual. It was necessarily formulaic because, like a drama, it had to be re-created each time it was celebrated. Only by making liturgy into a rigid formula could the Church ensure that it would be properly re-created in different locations and different ages.

Is film a modern equivalent of medieval liturgy? Like liturgy, film transcends barriers of geography, and like it, film has a deep mass appeal that does not depend on literacy. Film is more various than liturgy, but underlying its dazzling variety are there not formulas that are as rigid in popular cinema as the formulas of the medieval Mass?

Behind the films there is a technological and entrepreneurial elite that communicates in the esoteric languages of science and technique. Is this elite comparable to the Latin-speaking elite of the Middle Ages? Is it the servant of the collective dream of the Noosphere, and are movies the materialization of the dream? Perhaps Teilhard de Chardin could tell us if he were alive. Perhaps Shakespeare, if he were alive, could make the dream more coherent.

11

Revising the Past

The first Shakespeare film owned by the Folger Shakespeare Library was a print of Max Reinhardt's *A Midsummer Night's Dream* starring Anita Louise, Olivia de Havilland, Mickey Rooney, and Joe E. Brown. The print was donated by Warner Brothers in 1936. Quite properly, it was promptly deaccessioned by the Library's director, Dr. J. Q. Adams. Eventually, it wound up in the film collection of the Museum of Modern Art in New York. It was on cellulose nitrate film. Under the best conditions this type of film is hazardous. Within a single year, 1978, there were fires in three American film archives. The worst occurred at the film storage facility of the Bureau of Archives. It consumed 27 million feet of outtakes of Universal newsreel film dating between 1914 and 1965 and destroyed the building in which the film was housed. If Dr. Adams had been less circumspect in 1936, William Shakespeare, Edmund Spenser, Sir Walter Raleigh, and John Donne might have gone up in flames along with Anita Louise and Mickey Rooney.

When the use of cellulose acetate made safe film storage possible following World War II, the Folger reentered the film business. As of 1980, its archive included thirty-one full-length silent and sound films, fourteen videotapes, and thirteen full-length adaptations such as *The Throne of Blood*, a Japanese version of *Macbeth*. The collection was augmented in 1978 by a donation of seven half-hour films on Shakespeare by the National Geographic Society, and in 1980 by videotapes of the first six plays in the BBC's ongoing presentation of the complete dramatic works on television. Obviously, the archive is growing at a healthy rate.

The existence of such an archive demonstrates the continuing vitality of the classic impulse in media art. As the preceding chapter has shown, such an archive is extremely useful in understanding what happens to the past when it is brought into the present. Another aspect of such an archive is equally interesting. The past exists in two ways: in its presentness through translations into current media, as when Olivier makes a film of *Hamlet*, and in its pastness as a collection of artifacts and documents, as Shakespeare continues to exist, in apparent indifference to movies, in quartos and folios and innumerable editions. If an archive of Shakespeare on film and videotape is taken as an example of the past as present, the question naturally arises of how the past as present affects the past as past. How, in other words, do the films in the archive influence the way the texts in their original written form are read and interpreted? The evidence for answering this question can be found in current Shakespeare criticism. It shows the mind in the process of re-shaping the record of the past, for the most part unconsciously, to accord with its own experience of the present.

In an article published in *Anglia* in 1978 titled "Shakespeare in Buch und auf der Bühne"—"Shakespeare in Book Form and on the Stage"—Werner Habicht observes that from the beginning Shakespeare studies have drawn on two quite different bodies of material. Scholars have analyzed text, sources, influences, conventions, and the like in an effort to provide definitive solutions to the problems posed by Shakespeare's plays. Although the goal of definitive solutions has receded in almost direct proportion to the energy expended to reach it, as an ideal it remains influential. It is the benchmark against which various degrees of failure are measured.

Meanwhile, directors and actors have to keep the plays alive at the box office. To do this they must plan each production in terms of the variables of current theatrical style, the talent available, and the character of the audience. Consequently, there is no such thing as a definitive production. Each production is different, each elicits a unique set of meanings from the text. Frequently, these meanings seem indifferent to, or actually scornful of, the meanings proposed by scholars. In the library the plays appear to be securely anchored to the page by rows of black letters; in the theater they are Protean, infinitely variable and elusive. Harley Granville-Barker, a theatrical producer as well as a scholar, described Shakespeare's text as "a score waiting performance." Sir Tyrone Guthrie, a director with a lifetime of theatrical experience, wrote in *Tyrone Guthrie on Acting* (1971):

> . . . only some, and by no means always the most significant, aspects of a great play reveal themselves to the reader. . . . The total meaning of a play includes sight and sound, not merely the intellectual apprehension of the symbols on a printed page.

There is nothing in Sir Tyrone Guthrie's comment with which the most hidebound Shakespeare scholar could disagree. The divergence between scholar and director is not caused by different modes of perception. It is created by the nature of scholarship. The imperative of scholarship is rigor. When it is not rigorous, it ceases to be scholarship and drifts into impressionism. Rigor, in turn, depends on documentation. It is possible to be rigorous when discussing one of Shakespeare's sources—say Sir Thomas North's English translation from the French of Plutarch's *Life of Marcus Antonius*—because that source has an objective existence. A reader who doubts an assertion about the source can go to the library and read it for himself.

Stage productions are ephemeral. After the curtain goes down on closing night, a stage performance ceases to have an objective existence. A scholar can refer to it, but the references have to be from memory, which is unreliable, or to secondary sources. There is no way for the reader to evaluate them unless he has seen the same performance and remembers it in exactly the same way as the scholar. This problem is troublesome even in a successful study such as Marvin Rosenberg's *The Masks of Macbeth* (1977). It is possible to attempt reconstructions of famous productions—witness the excellent work of Charles Shattuck on productions by Booth and Kean and Kemble—but the most meticulous reconstruction is only a pale and uncertain shadow of the performance itself.

The advent of film has changed this situation fundamentally. Unlike stage drama, film has an objective existence. Films can be preserved like books and kept in archives for anyone who needs to inspect them. They thus open to the scholar a whole spectrum of insights into Shakespeare that reveal themselves only in performance.

Although the Folger archive is still incomplete, it already holds eight full-length versions of *Hamlet*, six of *Macbeth*, and ten of *Romeo and Juliet*, to name only three plays. Fewer than half of these films—perhaps ten out of the total twenty-four—are worth intensive study, but ten plays are a quantum advance over no plays at all. They permit the scholar to place variant productions of the same play under a microscope and to document observations as precisely as a quotation from the 1604 quarto of *Hamlet*. Since variant productions involve variant interpretations of the text, this is equivalent to making accessible to scholarship an expanded range of meanings latent in the text. And because many of these meanings are both mutually exclusive and entirely valid within their productions, they raise questions about the validity of the concept of unitary interpretation.

A qualification is needed here. The basic grammar of film is cut, fade, and dissolve, and long shot, medium shot, and close-up; and the rhetoric of film includes voice-over, musical continuo, unusual camera angles, trick photography, and special sound and lighting effects. There are no one-to-one equivalents of these devices in Shakespeare's text, which was intended for the stage. When scholars use films to probe traditional areas of scholarship, they must recognize that many characteristics of film, often those most typical of film art, have only an indirect relevance to their interests. However, even indirect relevance can be useful. Cinematic devices can be employed expressionistically to make thematic points. The Russian director Grigori Kozintsev, for example, created a splendid Heathcliff-like ghost for his film of *Hamlet* by posing the actor in silhouette against a dark sky and photographing his billowing robes in slow motion. The technique distances the ghost from the generally realistic setting of Kozintsev's Danish court and thus retains the suggestion offered by Shakespeare's Horatio that the ghost may be an hallucination rather than a true spirit. Richard Burton could not use slow-motion photography in his stage production of *Hamlet* (which is preserved in a 1964 videotape), but he conveyed the same idea about the ghost by limiting its presence to a gigantic helmet-clad shadow projected on the rear wall of the theater.

The two areas in which the record preserved on film contributes most obviously to the interpretation of Shakespeare's text are thematic interpretation—understanding the point of view of the play as a whole—and interpretations of individual scenes, lines, and words. Ideally, the two should be complementary—the part and the whole should harmonize. However, it sometimes happens that a given production is disappointing *in toto* but has brilliant moments that deserve attention in spite of inert material surrounding them.

A simple example of the way a film can contribute to thematic interpretation is provided by Laurence Olivier's *Henry V*. Olivier based his film on the common interpretation of Henry as an ideal warrior-king and the play as an epic celebration of English valor. This is the interpretation popularized by E.M.W. Tillyard in

Shakespeare's History Plays. The fact that Olivier made his film in 1944 and dedicated it to "The Commandoes and Airborne Troops of Great Britain" must have made the interpretation seem especially appropriate. The two central scenes in the film express this interpretation perfectly. They are the night before the battle of Agincourt when Henry walks in disguise among his disheartened troops, a scene that recalls the British experience after Dunkirk, and the battle itself with its sweeping images of the triumph of stouthearted English yeomen over the confident, heavily armed knights of France.

There are, however, problems of interpretation in Olivier's film, and those problems point directly to a revisionist view of the play. In the first scene of Shakespeare's play, Ely and Canterbury argue that if they do not divert Henry's attention from domestic to foreign affairs he will expropriate "All the temporal lands which men devout/By testament have given to the Church" (I, i, 9–10). When Henry decides to invade France, should we regard him as a dupe of the clergy or an intelligent and dedicated patriot?

Olivier eliminates the first possibility by making clowns of Ely and Canterbury. As noted in Chapter 10, during the speech on Salic Law they drop their papers, lose their place repeatedly, and start to bicker with one another. These idiots could not dupe anyone, much less the noble Harry. The Globe audience, which is still part of the film at this moment, breaks into loud guffaws and catcalls. Olivier has not merely slanted Shakespeare's text, he has intentionally made a travesty of it in order to preserve Professor Tillyard's unsullied hero. The film is not perverse. It is simply less complex than the play as written.

In two other Shakespeare films, Olivier draws on interpretations that do seem perverse rather than oversimplified. His *Othello* relies heavily on F. R. Leavis's essay "The Diabolic Hero and the Noble Intellect," in which Othello is described as a "ferociously stupid" egoist. In the words of John Dexter, who directed the film, he is "a pompous, word spinning, arrogant black general." There is a hint of racism here, and it is reflected in Olivier's performance in the title role. The result is an Othello who is brilliantly acted but who is almost the antithesis of Shakespeare's noble protagonist, not to mention common sixteenth-century ideas about Moors. By its failure, the film refutes the Leavis interpretation on which it is largely based.

Olivier's *Hamlet* is a much more complex mixture of goods and bads. One strand, however, is easy to identify and highly instructive. This is the Freudian interpretation of the play which Olivier drew from Ernest Jones's *Hamlet and Oedipus*. As Jack Jorgens observed in *Shakespeare on Film*, the Jones interpretation makes Hamlet into a mental cripple: "The contradictions seem ingrained not so much in the world as in the imaginings of a diseased, unschooled mind." Is Hamlet or Denmark out of joint? Claudius undoubtedly thinks that the problem is Hamlet's, at least until the play scene, but does Shakespeare? Evidently not. Whatever Hamlet's mental state, the moral problem that he confronts is real, not imaginary. It is the dilemma of acting justly in a corrupt world. Two scenes illustrate Olivier's sacrifice of this theme to trendy psychology.

In the play's most famous scene Hamlet considers suicide ("To be or not to be"), decides against it, then meets Ophelia. Suicide is a sin. Contemplation of it leads to "the fear of something after death"—i.e., damnation. Hamlet rejects suicide on entirely valid moral grounds, even though he remains suspicious of his own motives ("Thus conscience doth make cowards of us all"). Having decided to live, he encounters Ophelia, who appears to him, at the moment of the encounter, as a symbol of redemptive purity.

Dissatisfied with this sequence of events, Olivier inverts the Shakespearean order, placing the meeting first and the soliloquy second. The implied motivation goes something like this: Hamlet is neurotically disturbed by his mother's sexual alliance with Claudius. He encounters Ophelia, who arouses all of his Oedipal frustration, and bitterly abuses her. Then, in a fit of revulsion against his own cruelty, he rushes off to consider suicide. The sequence may be good Freud, but it is cheap melodrama in comparison to Shakespeare's Folio text.

The clash between Freud and Shakespeare is also evident in Olivier's handling of the bedroom scene. Shakespeare's Hamlet is worried about his mother's conscience, a theme that has just been emphasized by the agonized effort of Claudius to repent in the prayer scene. In Olivier's film, however, Hamlet's summons to his mother to repent takes second place to the photography, which shows Hamlet gaping down Gertrude's ample décolletage. Forget what Hamlet is saying. The images on the screen show that his words are irrelevant. He is being overwhelmed by lust, not filial love. Much of the scene takes place on Gertrude's bed with the camera constantly hinting that Hamlet is on the verge of rape. Again the effect is melodrama, a kind of seventeenth-century *Mary Hartman, Mary Hartman*, rather than tragedy.

Of course, many films draw on interpretations that are closer to Shakespeare than F. R. Leavis and Ernest Jones. In such cases, analysis of the films can often sharpen the scholar's understanding of the interpretations used. *Macbeth*, for example, is filled with references to blood and violence. It has often been described by scholars as a "tragedy of blood" in the tradition of plays like *The Revenger's Tragedy* and *Titus Andronicus*. Is this interpretation valid?

Roman Polanski's *Macbeth* takes this approach. It is evidently the result of three convergent influences: the idea that much Elizabethan theater was, in fact, a "theater of blood," the brutal murder of Polanski's wife by the Charles Manson gang, and Jan Kott's grim view of the political process in *Shakespeare Our Contemporary*. According to Kott: "Everyone in [*Macbeth*] is steeped in blood, victims as well as murderers. The whole world is stained with blood. . . . A production of *Macbeth* not evoking a picture of a world flooded with blood would inevitably be fake."

Whichever influence was ultimately most important, there is

blood in abundance in Polanski's film. At the beginning, the three witches are shown burying a severed arm in a pit. As the credits appear, the sound track carries the noises of a battle. The camera then pans on a battlefield littered with mangled corpses. When one of the bodies moves, the nearest soldier smashes it repeatedly with a spiked mace. The captain who reports the defeat of the Norwegians speaks through a mask of blood. Cawdor is dragged forward lashed to rails, covered with more blood. The potentiality of technicolor film for gruesome close-ups is obviously a key element in making Polanski's effects immediate and terrifying.

These scenes establish a point of view that is sustained throughout the film. The Scotland it depicts is a savage tribal society ruled by brute force and trickery. Morality is useful only to trap those stupid enough to believe in it. Polanski invented the last scene of the film, in which Donalbain leaves his brother clutching Macbeth's bloody crown and rides to the same ruined cottage where Macbeth met the witches at the beginning. The cycle of blood is about to begin again.

Is this a legitimate extrapolation from Shakespeare's text or something else? Consider Polanski's treatment of Cawdor. In Shakespeare the execution of Cawdor is reported, not shown. In Polanski it is presented directly through a long, mostly silent photographic excursus. Cawdor is shown chained to the stone floor of the courtyard of Forres castle. He is released and brought to a ledge on the castle wall, where he is again chained. After a sullen "Long Live the King" (Polanski's interpolation), he leaps forward. The chain jerks; the shattered body swings at its end.

Polanski's insertion of photographic excurses like the Cawdor episode between segments of Shakespeare's dialogue is an example of the use of film technique to express values—or possible values—in the play. It is not in itself a betrayal of the text. In fact, it is one of the more interesting aspects of the film. Evidently, Polanski regarded *Macbeth* as a series of vignettes, a little like time-lapse photographs, of a society gradually sinking

into chaos. The excurses slow down the action by dividing movements of dialogue into isolated units. These underscore the time-
lapse effect of the dialogue. Because of the brevity of the text of
Macbeth, most productions seem to move very rapidly. Polanski's
treatment creates the opposite effect. The film has the leisurely
inevitability of a nightmare. While many other treatments are
possible, Polanski's is both fascinating and effective.

The problem is not that the Cawdor scene is invented, it is the
content of the scene. Polanski's Cawdor is bitter and unrepentant
as he dies. Shakespeare, conversely, goes out of his way to make
Cawdor's death a symbol of the redemptive forces present in
Macbeth's world. According to Malcolm:

> . . . I have spoke
> With one that saw him die; who did report
> That very frankly he confess'd his treasons,
> Implor'd your Highness' pardon, and set forth
> A deep repentance. Nothing in his life
> Became him like the leaving it.
>
> [I, iv, 3–8]

Either these lines contain the archest irony or Polanski's version
of Cawdor's death is a falsification. It *is* a falsification. Polanski's
obsession with violence has caused him to miss the significance
not only of Cawdor's conversion but of the whole side of the
play that comes into focus in Malcolm's description of Edward
the Confessor's miraculous gift of healing. Polanski's Scotland is
so hopelessly savage that no redemption is imaginable.

Polanski's Scotland is undoubtedly a symbolic expression of his
view of the twentieth century. It is not, however, Shakespeare's
Scotland, and Polanski's film makes the fact obvious. The Shakespeare scholar Herbert Coursen described the film as "a multi-
million dollar disaster." This appraisal fails to recognize Polanski's
frequently brilliant insights. However, Polanski has demonstrated
once and for all that *Macbeth* is not a "tragedy of blood" in either
the Elizabethan or the twentieth-century sense.

A. C. Bradley remarked that in comparison to the sprawling

structure of the more typical plays, *Macbeth* is almost Aristotelian. It is, he wrote, "less unlike a classical tragedy than *Hamlet* or *Othello* or *King Lear*. And it is possible that this effect is, in a sense, the result of design." In good classical fashion, *Macbeth* suppresses secondary plots and locates much of the violence—Cawdor's death, the murder of Malcolm, and the suicide of Lady Macbeth, for example—off stage. Its economy permits it to focus on a single titanic figure who is brought low by a tragic flaw that is also an instance of emotion (ambition) overwhelming reason—precisely the situation that is explored by Lily B. Campbell in *Shakespeare's Tragic Heroes: Slaves of Passion*. More than any of the other tragedies, *Macbeth* is a star vehicle. It is all the more attractive for having a major woman's part complementing that of the protagonist.

Although there have been many stage versions based on this view, including two recent revivals at Stratford, Ontario, only one movie uses it. Unfortunately, this movie is a mixed bag. It was made at Bob Jones University in 1950 and stars Bob Jones, Jr., as Macbeth and Bob Jones III as Fleance. It was, however, made with care and serious artistic intent. It presents Macbeth as a giant among men. No other character in the film is remotely as interesting. His elemental force is projected in part by Shakespeare's dialogue but even more emphatically by the fact that his image dominates the camera. As the film moves from temptation to triumph to death, Macbeth becomes more—and the secondary characters less—prominent. The result is rather close, one imagines, to a production "in the school of" Edwin Booth.

While the Aristotelian reading of *Macbeth* is attractive, none of Shakespeare's other tragedies fits the Aristotelian pattern. In each of them, the central action shades off into a maze of secondary plots and minor characters. This technique is usually called "spatial form." It creates a social dimension in the plays that complements the psychology of the protagonists. The Danish court in *Hamlet*, for example, is both a real court and a visible symbol of the corruption that troubles Hamlet. In the same way, in *Antony and Cleopatra* Rome and Egypt are symbolic expressions of the motives, respectively, of duty and love—or reason and sensuality—that clash in Antony's mind and that are also symbolized by Octavia and Cleopatra. Spatial form also creates what could be called social verisimilitude. It allows Shakespeare to introduce characters who are busy with their own concerns and quite indifferent to the great matters of state that are at the center of the tragic action. They have a stubborn reality that resists the neat designs of the artist.

Polanski's *Macbeth* takes full advantage of Shakespeare's spatial form. His Scotland is an impressively realized, visible symbol of the savage motives that guide the principal characters. At the same time, Polanski is willing to turn away from the main action to dwell lovingly on Shakespeare's drunken porter urinating on the wall while Duncan's corpse lies bleeding in the royal bed. Conversely, the Bob Jones film ignores the play's social dimension in order to concentrate on the protagonist, and its minor characters remain minor. The porter is worse than a minor character from the Aristotelian point of view: he is a digression. He was excised from the Bob Jones script. The end result is a film more reminiscent of *Richard III* than of the major tragedies. It is an interesting film when allowances are made for its technical limitations, but a shallow one compared to Polanski's. Better technique might only have made the problem more obvious. Evidently, *Macbeth* is less classical than Bradley believed.

A final instance of the relation between interpretation and enactment is provided by Orson Welles's *Macbeth*. This film is neither a study of violence in the style of Polanski nor a film about a hero who is brought low by ambition. Like Polanski, Welles creates a full social context for his action, but that social context preserves the balance found in Shakespeare between redemptive and daemonic forces. To give adequate emphasis to the redemptive forces, in fact, Welles creates a new character, a Christian priest, from bits and pieces of Shakespeare's dialogue plus invented material. The Weird Sisters are the antithesis of the priest. They are relics of the paganism which Christianity is slowly replacing in Welles's Scotland but which is still widespread and powerful. The stark contrasts inherent in this view are underscored by the use of black-and-white rather than color film.

Being the child of an ambivalent culture, Welles's Macbeth responds to both forces. Because he is semi-pagan, his responses are mythic rather than analytic. He does not think rationally about evil, he imagines it. It appears as a series of hallucinations —as the malign apparition of the witches in the forest and as the imagined dagger that leads him to Duncan's chamber. Guilt appears in the shape of Banquo's ghost and in the nightmares— only slightly less vivid than the ghost—the prevent him from sleeping.

If Polanski's film is leisurely, time accelerates in Welles's film. At first Macbeth seems to be in control of events. Soon, however, they are moving so rapidly that he must improvise to keep up with them. In Welles's presentation, the dialogue becomes increasingly fragmentary, like bits of conversation heard from the windows of an accelerating train. Eventually things happen too fast to be fully understood, much less controlled. Macbeth does not act, he can only react, and in the end he becomes the puppet of the forces he has released. This loss of control nicely explains his complaint that life is meaningless chaos—the famous tale told by an idiot signifying nothing.

The impression of accelerating time created by Welles's film makes the characters seem progressively more isolated. We first see Macbeth in the midst of a group of admiring soldiers. At the beginning of the witches' prophecy, Banquo is his friend. When Macbeth remarks "Your children shall be kings" (I, iii, 85), however, a shadow falls between the two men. His words are not an exclamation or an expression of wonder but a deadly accusation. Banquo's hasty response "You shall be king" (86) is equally ominous. The two friends have already been divided.

Welles emphasizes the point by having Macbeth and Banquo drift constantly into asides during the ensuing conversation with Ross.

By the time Duncan arrives at Inverness Castle, the infection has spread. Banquo confesses that he has dreamed of the witches, and Macbeth suggests that they discuss the matter further, promising "It shall make honor for you" (II, i, 24ff). The promise is a tacit bribe. Banquo's reply, "At your kindest leisure," is an already unctuous acceptance of the bribe, and his comment "so I lose [no honor]" is—in Welles's treatment— an afterthought showing that he already knows what Macbeth is planning.

The banquet scene carries the theme of isolation further. A banquet is usually an affirmation of community. Yet Macbeth's behavior shatters the illusion. "You have displaced the mirth, broke the good meeting," says Lady Macbeth (III, iv, 109). Welles makes it clear that she has a deeply feminine interest in the banquet. She wants to be a gracious hostess moving among admiring guests. Instead, she endures the humiliation of having her husband break down in public; she must order her guests to leave. There is a domestic quality in Welles's version of the scene that is quite moving. At the end, like many other married couples following a social disaster, Macbeth and Lady Macbeth are too tired for recriminations. Lady Macbeth's only advice is that they go to bed. The good meeting has, indeed, been broken. Everyone has gone. Eventually, Lady Macbeth will leave too. When the rebels break into his castle, Macbeth will be totally isolated.

For all of the criticism it has sustained, Welles's film goes more deeply into Shakespeare's text than any of the other film versions. New views of *Macbeth* will undoubtedly be offered by other directors, but Welles's image of a half-pagan, half-Christian society and a protagonist who is trapped and isolated in an accelerating catastrophe of his own making serves Shakespeare remarkably well.

❊   ❊   ❊

An actor can never be satisfied merely with the meanings of the individual words comprising a line. He has to ask how the words add up. What is the intention of the character who speaks the line—serious, ironic, amused, or hostile? Should the actor speak continuously or pause, and if so, where? Does he address the audience or another character or several characters? Does he use stage props or gestures? And so forth. The variations are innumerable, and each one gives a different meaning to the line. A film archive of Shakespeare is, among other things, a dictionary of possible variations.

Take a simple example. The first speech of Claudius in *Hamlet* is a summary of the facts about the political situation in Denmark. In Olivier's film it is delivered in a half-drunken slur to a group of indifferent courtiers at a riotous banquet. In Kozintsev's film it is delivered in part as a formal proclamation to a mixed group of soldiers and nobles in the courtyard of Elsinore. In Burton's *Hamlet* it becomes part of the deliberations of the Royal Council, which has assembled *in camera* to advise the new ruler. In Olivier the speech means that Claudius is weak and corrupt. In Kozintsev it means that he is a ruler in full control of events. In Burton it means that he is a careful politician making sure his fences are mended. None of these interpretations is inconsistent with the text. When taken together do they not then show that the text has several meanings rather than a single one?

Another example: when Macbeth sees Banquo at the beginning of Shakespeare's Act III, he asks, "Ride you this afternoon?" Is the question an offhand show of cordiality? Or is it an effort to pin down Banquo's whereabouts so that the murderers can find him? Or is Macbeth worried that, once mounted, Banquo will continue riding, as Donalbain and Malcolm have already done? Polanski's Macbeth has already planned the murder. His tone is affable but carries sinister emphasis. Welles's Macbeth, conversely, speaks in a nervous, almost whining tone. Having already lost several retainers, he is worried that Banquo plans to desert him. The idea of murdering Banquo apparently comes later, another improvisation. Welles's interpretation seems more dramatic and more psychologically interesting than Polanski's. However, both have merit. Again, the contrast shows that there is a range of meanings latent in the text.

In some instances, one reading is clearly better than another. To cite *Macbeth* once more, when Lady Macbeth departs to paint the sleeping grooms with Duncan's blood, she advises her husband, "Go get some water/And wash this filthy witness from your hands" (II, ii, 46–47). In Welles's film Macbeth stares at his hands and begins rubbing them together. However, Polanski's Macbeth walks to a well, draws a bucket of water and begins to wash. The use of this stage prop makes sense of his question, "Will all great Neptune's ocean wash the blood/Clean from my hand?" (60–61). When Lady Macbeth returns from Duncan's chamber, she, too, washes her hands. The action fits her lines: "A little water clears us of this deed./How easy is it then!" (67–68). It also prepares the audience for the sleep-walking scene when Lady Macbeth compulsively washes her hands in an imaginary basin. The stage prop therefore seems desirable on an absolute basis. Since a bucket was well within the capacities of Shakespeare's company, is it not possible that one was used by the King's Men when they performed the play for James I?

A final example: when Hamlet meets Ophelia in Shakespeare's Act III, scene i, he speaks the lines:

> . . . Soft you now!
> The fair Ophelia! Nymph in thy orisons
> Be all my sins remember'd.
>
> [88–90]

These lines are usually spoken continuously. Their meaning appears to be obvious. Hamlet is depressed. He has been considering suicide, and only his fear of "something after death" has persuaded him to go on living. When he sees Ophelia she seems for the moment to represent purity and grace. Acutely aware of his own failures, Hamlet feels that her prayers may help him.

Olivier has a much more complex interpretation of Hamlet's lines. Hamlet is revealed in an archway. As the audience knows from previous scenes, he suspects that everyone in the court is spying on him. When Ophelia makes a noise, he is certain that yet another spy is trying to surprise him. His "Soft you now" is spoken to himself. It means "Be careful; something suspicious is happening." After a brief pause, Hamlet walks forward to determine the source of the noise. He sees Ophelia, who is apparently unaware of his presence. He exclaims, "The fair Ophelia!" It is an expression of surprise and pleasure. He then approaches her. She is standing by an altar holding a book. When he is close to her he sees that the book is a collection of prayers. The audience knows that Polonius has forced it on her—it is part of his plot to expose Hamlet—but to Hamlet it seems confirmation of Ophelia's goodness. He passionately exclaims, "Nymph in thy orisons—Be all my sins remember'd."

Delivering the lines in this way requires perhaps 45 seconds rather than the usual 15. It changes a bland transition passage into a moment of intense, psychologically revealing drama. To quote Hamlet's formula for good acting, it "suits the action to the word, the word to the action." It could not be done as effectively on the stage, however, as on film, since the camera emphasizes the element of surprise by revealing only one part of the action at a time.

If Olivier's interpreation here is better—more revealing—than the conventional interpretation, is it also closer to the intention of Shakespeare's text? Although there is no way to answer this question, the existence of a dictionary of variant strategies for interpreting key passages may well allow us to glimpse, if fleetingly, performance strategies used in the original productions. Whether it does or not, it makes a range of valid interpretations available to scholars as well as to actors and directors. Consequently, it makes Shakespeare's text more plastic, more open, more rich in potential meanings than it appears to be on the page. To put the idea another way, the meanings that are revealed in a film are no longer transient as they are in a play. Film and videotape capture them permanently. They can therefore be treated with a degree of rigor that was formerly possible only in connection with the printed text. If they *can* be treated in this way, they must be. If the critic ignores them, he fails in his responsibility to use all of the available information.

One implication of the preceding observation needs to be stressed because it is not immediately obvious. It is a truism of film criticism that the only definitive text of a film is the film itself, preferably the master negative. When several different films of the same play are available, as is already the case for *Hamlet, Macbeth*, and other Shakespeare plays, does the "definitive text" of the play consist of all of these versions? From one angle the question is absurd. From another it is significant and disconcerting. The text of a Shakespeare play is only nominally in printed symbols; in reality it is the living meaning that those symbols convey. A reader creates meaning in his imagination and the meaning changes with each reading, but it is a private meaning. A playgoer experiences many different meanings, but he has no way to fix them. A few may stick in his mind, but between one production of a given play and the next, most of the meanings are irretrievably lost even to memory. Film is different. A single film of a play is limiting, but when several films of the same play are available, contrasting interpretations of the same passage can always be found that are consistent with the printed text but inconsistent with each other. Moreover, they are public interpretations that can be documented. Film is therefore pushing Shakespearean scholarship inexorably from unitary interpretation to recognition that the language of Shakespeare's drama is Protean; that the printed word is not an end but the beginning of a territory whose boundaries are constantly growing. This introduces what might be called a Heisenberg uncertainty principle into the modern understanding of Shakespeare. In doing so, it changes the meaning of the past.

12

Hitchcock's Formulas

Alfred Hitchcock was one of the great professionals in the movie business. The word "professional" is used here in its most favorable sense: movies are entertainment. No one entertained more or more consistently than Hitchcock. What the Lincoln Continental is to the Ford Pinto, the Hitchcock film is to the standard production-model Hollywood thriller. The public recognizes this. Hitchcock is one of a very few directors whose name is as important at the box office as the names of his stars. In the brief annals of film Hitchcock has made it. His films are touchstones of the art.

There are other filmmakers whose work is more artistic in the traditional sense than Hitchcock's. Eisenstein, Chaplin, Bergman, Olivier, Fellini—the list could easily be expanded—make films that *look like* art. This may be less of a compliment than it seems. It may be a way of saying that they are creating films that imitate the classics of other media and that their audiences are conservatives who are uncomfortable with the realities of contemporary life. Probably not. It is certainly true, however, that the self-conscious artists of film are making movies for a coterie, whereas

Hitchcock always made films for a mass audience in a style fully at home with the medium. His films are thus well suited to illustrate the expressive phase of film art in contrast to the classic phase as manifested, for example, in translations of Shakespeare's plays from the stage to the movie screen.

Consider the film artist a rhetorician. The purpose of art, says Aristotle, is to give pleasure. Not any kind of pleasure but the sort that comes from learning. The experience of art is an insight, an illumination of the action being imitated. Rhetoric, on the other hand, is oriented toward the marketplace. It succeeds by popularity rather than by approval of the few; and it is transient rather than permanent. Its immediate purpose is not illumination but persuasion, and its governing concept is that the work produced must be adjusted to the appetites of the audience. Rhetorical art succeeds by saying what the audience has secretly known (or wanted to know) all along. Its language is disguised flattery, and its symbols are surrogates for unconscious cravings. Given the passionate desire that everyone has to suspend disbelief, almost anything works, as witness the comic book and the exploits of Mike Hammer and James Bond; but some kinds of rhetoric work better than others. Just as there is good and bad art, there is good and bad rhetoric.

In the traditional formulation, a work of art produces insight. To experience it is to become different—if not wiser, at least more human. Since a work of rhetoric is shaped by its audience, it does not produce insight; but its data, when analyzed, can lead to certain useful understandings. We study a work of art aesthetically, but the study of entertainment is a branch of sociology or mass psychology.

Entertainment tends to go according to formula. A formula is simply a way of doing things that works, a way that has been tried and found successful in the marketplace and is therefore repeated as long as it retains its appeal. For this reason, a formula can be understood as a psychological category created by the needs and anxieties of the audience. In a sense, it is a collective dream. Crude rhetorical art, like that of Mickey Spillane or Ian Fleming, is almost pure formula, and it is fantastic because it approximates the uninhibited daydream. Adolescents, by and large, can take their fantasy straight. They provide the economic base for the comic-book industry and its relatives. Grown-ups, on the other hand, want their fantasy to be credible because they have to balance their appetite for fantasy against their social conditioning. Their appetite both shapes and supports Hitchcock's work. They can enjoy Hitchcock without being ashamed, whereas they feel apologetic or vaguely guilty about enjoying what their children like.

Intellectuals tend to be the most inhibited of all groups. In the thirties they generally scorned movies, just as there are still a few people here and there who refuse to watch television. The fad for formula entertainment with built-in satire—*The Man from U.N.C.L.E.* or *Batman* or *The Rockford Files*—shows that the predicament of the intellectual is real. It is, in effect, a mild schizophrenia, since the entertainment it summons into being must provide both a fantasy to which one can surrender and a hostile critique of that fantasy. Evidently, the needs that modern society creates are at war with the values it has inherited from traditional culture.

How does one become a master rhetorician? There are doubtless any number of ways, but two or three things definitely help. First, it is good to know one's audience. It is best, in fact, to have been one of them. There is a famous passage in Henry James's "The Art of Fiction" that explains how a lady artist (it was George Eliot) was able to deduce the whole milieu of French Protestantism from a glimpse of some young Protestants finishing a meal with their *pasteur*; but James was talking about art and, in particular, about a moment of insight. A rhetorician does not need moments of insight. To the extent that a moment of insight suggests departure from formula, it may prove an embarrassment. The rhetorician needs a sense of the formulas themselves, and this sense will be surest if he has grown up amid the conditions that produced them. Being ingrained, it will seem to emerge spontaneously in later life as talent.

But talent is not enough by itself. It must be shaped and disciplined by experience, and for the rhetorician the only relevant experience is the marketplace. Mastery of rhetoric, like mastery of any other skill, comes slowly. The rhetorician needs a long career allowing for experimentation, some failure, but mostly a polishing to perfection of the formulas that work and a pruning away of those that do not.

Alfred Hitchcock was fortunate on both counts. No pedagogue could have invented a curriculum better suited than Hitchcock's career to the training of a master of film rhetoric. George Perry's survey (*The Films of Alfred Hitchcock*) describes his as the ideal childhood. His father was a poulterer and greengrocer, a Catholic, and a rigid disciplinarian who once had the five-year-old Alfred locked up in the local jail for misbehaving. The lower-middle-class background is as close as possible to the average background of movie audiences of the twenties and thirties. The rigidities of pre-World War I class distinctions, of fin-de-siècle Catholic dogma, and of compulsive parental discipline are a paradigm of the dull, routine, boss-ridden, money-tormented environments from which the Walter Mittys of this world forever plot their fantasy escapes. If they explain the flight of the young Alfred from the grocer's shop to the Bohemia of the early film industry, they also explain the recurrence (and recurrent success of) the "flight from normalcy" motif in the mature thrillers.

The motif first proved itself in popular fiction like Robert Louis Stevenson's *Kidnapped* and John Buchan's *The Thirty-Nine Steps*, which Hitchcock made into one of his earliest thrillers. There is more than a trace of it in James Joyce's *A Portrait of the Artist as a Young Man*, which, however, is art in the traditional sense, a study of psychological imprisonment rather than high adventure. Stephen Daedalus left Ireland to forge the uncreated consciousness of his race. Alfred left the grocer's shop, one might say, to ease the already created and very uncomfortable subconscious of a world audience. In one way or another, Hitchcock's early background projects itself into all of his best-known films. Since it is also the background of his audiences, it authenticates his formulas and helps to account for their appeal.

Hitchcock arrived on the seacoast of Bohemia in 1921. He was continuously involved in making films after that time. His first thriller was a silent (*The Lodger*, 1926); he directed the first British talkie (*Blackmail*, 1929); and he was making films until his death in 1980.

Hitchcock learned the lesson of silent films well. *The Lodger* is so eloquent visually that it was shown with only about eighty titles, against an industry average of about two hundred per picture. Its eloquence is partly a matter of baroque camera effects. Its most famous scene, for example, is one in which the hero (Ivor Novello) paces his hotel room while being photographed from above through a transparent ceiling. Hitchcock's later fondness for striking camera effects may thus be traced to lessons imposed by the silents. His technique capitalized from the beginning on the hallucinatory effects—the spatial disorientation of the viewer—that are characteristic of the medium.

Another lesson that Hitchcock learned early was the importance of tone. Tone is to rhetoric what unity is to art. It creates the illusion of continuity whether continuity is there or not. It is primarily a visual quality in film, but it is unquestionably related to the audible tone provided by the musical accompaniment that has been standard in movies since the silents. In the best movies, tone becomes a pervasive element all the more effective by being subliminal—the epic tone of the photography in John Ford's movies and the grainy, newsreel tone of the early Rossellini films are cases in point. Hitchcock learned the secret of tone during the days of the silents and applied it with increasing skill throughout his career.

Since tone is hard to define, perhaps "authority," "quality," and "precision" will suggest the central qualities in Hitchcock's work. Authority—the sense of complete mastery of technique—is central to his success. By suggesting hidden but omnipotent control, it insulates the spectator from the implications of the thriller plot, reassuring him that no matter how terrifying the present may seem, sanity will prevail in the end. "Quality" (which means quality film, quality camera work, quality lighting and sound, quality sets, and the like) makes its contribution by separating a Hitchcock film as far as possible from the cruder forms of popular entertainment to which it is generically related. Finally, "precision" seems to have a double function. On the one hand, it underwrites the reality of the fantasy world. The images are sharper than life, just as the situations that they reveal have a mathematical neatness unknown in ordinary experience. Like Platonic ideas, they are more real than reality. The extra sharpness, the unnatural clarity, may also contribute, like "authority," to the protection of the spectator by suggesting: "This is real, but it is not your reality; therefore, you can maintain your separateness from it."

Incidentally, Hitchcock's understanding of tone helps to explain his ability always to adjust to the technological revolutions in filmmaking that eliminated so many of his competitors. For Hitchcock each new technical advance was an added tool, a new means of controlling tone. After bridging the gulf between silents and talkies, he continued to show a remarkable ability not only to assimilate but to use positively such advances as faster, less grainy film, more versatile cameras and sound equipment, and color.

Hitchcock's experience can be measured by the fact that after 1926 he directed and produced more than fifty full-length films. Several were experiments that took him outside his usual territory. *Easy Virtue, Champagne,* and *Jamaica Inn,* while they have interesting moments, can be discounted. *The Lodger* was Hitchcock's first triumph. It was a thriller, and all of his best films after that were variations of the same genre. This form offers the most interesting lessons to a student of his work.

First of all, the thriller is different from the detective story. Whereas "purgation of guilt" is involved in both, the methods of purgation and the environments in which they operate make all the difference. W. H. Auden has outlined the English variety of the detective story in "The Guilty Vicarage." The English detective is an intellectual. He solves problems rationally. He is a descendant of Locke via Monsieur Dupin and Sherlock Holmes, which is to say that he is a child of the Enlightenment. Like the Newtonian universe, his world is sane and ordered—in the typical country house all the guests seem innocent, and only one is guilty. The problem is to identify and banish the interloper, after which the remaining guests can get back to their tea, tennis, and evening bridge. Reason restores paradise.

The thriller is both more primitive and more in line with twentieth-century experience. Its milieu is a dream world in which the normal rules of reason no longer apply, and its hero is often closer to a buffoon than an intellectual. The thriller explores a spectrum of realities having the common characteristic of "strangeness" and varying from the comic through the absurd, the sinister, and the daemonic to the explicitly insane. The theological type of this world is the Calvinist City of Man, a league of the Reprobate through which the few Elect muddle, not by reason or good works but by a divine thrusting on. It is the world of *Bleak House* and *Our Mutual Friend*, of *The City of Dreadful Night*. If Hitchcock's popularity shows anything, it is also the psychological world of twentieth-century man.

Two defining characteristics of the thriller are its setting, which is alien, and its hero, who is typically a victim rather than an agent. The third characteristic follows from the first two: the hero must be invisibly supported during his adventures. In mythic and religious literature (e.g., the *Aeneid, Paradise Lost*) the support is visible. Vulcan provides Aeneas with impregnable armor, and God sends Adam prevenient grace even before he asks for it. The twentieth century, however, is too much a product of the nineteenth to admit publicly to a belief in Providence. Only the crudest forms of popular entertainment, the comic books, permit impregnable skins and X-ray vision, and even these try to hide the supernatural under a veneer of rational explanation: Superman is "a visitor from another planet." More sophisticated forms of popular entertainment, the western for example, work things out by chance: the assassin's bullet always misses, the rope is never tied quite tightly enough, at the last minute the chief's daughter betrays the plan of the Indian raid to her paleface lover, and so forth. Whatever the form, from *Superman* to *North by Northwest,* the hero is one of the Elect. This does not mean that he cannot make mistakes; he is often, like James Bond, absurdly incompetent. Rather, it means that no matter what he does, it turns out all right in the end. This is an exact plot equivalent of the Calvinist doctrine of Election.

Heroic invincibility must be considered the most important characteristic of the thriller plot. (In the classic detective story the detective is often aloof. He does not need invincibility because he is seldom in danger: he is an observer, outside the plot just as Newton was outside Nature.) The audience of the thriller identifies with the hero as he seeks a way out of the nightmare in which he finds himself. His eventual success—the eternally satisfying happy ending—is the payoff. It is a way of saying that no matter how terrible the world may seem, there is a hidden benign force at work that guarantees the eventual triumph of good—the Reprobate will be punished, and the Elect will live happily ever after.

To deprive the hero of invincibility would be to move from fantasy to reality, from rhetoric to art, and this is exactly what popular entertainment must not do. Hitchcock showed occasional insensitivity to this rhetorical imperative. In *The Lodger, Blackmail,* and *Suspicion* he originally planned unhappy endings but eventually changed his mind in all three cases in the interest of commercial success. This suggests the existence of a frustrated artist somewhere in the psyche of the master rhetorician, an artist who emerged from time to time in Hitchcock's television program. But surely in the case of the three movies the public was right and the artist wrong. None of the three films is art in the traditional sense, but all three are splendid rhetoric.

The alien milieu in which the hero's adventures occur is as important to the thriller as the hero himself. Hitchcock's films illustrate most of the possible variations. In *To Catch a Thief* the milieu is simply comic. In *The Thirty-Nine Steps* and its 1959 twin *North by Northwest* it alternates between the absurd and the sinister without ever becoming frightening. In *The Lodger* and *Psycho* it is daemonic, but, from the dominant point of view, that of the hero, it is still sane. In the group of films including *Spellbound, Rope, Vertigo,* and *Marnie* insanity becomes overt, and, at least in *Spellbound,* the visual image disintegrates into surrealistic dream sequences produced with the help of Salvador Dali. Each milieu is realized in meticulous detail. Several are underwritten by the use of well-known landmarks such as the dome of the British Museum (*Blackmail*), the Forth Bridge in Scotland (*The Thirty-Nine Steps*), and the Mt. Rushmore Memorial (*North by Northwest*). But in every case the spectator is insulated from the milieu by Hitchcock's slick photography, by comic interludes, and by such tricks as the traditional appearance of Hitchcock himself, which, like a stage aside, engages the spectator in a private joke with the director at the expense of the drama.

Hitchcock was at his best in the range between the comic and the sinister. Whatever its disguise, the thriller is, after all, a variant of the comic epic, and comic action goes best with comic or mock-sinister settings. Moreover, the comic is a valid way of seeing experience. Cary Grant as an international jewel thief must provide the same sort of innocent Saturnalia for modern audiences that Falstaff provided for the Elizabethans. The darker the comic world becomes, the greater the temptation to take it seriously. Probably one of the delights of being a master rhetorician is seeing how far you can bend a formula without breaking it. Hitchcock's spy stories balance between the comic and the terrible with breathtaking virtuosity and never a false step. Their villains are bad without being evil, their heroes are good without being virtuous or wise, and their situations are absurd without being ridiculous. In *The Holy Sinner* Thomas Mann commented on God's habit of involving His saints in impossible predicaments in order to display His omnipotence by extricating them. The same might be said for the Hitchcock of *The Thirty-Nine Steps, The Lady Vanishes,* and *North by Northwest.* In fact, the parallel is exact because the unstated point of the hair-breadth escape is the operation of Providence.

Rope and *Psycho* carry the thriller world about as far as it can go without being taken seriously. Actually, both films received a good deal of criticism (i.e., some people took them seriously)—the first for its rather crude reworking of the Leopold and Loeb case, and the second for the brutality of the initial murder scene. The criticisms of *Rope* were justified. Hitchcock's effort to make his characters credible by equipping them with cut-rate Nietzschean philosophy introduced a lump of serious material that his formulas simply could not assimilate, a point that becomes perfectly clear when *Rope* is contrasted to *Compulsion. Phycho*, on the other hand, is reasonably good fun if one can get over the murder scene, which, like Nietzschean philosophy, calls for a more serious follow-up than the movie wants to deliver.

The psychological thrillers, in which the milieu varies from daemonic to insane, are the weakest. Ingrid Bergman's flimsy Freudian ministrations to Gregory Peck's equally flimsy symptoms provide a rationale for the providential cure that climaxes *Spellbound*—a scientific equivalent of prevenient grace in *Paradise Lost.* The formula is followed, but it fails precisely because Hitchcock has gone to such tedious lengths to make it convincing. Anybody who knows enough Freud to appreciate what Hitchcock is doing knows that his psychologizing is sentimental and false. The same can be said for the miraculous cure at the end of *Marnie*. In the thriller, guns, spears, fists, rocks, broken bottles—anything, in fact—are better than understanding. Success should come in spite of intelligence not because of it. In the wars between good and evil, it is the enemy who is supposed to have all the brains.

Hitchcock's protagonists are a various lot. Most of them have sexual consorts. In the earlier films the relations between the sexes are generally orthodox. In the later films they become more exotic. The woman is dominant and maternal (*Spellbound*), a seasoned predator and sexually more experienced than the hero (*North by Northwest*), alternately frigid and passionate (*To Catch a Thief*), or frigid and dependent (*Marnie*). This may simply reflect the relaxation of censorship after World War II, but since the unorthodox sexual relations are correlated to an increasing obsession in Hitchcock's movies with the daemonic and the insane, their appearance may be related to new appetites on the part of the audience. Heterosexual fun and games have always been a part of the comic epic and its variants, as in *Tom Jones*. The sudden change of a female character from prude to wench is also familiar and particularly effective when portrayed by an icily refined actress. The more unorthodox relations explored by Hitchcock, however, raise the same question as his psychologizing. Do they come from the artist still buried in the rhetorician? Or do they simply ring the changes on the Oedipal situation to make sure that everybody has his share?

Another feature of Hitchcock's protagonists is their strong class identity. The class theme emerges first in *Murder* (1930). The hero is titled and is played by Herbert Marshall, whose public image has always been that of an aristocrat. Marshall plays a "good' aristocrat—he saves the heroine from being executed for a crime she did not commit. On the other hand, there is considerable undercutting of the image. Marshall plays an actor (a hint of self-parody), and in two scenes he wantonly insults lower-class characters. The treatment reveals a mixture of admiration and hostility and doubtless reflects attitudes toward his betters that young Alfred took with him from the grocer's shop. *The Thirty-Nine Steps* is less ambiguous. It toys with the same class attitudes explored by Graham Greene in *This Gun for Hire*. Although he is not a lower-class character like Greene's gunman, Hitchcock's hero is definitely an outsider, while the villain is an artistocrat and inhabits a baronial country house in Scotland. *Murder* defines one standard type of Hitchcock thriller —noblesse oblige—while *The Thirty-Nine Steps* defines its antitype, which might be called "local boy makes good." In the first type the upper class is benign, a source of deliverance; in the second it is malign, a source of evil, and must be destroyed by the middle-class hero.

That the class theme remained strong in Hitchcock's American films is evident from his choice of leading players. The noblesse oblige roles were consistently given to actors whose upper-class identity was established by accent (modified British) as well as publicity. Ray Milland and Cary Grant were Hitchcock's favorite male stars, with Cary Grant clearly running first. Grant has both class and *sprezzatura*. He embodies what every grocer's clerk wants to be. (Hitchcock's malign aristocrats, identified by lack of *sprezzatura*, have been played by such Hollywood heavies as Joseph Cotten, Claude Rains, and James Mason.) The class interest is equally evident in Hitchcock's female leads. Madeleine Carroll, Joan Fontaine, and Ingrid Bergman are all typed as ladies by casting and publicity.

The class tagging is especially obvious in his choice of Grace Kelly, who might almost be called Hitchcock's invention. Miss Kelly's credentials include main-line Philadelphia, family wealth, and a successful career as a fashion model. (She has since, of course, justified Hitchcock's casting instincts by becoming a real-life princess.) Her modeling career is especially significant; Eva Marie Saint (*North by Northwest*) and Tippi Hedren (*Marnie*) also came to Hitchcock via modeling. High fashion is unabashedly snobbish, and its models must consciously learn to project the upper-class image in posture, gesture, and expression as well as in dress. (Since high fashion is projected by stills, speech and accent are unimportant; thus Hitchcock's heroines lack the hint of British inflection characteristic of Milland and Grant.)

The pairing of the ideal Hitchcock leads, Cary Grant and Grace Kelly, in *To Catch a Thief* helps explain its near-perfect finish. Interestingly, the film also projects an entirely benign image of class relations. Grace Kelly plays a true blue blood and Cary Grant a self-made thief (an echo of local boy makes good?). Miss Kelly's initial frigidity carries with it a suggestion of class hostility, and her capitulation to Grant a trace of middle-class wish-fulfillment or class revenge (the Lady Chatterley motif). But Grant is himself so much the complete gentleman that it is impossible to take his criminal background seriously. The picture is simply a romp, luxuriating in fantasies of Riviera high life and beautiful people whose only worry is the whereabouts of the family diamonds.

Additional variation on the thriller formula is provided by dominance of either the male or female lead. In *Murder* and *Blackmail* the male is dominant while the female is helpless. Hitchcock took this stereotypical situation from melodrama. It is a perfectly satisfactory arrangement. But just as he explored new twists to the thriller plot, early in the thirties he began to experiment with more original deployments of characters. In *The Thirty-Nine Steps* the male-female relationship is equalized, and there are several episodes where the equality becomes overt antagonism. This is a reworking of the Beatrice-Benedick theme, so it cannot be called an innovation, but it is certainly less commonplace than the melodrama convention. Predictably, the antagonism eventually turns to love and hence to the surrender of the female.

Spellbound and *To Catch a Thief* shift the balance of the relationship still further. In both films the female is dominant and the male dependent. Particularly in *Spellbound*, the female has an Oedipal function, being both mother surrogate and object of sexual desire. The Oedipal basis of the fantasy becomes overt in the scene in which Gregory Peck stands over the sleeping Bergman with an open razor, and the spectator is left in suspense as to whether he will make love to her or cut her throat.

In *North by Northwest*, Cary Grant again plays a dependent part. He is equipped at the beginning of the film with a domineering mother, a nagging secretary, and not one but two ex-wives with alimony claims. When the chase begins, mother, secretary, and wives are replaced by Eva Marie Saint, who first saves him by concealing him in the upper berth of a Pullman compartment and then seduces him. Later, she is shown to be the mistress of the villain, who, in this situation, can only be understood as a father surrogate. Although Grant eventually bestirs himself enough to rescue Miss Saint from the villain, he resumes his dependent role in the final scene, where she is shown climbing into the upper bunk with him, evidently preparing for that special kind of erotic fun known as Turkish Delight.

Hitchcock's film *Marnie* appears on first inspection to be a return to the melodrama formula of the dependent heroine and noblesse oblige. Outwardly, Marnie seems to be a self-possessed, sexually experienced, and highly successful thief, a female counterpart of Cary Grant in *To Catch a Thief*. Having been caught in the act of theft by the wealthy hero (Sean Connery of James Bond fame), she agrees to marry him. He soon discovers that she is virginal and sexually frigid, that her thieving is a neurotic compulsion, and that she comes from a lower-class background. As in *Spellbound*, an informal psychoanalysis ensues. Her trauma is duly discovered (her mother was a Baltimore prostitute, and Marnie was involved in the killing of one of her customers), and she is restored, as the analysts say, to a full and normal life. George Perry has already observed, however, that this apparently innocent fantasy has perverse undertones. The hero's marriage to a woman whom he knows to be a thief is curious, to say the least. The suggestion of perverse relations is further underscored by the overt jealousy of the hero's sister. If the film is considered as fantasy, it is a playing out of the Electra complex. But if it is judged on any other basis, the hero is at least as sick as the woman he is trying to cure.

Because Hitchcock continued to produce successful thrillers for over forty years, his films are a kind of contour map of the middle-class mind during this period. The early films indicate an audience restless, in search of escape, fascinated with crime and sudden death, and subconsciously considering its environment absurd or sinister. This is not, in itself, surprising or unique to the twentieth century. What is interesting is the increasing morbidity of Hitchcock's handling of the formulas. In the fifties and sixties—that is, in the period following World War II, which one would like to consider a period of relaxed social tensions— the Hitchcock world becomes darker. The dominant movement is away from the comic and toward the daemonic or the overtly insane. For the most part, the daemonic and insane are still held in the frame of the comic epic, but there is an increasing challenge to the frame itself, as demonstrated in *Rope, Psycho*, and *Marnie*. The evil threatens to become real, the brutality becomes ugly, and the source of deliverance turns out to be as corrupt as the forces that it is opposing.

To the degree that the controlling force of the thriller plot is Providence, this pattern of development suggests an erosion of faith. The fantasy is becoming progressively harder to accept; a reality principle constantly threatens to destroy it. And to the degree that the thriller involves audience identification with the hero, it suggests a kind of self-revulsion. In spite of obvious tendencies toward sadism and masochism, Mike Hammer remains officially innocent in Mickey Spillane's novels. Because he is of the Elect, acts that would be evil in others become sanctified in him. This is not the case in *Marnie*. Here, Hitchcock's undercutting is too plain to be missed. The heroic image is intentionally tarnished. Instead of seeing an idealized version of his ego, the spectator finds something deformed and rather ugly. Something, perhaps, much like himself.

These threats to the comic epic frame of the thriller become explicit in *The Birds*, which may be Hitchcock's most honest examination of his themes. Based on Daphne du Maurier's novel, *The Birds* is an art film in the sense that it brings into the open both the assumptions and the trends evident in the thrillers. Instead of being concealed, the supernatural operates overtly: the birds suddenly become hostile (no rational explanation is offered) and attack the inhabitants of a small California village. The transformation of protagonist to villain is also evident. Tippi Hedren, the female lead, plays a wealthy, restless girl in search of sexual adventure. It is her arrival at the village that triggers the attacks of the birds, and she is the most obvious focus of their hatred. In one scene she is brutally pecked and clawed. The motif of self-revulsion which is only a suggestion in *Marnie* is the main point of *The Birds*. Nature becomes the agent of an avenging Providence. Only man is vile, and before being destroyed he must be stalked, terrorized, and physically tortured to expiate his sins.

One can only assume that like most well-informed members of contemporary society, Hitchcock was deeply worried about the gathering crisis in the world community: a crisis of greed—of modern man's refusal to face up to long-range consequences of uncontrolled exploitation of Nature. In the world of the collective dream that is film, this anxiety emerges as a plot in which Nature turns on human society.

All this being fairly clear, the movie ought to be a good one. Unfortunately, it is not. The problem is tone. The tone of *The Birds* is too much that of the thrillers, and for this reason the film's denotation jars badly with its connotation. In the end, the chief interest of *The Birds* is the light it throws on Hitchcock's other work. *The Birds* made a poor showing at the box office. Audiences who went expecting rhetoric were disappointed, while audiences accustomed to Bergman and Rossellini could not take its pretensions seriously. As a dream the film was a failure.

The increasing threat to the thriller formulas that was evident in Hitchcock's work of the fifties and sixties is significant. That Hitchcock continued—except for *The Birds*—to use the formulas until his death, and that they continued to work at the box office, is also significant. A dream, Freud discovered, is a device to keep the dreamer from waking up. It is benign, curative. Subjects experimentally prevented from dreaming experience a rapid deterioration of personality, leading eventually to psychosis.

A culture is like an individual. It needs its dreams as well as its waking periods. They are supplied for modern world culture by the rhetoric of popular entertainments like Hitchcock's thrillers. If it was becoming harder to dream in the 1960s because of increasing social tensions, Hitchcock bent his formulas so that dreaming remained possible.

There may not be a pot of gold (or a virginal concubine) at the end of the rainbow. It may be that the City of Dreadful Night is truly dark and truly possessed by daemons and that there is nothing to distinguish the Elect from the Reprobate. It may be that civilization is coming to the end of the road. In an absolute sense, modern man is probably more like Sisyphus than stout Cortez with eagle eye, but if he truly believed this, it is hard to see how he could continue to push the stone up the hill. In the psyche the instinct for survival has to be a little stronger than the death wish, and no matter how modern man plots his situation on the charts of reason, his subconscious mind needs to view life as a fantastic quest through alien territories and the domains of strange gods, underwritten by Providence and with a payoff guaranteed.

Film is ideally suited to expressing this fantasy through characterizations that draw on the personalities of well-known stars, plots that utilize the fluidity of movie action, and, above all, images that transcend the limitations of the world of causality and have the freedom of dreams along with the immediacy of direct experience. Hitchcocks films are brilliantly successful because they take full advantage of the innate capacities of the medium. They do not imitate classic art forms; they express their own characteristics.

THE THREAD OF ARIADNE

13

The Next Frontier

In history books the American Revolution begins with the approval of the Declaration of Independence on July 4, 1776. It was the first in a series of revolutions, some violent and some constitutional, that have continued in an unbroken sequence to the present day. The world has not seen the last of them. Thomas Jefferson believed that "a little rebellion, now and then, is a good thing, and as necessary in the political world as storms in the physical." He understood, too, that the American experiment was more than a local issue—that it would be an example for the future. "While we are securing the rights of ourselves and our posterity," he wrote in 1790, "we are pointing out the way to struggling nations, who wish like us to emerge from their tyrannies also."

Two centuries later, Jefferson's comment remains acceptable, with a single reservation. From the vantage point of the late twentieth century, to consider the transfer of power from a British to a colonial elite that occurred in the wake of the uprising of 1776 a revolution is an exaggeration. From time to time, economic historians have asked whether the colonists were fighting for a new way of life or for larger profits than the British government was allowing them. This economic interpretation of the American Revolution is too simple. However, when one considers the intellectual basis of the American Revolution, knottier questions arise. By the late eighteenth century the theory of the Rights of Man was anything but revolutionary. Its immediate sources were John Locke and the French *philosophes*. Behind them were the English Commonwealth and the Reformation of the sixteenth century. And behind them, at a still more distant remove, were English common law and the political theories of Aristotle and Cicero.

The intellectual foundation of the new American government was traditional and conservative. Plato could have understood the Declaration of Independence, although he would have disagreed with most of its positions. It does not claim to offer a newly invented set of human rights or even new arguments to justify those rights. Instead, it rests its case on the plan that God devised for mankind at the beginning of Creation. Far from being controversial, God's plan is so widely understood, according to the Declaration of Independence, that it is self-evident to all right-thinking men. Thomas Jefferson described the plan in the harmonious language of the eighteenth-century deists:

> We hold these truths to be self-evident: that all men are created equal; that they are endowed by their Creator with inherent and unalienable rights; that among these are life, liberty, and the pursuit of happiness; that to secure these rights, governments are instituted among men. . . .

Writing to Henry Lee in 1825, Jefferson remarked: "This was the object of the Declaration of Independence. Not to find out new principles or new arguments never before thought of, not merely to say things which had never been said before, but to place before mankind the common sense of the subject."

As Jefferson was writing the "common sense of the subject" of independence, forces were gathering that would decisively change society's definition of common sense. These forces were born from technology. That is to say they depended on habits of thought quite foreign to the tradition inherited by Jefferson. The Jeffersonian tradition is centered on human beings. It seeks to define man's basic physical and spiritual needs and then to create a social structure that meets those needs. It views Nature as an abundant reservoir of food and raw material and a pleasant backdrop for human activity, and its image for Nature is a garden. Conversely, technology is oriented toward the material world. It does not view Nature as a reservoir or a pastoral backdrop but as a mystery to be solved or an adversary to be conquered or a resource to be exploited. Its immediate object is the creation of wealth through knowledge. It justifies its activities on humanitarian grounds—scientific discovery will increase the well-being of society as a whole—but it is indifferent to the immediate social consequences of its activities. Any short-term suffering will be more than offset by long-term benefits.

Jefferson was a philosopher and a rationalist. He had read his Newton, his Locke, and his Montesquieu. But he was not a scientist in the sense of d'Alembert or Priestly or Euler or Dalton. He was an *amateur* of gadgets, but he was not even an engineer on the model of Watt or Fulton. There was little in the human-centered tradition he inherited that was remotely adequate to explain the forces already reaching critical mass during his lifetime. Although he admired science, he was repelled by the industrial revolution that science had made possible. As his letters state the case:

> The English have been a wise, a virtuous, and truly estimable people. But commerce and a corrupt government have rotted them to the core. Every generous, nay, every just sentiment, is absorbed in the thirst for gold. I speak of their cities, which we may certainly pronounce to be ripe for despotism, and fitted for no other government.
>
> Letter to Ogilvie, 1811

Again:

> Carpenters, masons, smiths are wanting in husbandry; but, for the general operations of manufacture, let our workshops remain in Europe. . . . The mobs of great cities add

> just so much to the support of pure government, as sores
> do to the strength of the human body.
>
> *Notes on Virginia* (1785)

And again:

> When we get piled upon one another in large cities, as in
> Europe, we shall be corrupt as in Europe, and go to eating
> one another as they do there.
>
> Letter to Madison, 1787

The point of view in these comments is closer to Sir Thomas More's *Utopia*, published in 1516, than to Friedrich Engel's *The Condition of the Working Class in England in 1844*, published in 1845, only nineteen years after Jefferson's death.

The basic concerns of the American Revolution were tangential to the technological developments that were emerging during the closing years of the eighteenth century. Precisely because the Founding Fathers did not—perhaps could not—understand the implications of these forces, they made few provisions in the charter of the new American nation to contain them. This is why time and again throughout America's history attempts to control the new technology and the economic forces released by it have ended in the Supreme Court. Lacking clear and explicit directives, the Court has had to proceed by inference from the nation's basic documents and has often, in effect, created legislation.

In the early history of the United States, the real American revolution, the revolution that shaped American society and pushed it willy-nilly into the modern world, was the first technological revolution, the Age of Steam. The revolution of steam created unimaginable accumulations of capital for those who controlled it. This capital sent the pioneers westward in a feverish effort to exploit new land even as it shifted the power base in society from the land to the cities. It created wealth beyond the imagination of Croesus and degraded laborers to the status of animals; it substituted the locomotive for the garden in the popular imagination; and it abandoned the tangible reality of transactions between man and man for the abstractions of banking and credit. For the intellectuals, who thought in terms of Plato and Cicero rather than Watt and Bentham, it was a confusing experience. Contemplating the railroad tracks from his sanctuary on Walden Pond, Thoreau saw the sleepers as gigantic weights crushing the backs of the Irish immigrants who laid them. On the other hand, when Walt Whitman learned of the completion of the Union Pacific Railroad in 1869, he celebrated the event, in his poem "Passage to India," as a triumph of the human spirit, a uniting of humanity. Whatever the intellectuals thought, the revolution continued. The railroads kept moving westward, and the Irish immigrants were joined by the Poles, the Italians, the Mexicans, and, in the fullness of time, Chinese coolies imported to California to push the railroad east from the Pacific.

Railroads are an apt symbol of the real American revolution because they are symbols of mobility as well as technology. England and France were as deeply affected as America by the technological revolution of the nineteenth century, but their experience was different. The unique feature of the American experience was its openness, due partly to the open social structure—the upward mobility—that is inherent in any expanding economy and that was encouraged by native political traditions rather than opposed, as it was in Europe. It was also encouraged by the fact that beyond America's urban centers the land extended in almost unimaginable openness from the Blue Ridge Mountains to the Pacific coast. The openness of the land complemented the openness of the economy. It created a special psychological tone that deeply influenced the American character, an optimism that Europeans often found shallow and a directness they often found coarse. If conditions became intolerable, there was always the option of moving west. E. E. Dole graphically illustrates the extent of the migration in his article "Turner: The Man and the Teacher":

Critics of the migration theory never have seen a territory such as Oklahoma grow in seventeen years from a population of a few hundred cowboys and Indian agency employees to 400,000 inhabitants, most of them homesteaders. They did not see 100,000 home-seekers rush into the Cherokee Outlet to people a region as large as a New England state within twenty-four hours. Perhaps they did not realize that in the two decades from 1870 to 1890 the population of the Dakotas rose from 14,000 to 719,000; Nebraska from a little over 120,000 to more than a million; and Kansas from slightly over one-third of a million to nearly a million and a half.

Even for those who chose to stay where they were, the sense of limits, the feeling of being trapped hopelessly in a physical place or a static social hierarchy, was less oppressive than in Europe.

The bias in the national character produced by this revolution is described in a classic passage in Ole Rölvaag's novel of pioneer life *Giants in the Earth*:

They threw themselves blindly into the Impossible and accomplished the Unbelievable. If anyone succumbed to the struggle—and that happened often—another would come to take his place. Youth was in the race; the unknown, the untried, the unheard-of was in the air; people caught it, were intoxicated by it, threw themselves away, and laughed at the cost.

Rölvaag's description touches on one of the enduring themes in American historical thought, formulated by Frederick Jackson Turner in "The Significance of the Frontier in American History." As noted in Chapter 1, Turner's conclusions seem strangely inconsistent with important aspects of American culture, but they were embraced warmly by American historians and continue to be influential today.

Turner believed that the frontier rather than the political theories of the Founding Fathers was the true explanation of what America had become. "The true point of view in the history of this nation," he wrote, "is not the Atlantic coast, it is the Great West. . . . What the Mediterranean Sea was to the Greeks, breaking the bond of custom, offering new experiences, calling out new institutions and activities, that and more the ever-retreating frontier has been to the United States." The frontier was more than a place for Turner; it was a "form of society," or in James Truslow Adams's phrase, "a state of mind rather than a place."

Turner drew his thesis from the Census of 1890. The phenomenon was not as original as he apparently thought, since it is obvious that the expansion of America and the mentality that expansion produced had counterparts in nineteenth-century European industrialism and the combination of *laissez-faire* economics and Comtean positivism that accompanied it. However, for Turner the key factor was open land, which America once had possessed in abundance. The Census of 1890 appeared to prove that the free land was gone. The best land had been occupied, only marginal land remained. Turner ended on a note of nostalgia that has been echoed frequently in history books, popular fiction, and movies: "The frontier has gone and with its going has closed the first period of American history." Later he accurately predicted that the individualism and *laissez-faire* economic tradition of the frontier would yield increasingly to government control.

Turner unquestionably slighted the influence of European tradition on American thought. It was—and continues to be—fundamental. However, he was certainly right about the buoyant psychological effect of open land on the national psyche. What he missed in his study of the frontier, in spite of the fact that he was awash in the evidence, was that in America the economic frontier complemented and reinforced the attitudes encouraged by the physical frontier. Throughout the century and in spite of periodic setbacks, the thrust of the American economy was upward. The economy grew predictably through expanding production and an increasing population. More important for the American psyche, it also grew unpredictably, with dazzling leaps forward, through windfalls created by the discovery of new raw materials and the development of new techniques and machines by nineteenth-century technology.

The California gold rush of 1849 typifies this windfall growth, but it is only one of a continuous series of events that transformed every aspect of American society. In its real consequences the gold rush was a minor episode compared to the expansion of railroads, the explosion of the Western cattle market after the Civil War, the introduction of the telegraph, the development of efficient knitting machines, the expansion of newspapers and publishing in the wake of the mass-production of cheap paper from wood pulp, the replacement of sail by steam, the discovery of the power of statistics and the related expansion of life insurance, ready-made clothing, modular building materials, and dozens of other activities that depend on statistical controls.

The frontier mentality never depended exclusively on free land. If 1890 marked the end of the physical frontier, it was only the midpoint in an expansion that was more or less continuous throughout the nineteenth century. The closing decades of the nineteenth century were the Gilded Age, the age of the entrepreneur, of the Morgans, the Rockefellers, the Carnegies, and the Mellons. If they were the age of Henry James, they were also and more deeply the age of Horatio Alger and the gospel of success.

Historians are a suspicious lot. They know enough about hard times to be skeptical about good ones. Probably it did not seem possible to Turner that the expansion of the nineteenth century could continue very far into the twentieth. The American people, however, spent their time reading *Tom the Bootblack* and *Acres of Diamonds* rather than *The Frontier in American History*. In spite of the Census of 1890, they continued to throw themselves blindly into the Impossible and accomplish the Unbelievable. The windfalls continued to occur at regular intervals. If anything, their novelty—and their economic impact—increased. In 1890 the telephone was a curiosity. Radio, aircraft, plastics, aluminum, synthetic fibers, movies, television, computers, wonder drugs, and space flight were all to come. Above all, the internal combustion engine was an infant whose effect on the whole fabric of American life, for good and for evil, could not be dimly imagined by its most ardent enthusiasts.

The mentality of the frontier survived the 1890 census. It blossomed. It confounded the skeptics. As physical limits threatened to stop expansion and curtail upward mobility in one sector, technology produced whole new industries and, with them, new human opportunities. The fact that only a small fraction of the population benefited directly is beside the point. As Henry Nash Smith concluded in *Virgin Land* (1950), the openness of America has always had the quality of a myth, a religious belief. As long as some Americans continued to prosper in the old frontier way, all Americans shared in their experience.

The myth has always had its critics—witness Thoreau. Since 1900 it has had especially hard going. As Turner foresaw, one of the battlegrounds has been government regulation. Measures extending government regulation of corporations and individuals have been bitterly attacked as un-American even when they have been aimed at correcting gross and grossly harmful abuses: the Sherman Anti-Trust Act, for example, the Hepburn Act which gave bite to the Interstate Commerce Commission, the Pure Food and Drug Act, the Income Tax Amendment, the Recovery Act of 1933, and the Wagner and Social Security acts of 1935. It is not surprising that corporations and bankers should have resisted those efforts at regulation. What *is* surprising is that the corporations and bankers have consistently rallied large numbers of the victims to defend, passionately, their own exploitation. Their success stems from psychology rather than from economics. Government regulations are announcements in the cold language of the law that American society is being hedged in by limits. They threaten the myth of the frontier. They proclaim that certain activities are not only impossible and unbelievable but illegal as well.

In addition to creeping regulation, there have been moments when the whole machine seemed to be breaking down. Two major and seven minor recessions since 1929 have given substance to the fear that the openness of American society may, indeed, be coming to an end; that the economic frontier may be going the way of the open lands in the West.

What were these recessions, really? Were they setbacks like the depressions of the nineteenth century or were they portents of harder times to come? Until 1960 the answer seemed plain. Every setback was balanced by a windfall. After the brief postwar depression of 1921, the American economy soared to dizzy heights, partly on the basis of real growth and partly on the stock market, which replaced Sutter's Mill as a symbol of thrusting blindly into the Impossible and accomplishing the Unbelievable. The two depressions of the thirties were a deeper wound. The first lasted from August 1929 to March 1933—43 months. It caused a 54.4 percent drop in production and a peak jobless rate of 24.8 percent. The second (in the opinion of many, a continuation of the first) lasted from May 1937 to June 1938—13 months —with a drop in production of 32.4 percent and a jobless rate of 20 percent of the labor force.

The doubts about the American Dream created by these events were profound and widespread. But things did eventually get better. Already historians look on the period between 1945 and 1965 in the same way that they look on the twenties. The postwar years were characterized by rapid economic expansion, upward mobility, and spectacular technological achievements. To say that Americans thrust themselves into the Impossible and accomplished the Unbelievable during the fifties and early sixties is an understatement. The driving force behind the economy during this period was high technology. Its achievements stagger the imagination. They began with antibiotics and nuclear fission and television. As the fantasies of the laboratory became the realities of the marketplace, they expanded to include jet airliners, polymers, computers, lasers, rockets, transistors, microelectronics, systems analysis, cost-benefit accounting, mind-altering drugs, tape recorders, steel-belted radials, body stockings, the aluminum beer can. Where would it end?

President Kennedy inherited all of this. It was almost too good to be true. He called it the New Frontier, honoring the past and making a promise of new marvels to come. As if to prove Henry Nash Smith's theory that the frontier is as much myth as reality, the media called the White House Camelot, treated Mrs. Kennedy like a reigning queen, and groveled in supine adulation before the new White House courtiers, who were, they agreed, the brightest and best that America had to offer.

There is no need to linger over the end of the story. The New Frontier became the Great Society and died on the floor of the Chicago Convention of 1968. Almost before it began, it showed signs of decay. By 1972 John Kennedy, Martin Luther King, and Robert Kennedy had been assassinated, Lyndon Johnson had declined renomination, and Hubert Humphrey had been defeated (with the assistance of Eugene McCarthy) by Richard Nixon. Los Angeles and Detroit and Washington had exploded in riots. Berkeley, Columbia, and Kent State had destroyed for our time the myth of the university as a sanctuary of contemplative thought in the chaos of social change. Viet Nam had become an international debacle, and light refused to appear at the end of the proverbial tunnel. The domestic programs of the Great Society, which were supposed to provide a decent income as well as education and medical care for all citizens, had drained the economy without accomplishing very much at all, let alone the Unbelievable.

Toward the end of this period, Americans had a new set of reminders of the limits within which they were living, and these were especially troublesome because they came from beyond America's borders. To the frontier mentality, America had always seemed protected from foreign threats by the Atlantic and Pacific oceans, and self-sufficient in basic raw materials. Intercontinental ballistic missiles shattered the idea that America was insulated, and the threat of the missiles was underscored by the international monetary crisis, the balance-of-payments problem, the bull market in gold, the decline of the dollar, double-digit inflation, and the lesson in interdependence provided by the rise of OPEC. The American sense of military superiority was eroded by Soviet penetration of the Near East, Ethiopia, Angola, and Afghanistan. Closer to home—in America's backyard—was Fidel Castro. In 1980, in fact, Americans were so upset by Castro that many of them considered the presence of 2000 Soviet troops in Cuba to be a threat to the entire North American continent, in spite of the failure of half a million American troops to change the political drift of Southeast Asia.

There is a vivid symbol from the sixties of the conflict between the frontier tradition and the sense of narrowing limits. By conscious choice, the chief impossibility that President Kennedy proposed to the American people at the beginning of his administration was space exploration. The commitment to put an American on the moon by 1970 had all the characteristics of a crusade. It was new, it was less complicated than civil rights, and it was more inspiring than economic expansion, which simply meant more of the same. Most important, it appealed to the frontier tradition in its classic form. The moon was territory in the literal sense of the word. It was Diana—virgin land. Beyond the moon lay the planets and the stars. Perhaps the frontier had only begun. In the words of Walter Rundell, a distinguished American historian:

> The American experiment in democracy has not failed, perhaps . . . because of the simple Western belief that it *cannot* fail. Now, as civilization appears to be on the brink of the supreme adventure of staking out new frontiers in space, students of history may well heed the advice that Carl Russell Fish gave in 1917. We should study the old frontiers so that we may comprehend the new.

"New frontiers in space." Only Rölvaag's language does justice to the atmosphere in which the quest for the new frontier was pursued: "Youth was in the race; the unknown, the untried, the unheard-of was in the air; people caught it, were intoxicated by it, threw themselves away, and laughed at the cost."

Unfortunately, they eventually stopped laughing. When the American astronauts finally reached the moon, it held no surprises. As astronomers had known for a century, the moon was a gray, dead, airless lump of rubble. It could be reached at enormous expense, but who would want to make the trip? It was not a new Peru or a California; it was not even a new Nevada.

Today most people have forgotten the puppet-like figure on the gray tube planting a tin flag in the lunar soil. The enduring image of the space program—the image that has become part of the deep psychology of modern culture—is the image of the earth that the astronauts saw when they looked back. This image may have been worth the entire price of the space program. It is not an image of unknown lands but of humanity. It has become the symbol of the ecology movement because it announces more plainly than any argument that man is small and fragile and alone. If man cannot learn to live on the earth he will die on it.

The smallness of the earth has obvious implications for the aspect of the frontier mentality that depends on the openness of the land. It is a restatement of the message of the 1890 census: *Use what you have because there is no more.* It also has implications, which are beginning to become apparent, for the aspect of the frontier mentality that has been sustained by economic growth. The earth is finite economically as well as physically, and its resources are already strained. Whether or not the fear that world resources are dangerously depleted is exaggerated, the elasticity of the supply of those elements that are critically important to human survival—energy, water, and food—has been declining. At the same time, population is increasing. The stress created by the world energy and food crisis is reflected in America in burgeoning immigration, mostly illegal, from Mexico and the Caribbean.

Clearly, America is not experiencing a momentary setback that will be canceled by a technological windfall. The next three decades will be a period of unprecedented strain and unprecedented frustration. In the end, since they cannot change reality, Americans are going to have to change their political goals and their personal expectations to conform to the world in which they live. They are going to have to accept periodic reductions in their standard of living as well as high unemployment before the economy reaches equilibrium—if an equilibrium is attainable at all.

In 1970, Americans were talking confidently about cleaning up their society and reforming the world. Today the mood has changed. Their government has stabilized or cut domestic programs for education, welfare, medical assistance, and civil rights. The public wants reduced taxes and lowered federal presence in local affairs. Beneath the superficial movement toward conservatism, more bitter and fundamental tensions can be felt: the hostility between rich and poor, black and white, Hispanic and Anglo, farmer and white-collar worker, public servant and private entrepreneur, and youth and age. None of these hostilities can be resolved without money, which is in short supply. Consequently, instead of preparing to reform the world, Americans feel the world pressing in upon them. When they look ahead they do not think in terms of accomplishing the Unbelievable, they think of muddling through. The Impossible no longer looks like a challenge: it only looks impossible.

Sometime between 1968 and 1972 the frontier died. Its obituary notice had been written in 1952 by Walter Prescott Webb in *The Great Frontier*: "As we linger in contemplation of the great tapestry of modern literature which has left us images of what the human imagination did with a New World, we know that it represents a special kind of experience, that it is done, and our last impression as we turn away is that to many of us it was as big as God." If Webb wrote the obituary, Don McLean wrote the funeral elegy of the frontier in his song "American Pie":

> I lost the three men I admired most
> The Father, the Son, and the Holy Ghost
> They took the last train for the coast
> The day the music died.

If open land and industrialization created the first American revolution perhaps it is time to recognize that the next revolution is in progress. It is a revolution created by the end of the first frontier. It is the revolution that will have to take place as Americans, along with the rest of the world's population, adjust to impossibilities.

Most writers who have thought about this have taken a pessimistic view of the outcome. Webb, who correctly identified the frontier with economics as well as geography, speculated that if American economic growth came to a halt, the historical period from 1800 to the present would seem to be "an aberration, a temporary departure from the normal, a strange historical detour in which men developed all sorts of quaint ideas about prosperity for all, freedom for all, and continuous progress."

There are, of course, even more ominous scenarios for what is coming. The Orwell-Burgess school foresees a police state based on the marvels of Skinnerian conditioning and electronic surveillance backed up by raw power. Throughout the world today democracies are on the defensive. Torture seems to be a more popular method of social control than Skinnerian positive reinforcement or bugs in every bedroom, but all methods are used. Can American democracy survive the coming turbulence, or will it opt for what is called "strong leadership" and rigid social controls?

The environmentalists predict with considerable justification that long before man creates the perfect tyranny, he will drown in his own pollution. The greenhouse effect, a rise in planetary temperature created by increasing amounts of atmospheric carbon dioxide, is sufficiently worrisome to be of concern to both national and international scientific groups. Meanwhile, radioactive wastes and chemical poisons continue to accumulate everywhere. Each year brings more acid rain and another headline announcing "the largest oil spill in history."

Population experts predict mass starvation rather than death by Strontium 90 or PVC. According to Robert McNamara, 30 million children under five years of age already starve every year.

General famine has occurred sporadically in several under-developed regions including Bangladesh, the Sahel, and Cambodia. Although in 1980 world food supplies were roughly in balance with demand, the balance depends on continuing high levels of food production in a few nations that produce food surpluses. A sudden change in world climate could lead rapidly to unprecedented disaster. Pessimists argue that nothing can save the hundreds of millions of human beings who live on the margins of modern society. They foresee a series of catastrophes that will reduce world population by attrition on the one hand and produce a new feudalism on the other. Short of the total annihilation of mankind, multinational corporations will become the feudal landholders of the new order. They will look after their dependents and leave the rest of mankind to its own devices.

According to this scenario, the state has lost its traditional authority. In the future it will become an increasingly transparent fiction. The multinationals, however, have adapted to the new, world-based economy. They will survive in the same way that small, agile warm-blooded animals survived the dinosaur when the world's climate suddenly changed.

But enough! In all this litany of gloom there is one comforting fact. Mankind cannot be destroyed by all of the catastrophes predicted by futurologists simultaneously. In fact, futurology is more closely related to astrology than to science. Whatever the future brings, it is sure to be different from what has been predicted. It might even be a pleasant surprise.

Thomas Jefferson was more interested in human beings than in technology. He drew his ideas from a tradition that extends back through the eighteenth century to the republican political thought of Greece and Rome. The point of view for which he spoke assumes that society will develop gradually, within limits defined by stable values. It seeks to identify those values and to shape social institutions in their image. It begins with man's humanity and deploys the limited resources of society and Nature around that humanity in the best possible manner. At its center is the idea of liberty—of the open society—since without liberty no other aspect of human life can develop naturally.

The most important task of Americans during the revolution of the eighties and nineties will be to preserve this tradition. Webb equated liberty with the individualism of the frontier. He therefore feared that the end of the frontier would be the end of liberty. In its place would come a drab conformity and an interest only in "the harmless nuances of the known." There is more nostalgia than reason in Webb's comment. The idea of liberty came from Greece not from Dodge City; and the practical application of the idea of liberty to human affairs was the work of the Protestants of the Reformation and the Puritans of the English Commonwealth far more than it was the work of Davy Crockett or Judge Roy Bean.

Beyond this, there is the fact that the known is never as simple or as obvious as it seems. Every advance in knowledge transforms the known into something strange and challenging. Today man has advanced so far into "the harmless nuances of the known" that he finds himself responsible for large areas of human life that were formerly in the hands of God. It is a frightening situation, but also an exhilarating one. The handmaid of knowledge is power. As modern man understands well, power can be abused. But even in the abuse of power something is learned. It is at least possible that man will learn to use knowledge and power benignly rather than for self-destruction.

After two centuries of preoccupation with economic growth, Americans are being forced to reconsider the problems of human nature that interested Thomas Jefferson. This is an extremely difficult task. It is always easier to cling to illusions than to face the truth. The story of Oedipus the King is a prime illustration. And it may be far easier for a society addicted to novelty to thrust blindly into the Impossible in hope of accomplishing the Unbelievable than to confront such "nuances of the known" as the preservation of an open society in a political climate that makes freedom seem an impossible luxury. In the words of Dostoevsky's Grand Inquisitor, "In the end they will lay their freedom at our feet and say to us, 'Make us your slaves but feed us.' They will understand at last that freedom and bread for all are inconceivable together."

Science is not the villain of the twentieth century. It has created the knowledge that is man's only hope for survival. The problem is learning to use technology to serve life rather than to threaten it. It is a problem that goes deeper than rational knowledge, all the way to the instinct for survival. Beyond instinct, it includes the values—irrational, absurd, sentimental, impractical, and outmoded though they may seem—that are suggested by the phrase "life, liberty, and the pursuit of happiness." To understand this phrase is to confront again the tradition that extends from ancient Palestine and Greece to Jefferson's Monticello and contemporary Washington, D.C.

The second American revolution, the one Americans are now living, will force them to decide how valuable their values really are. They will have to decide between Thomas Jefferson and the Grand Inquisitor. It may be that Thomas Jefferson will have more to say to the generation of the eighties and nineties than to any previous generation since the first American revolution. Jefferson believed that revolution was not only a right but a duty. He wrote: "The Creator has made the earth for the living, not for the dead." It would be good to think he was right, since many of us are going to live long enough to find out.

14

A Possible Self

Goethe is sometimes described as the last universal man. He was a passionate amateur biologist as well as a statesman, poet, dramatist, essayist, and critic. He wrote on geology, the metamorphoses of plants, color optics, and crystallography, as well as literary topics. His discovery of the intermaxillary bone in the human skull was an important contribution to the evidence linking man to other forms of animal life. His theory of art was decisively influenced by the biological concept of organic form, the idea that the part is determined by the whole to which it belongs. He was also one of the first major European artists—perhaps the first—to apply the transnational, universalist view of science to culture. He imitated Persian poetry in the collection titled *Westöstlicher Diwan* and proposed world literature (*Weltliteratur*) as an alternative to the exclusively European bias of the literary study of his age. "National literature," he remarked in his conversations with Eckermann, "is now rather an unmeaning term; the epoch of World Literature is at hand, and everyone must strive to hasten its approach." Goethe's announcement of the arrival of world literature anticipates the enormous expansion of human consciousness that technology has caused in the twentieth century. It confirms his standing as a prophet of modern humanism.

Goethe's close friend Friedrich Schiller was as much a philosopher as a poet. His *Letters on the Aesthetic Education of Man* (1795) applied Kantian philosophy to the problem of achieving lasting improvements in human society. At one time Schiller believed that human society could be improved by political means. His studies of the German Peasants' Revolt and the Thirty Years War, however, made him skeptical of the ability of politics to solve human problems. The failure of the democratic reforms of the French Revolution confirmed his skepticism. He concluded that attempts to legislate one form of oppression out of existence frequently end by creating another more virulent than the one being abolished.

In Johann Winckelmann's *Reflections on the Paintings and Sculpture of the Greeks* (1787), Schiller felt he had discovered historical proof that art can achieve what law and the force of arms cannot. The *Letters* generalize this idea. Art is a form of play in which the spirit freely objectifies itself in material creations. These creations—paintings, songs, statues, and the like —in turn, educate and liberate the individuals who make up society. The process is gradual and peaceful rather than revolutionary. It occurs because the self remains potentially free and undetermined in spite of the cultural and political forces that limit its freedom at any given moment. Schiller's humanism is thus, like Goethe's, open and affirmative and deeply committed to the idea of a possible self that transcends the actual self and gives it meaning.

The main current of nineteenth-century humanism was neither philosophical nor affirmative. It was a classical humanism oriented to the past and attached to the didactic theory of art. When it confronted the present, its typical themes were the in-humanity of industrial society, the contrasting beauty of the vanished past, the divorce of body and soul caused by science, and the crudity of the culture brought into existence by egalitarian politics. To all of these negative trends it opposed the sanity and objectivity of the classics.

Sainte-Beuve and Matthew Arnold were among the chief nineteenth-century spokesmen for this classical humanism. In a world he felt was rapidly being dehumanized by science and religious and political factions, Arnold turned to art—particularly poetry—for consolation. His essay *The Study of Poetry* begins with the famous suggestion that poetry may eventually have to take the place of religion for modern man:

> Our religion has materialized itself in the fact, in the supposed fact; it has attached its emotions to the fact, and now the fact is failing it. But for poetry the idea is everything. . . . The strongest part of our religion today is its unconscious poetry.

The instinctive sense in this comment of the kinship between art and religion is fascinating, but as T. S. Eliot, among others, has argued, Arnold asks too much of poetry. Religion and art may satisfy similar human needs, but one is not a substitute for the other in any simple sense.

Arnold anticipates the hostility to modernism that is typical of much that passes for twentieth-century humanism—a hostility that would have been incomprehensible to Goethe. He also anticipates the widespread idea that a fracture or "dissociation of sensibility" (Eliot's term) occurred in European culture in the seventeenth century when scientists like Francis Bacon and René Descartes drove a wedge between the spiritual and material worlds. Arnold sought the wholeness that had vanished from his own culture in the classics of antiquity and in the medieval Catholicism of Dante. Dante's line "In Your will is our peace" was Arnold's favorite touchstone for great poetry and, evidently, for great philosophy as well.

In *The Idea of a Christian Society* (1938), in his own quest for wholeness, T. S. Eliot momentarily took a sympathetic view of German National Socialism or, to put it more accurately, what he then imagined National Socialism to be. More typically, he looked to the Christian and feudal world of the Middle Ages for the model of a healthy society. His contemporary William Butler Yeats celebrated the heroic world of Gaelic legend in his early poetry; later he used the exotic, half-historical and half-mythical culture of Byzantium to symbolize the kind of society in which a full spiritual life is possible.

Similar attitudes can be found in French and American humanism. The *Action Française* movement idealized the French monarchy and Roman Catholicism. In America the Fugitive-Agrarian group decided that the Good Life had last been seen on antebellum Southern plantations. The new humanists of Boston, New York, and Princeton agreed with the Fugitive-Agrarians concerning the evils of science, industrialism, and romantic freedom in the arts. Although they were notably un-enthusiastic about Southern plantations, they also agreed that egalitarianism has its limits—that the good society is one in which the many are governed by the enlightened few.

Reinforcing the humanist attack on modernity, E.M.W. Tillyard and C. S. Lewis (both British scholars) and Douglas Bush (an American scholar) offered a reading of the history of Western culture that made the early seventeenth century the dividing line between the age of wholeness ("the Elizabethan world picture") and the age of fragmentation. In this reading, the transition begins with the appearance of such works as Machiavelli's *The Prince* and Bacon's *Novum Organum,* and the heliocentric astronomy of Copernicus. Theodore Spencer argued in *Shakespeare and the Nature of Man* that the tensions created by the trauma of the decay of the old culture explain the resonance of Shakespeare's tragedies for the modern reader.

In 1951 Jacques Ellul summed up the discontents of classical humanism in a massive indictment of modern culture titled *La Technique: L'enjeu du siècle.* According to Ellul, technology and the social organization needed to make the technology work (which he called "technique") are destroying humanity. His book is the forerunner of a series of attacks on technological society that began appearing in the mid-1950s and are still pouring from American and European presses. His conclusion is gloomy. In spite of all the ills the technocrats have visited upon mankind, they have won:

> What good is it to talk to motives? Why? All that must be the work of some miserable intellectual who balks at technical progress. The attitude of scientists, at any rate, is clear. Technique exists because it is technique. The Golden Age will be because it will be. Any other answer is superfluous.

As public anxiety has mounted because of pollution, depletion of resources, population growth, the spread of nuclear weapons, the dehumanization of workers by the techniques of modern production, and increasingly severe economic problems, an international coalition of the disaffected has emerged that includes neo-humanists, environmentalists, advocates of a "steady-state" economy, and radical political theorists of the right and the left. Beneath the immensely various points of view that are evident in this coalition, the themes of classical humanism persist like the ground accompaniment to melodies in a musical composition: modern culture is inhuman, man is bent on self-destruction, the clock of progress somehow must be turned back, the masses cannot be trusted and therefore must be led by those who understand what needs to be done.

While it is certainly true that modern culture faces innumerable problems and that many of them have been caused by the use and abuse of technology, the blanket condemnation of modernity is little more than a council of despair and a confession of the sterility of the ideas on which classical humanism is based.

After two hundred years, the lament for the good old days has begun to grow tiresome. It is by no means certain that the good old days, which so often turn out to be the days of serfs and barons and laity and bishops and black slaves and white masters, were all that good. And, no matter how good they were, they are over. There is no going back. Modern man lives in his own world and will make his own accommodation to it. What is needed is a humanism that can confront the past without sentiment and the present without fear, a humanism, in other words, in the tradition of Goethe and Schiller.

Curiously enough, the Renaissance ancestors of the classical humanists were radicals rather than conservatives. They wanted to break once and for all with what they believed to be the deadening traditions of the Middle Ages. In the sixteenth century the historical alternative to scholastic culture was the culture of Greek and Roman antiquity. Consequently, Renaissance humanists idealized the ancient world—not because it was like what they knew of their own world but because it was different. They searched avidly for manuscripts of lost classical authors, published new editions of the classics and of the early Church fathers, developed new theories of style based on imitation of classical models, and sought to institutionalize their revolution through an educational curriculum based on intensive study of those models. The excitement of revolutionary discovery can still be felt in their literary and critical works.

By the nineteenth century, however, the sense of discovery had been lost. The legacy of the Renaissance humanists survived as a list of approved Greek and Roman classics supplemented by more modern classic authors like Dante, Shakespeare, and Montaigne. Analogous lists can be found in the nineteenth-century canon of visual art and music, but they are less significant because before the twentieth century both education and higher culture were language-oriented. The study of the classics (including those of painting, sculpture, and music) had ceased to be an adventure and had become, when it had any intellectual content at all, a means of indoctrinating students in what Matthew Arnold called "the best that has been thought and said in the world." Arnold's phrase betrays itself. The classics were not valued because they are different and hence liberating but because they are familiar and hence reassuring. To study them from this point of view was not to discover something new but to confirm what was already known.

Ironically, it was the effort to make the universality of the classics fully intelligible that exposed the historical naïveté of the classical humanists. Because the classics often present archaic customs in unfamiliar languages, a good deal of historical research was necessary to explain them. As this research became more sophisticated an odd fact began to emerge: the more diligently and expertly the past was studied, the farther it receded from the present and the less tenable the idea of universal values became.

Historical criticism began with the study of language since the subjects to which it was first applied in a systematic way were texts in archaic languages—Hebrew, Greek, and Latin at first, and later, languages like Gothic, Old French, Gaelic, and Provençal. Linguistics was soon joined by studies of the historical contexts within which various works of art were produced: the biographies of artists, the political circumstances that shaped the works, the history of the genres to which they were assigned, contemporary tastes, the nature of the materials from which the works were created, the conditions of performance in the cases of drama and music, the economics of patronage or of the art market, and so forth. While precedents for all of these approaches can be found in every period of Western culture, they became formal disciplines in the nineteenth century and began to take on lives of their own as philology, textual criticism, art history, musicology, and the like. And as they became formal disciplines, they developed methodologies that, in the opinion of many of their apologists, produced scientifically objective results.

The consequences of historical criticism are easy to illustrate. Today, Shakespeare is considered the foremost classic English author. There is general agreement that his plays exhibit universal truths of human nature and that his use of the English language sets the standard by which all later authors using that language are to be measured. Precisely because of Shakespeare's classic status, his world has been studied more intensively than that of any other English author. His theater has been reconstructed; the organization of the English acting companies of his time has been excavated from Elizabethan records; Elizabethan grammar, spelling, handwriting, and pronunciation have been scrutinized; the influences on Shakespeare of other dramatists, of political, social, and religious sources, and of current events have been evaluated; his characters have been analyzed in terms of Rennaissance faculty psychology as well as in Freudian terms; his puns have been explained; and the meager facts of his life have been collected and recollected.

All of these efforts should, theoretically, have made it easier to read Shakespeare. This is not the case. Instead of making Shakespeare more accessible, historical criticism has deposited a huge mountain of controversial, problematic, sometimes illuminating and sometimes plain silly scholarship between Shakespeare and his would-be reader. In the process, the scholar has almost inevitably come to be regarded (and to regard himself) as the keeper of a sacred flame. Having explored the mountain and become familiar with its topography, the scholar claims a special, almost priestly, authority in matters of interpretation. As Shakespeare scholarship has accumulated, Shakespeare has therefore become more and more remote. This exemplifies the general effect of historical scholarship. The knowledge that is supposed to be the precondition to appreciation becomes a demonstration that the values of the classics are not universal. They are strange and alien. If the historical scholars are right, the classics are fenced with signs: "Laymen, Keep Out."

This is not the result of a plot by the clerks of the modern establishment to rob humanity of its heritage. It is the by-product of an irresistible cultural movement. Nevertheless, the quest for historical understanding has left classical humanism in an untenable position. The idea that a classic exhibits universal values or that a "perennial philosophy" can be discovered in the classics of every age and language is wishful thinking. This does not mean that works of art are not in some sense universal, nor does it mean that it is impossible or improper to make a collection of works of art that express a common tradition. It does mean that classical humanism has ignored the otherness of the past in its eagerness to put the past to current uses, including the use of nostalgia.

Is anything perennial? If so, in what sense? A thought-experiment based on two scientific discoveries may be useful here.

Toward the end of the seventeenth century Sir Isaac Newton formulated the law of universal gravitation. His idea was not entirely new. It drew heavily on Galileo's study of pendulum motion, on Descartes's analytic geometry, and on Kepler's discovery of the elliptical orbits of planets. Newton is rightly given credit, however, for bringing earlier scientific theory into focus and expressing the result in precise mathematical language. Before the publication of *Principia Mathematica* in 1687, gravity was an empirical observation. After 1687 it was a precise concept that could be applied to a whole range of phenomena from the trajectory of artillery shells to the orbits of planets.

Was gravity invented by Newton? In other words, does a change in the understanding of a fact change the fact itself? Fortunately, the question does not have to be answered with philosophical rigor in the present instance. When stones were dropped off the cliffs of Piraeus, they accelerated toward the sea at 32 feet per second squared. Nothing has happened in later history to change this. They still accelerate at 32 feet per second squared. Newton did not invent the law of universal gravitation, he discovered it. He did not change Nature, he only changed man's understanding of Nature. For normal purposes, it is safe to say that gravity is perennial.

The problem is more difficult for phenomena that relate to the mind. In human affairs a kind of sociological uncertainty principle always seems to operate, and the results, in turn, change the human relations being observed.

Freud published *The Interpretation of Dreams* in 1900. Freudian psychology may be said to have begun with this event. Freud was a scientist, a physician, and was interested in the universal patterns underlying behavior. He is often accused of being reductive in his methods because he sought to explain the enormous diversity of human personality in terms of a small number of basic principles. Freud believed these principles to be universal; they could be applied to the past as well as to the present. He named the most fundamental personality warp—the Oedipus Complex—after a character in a play by Sophocles, and he subjected historical figures who lived long before the twentieth century to psychoanalysis. He even extended his principles to fiction. He wrote brilliant studies of Shakespeare's *Merchant of Venice* and Ibsen's *Rösmersholm* and sketched out an interpretation of *Hamlet* that was later extended by his disciple Ernest Jones in a classic study titled *Hamlet and Oedipus*. His *Moses and Monotheism* (1939) is a blend of psychoanalysis, history, and religion that has had considerable influence in all three fields. His followers have continued this work. Psychoanalytic art criticism has been commonplace since the 1920s, and the use of psychology for biography pioneered by Erik Erikson has produced a distinct branch of history called psychohistory.

Are the principles of behavior discovered by Freud perennial in the same way that gravity is perennial? As psychoanalytic criticism and psychohistory have gained popularity this question has been raised repeatedly. It has been answered with as many *yeses* as *noes*. From the present perspective, the *noes* are more convincing. An uncertainty principle is operating here. People's behavior is influenced by what they think their behavior ought to be.

Since 1900, Freud's powerful and comprehensive theory of behavior has had an influence that extends far beyond the medical profession. In effect, it has encouraged new norms while examining traditional ones. Many forms of behavior that were repressed in the nineteenth century because they were considered deviant or evil are now expressed freely and considered normal. Family relations, patterns of child-rearing, sexual habits, attitudes toward aggression, and responses to social problems like crime and insanity have changed because of Freud. Art has changed. Perhaps even the modern way of dreaming has changed. If changes of this sort have occurred, it follows that individuals who lived before Freud's influence became widespread behaved in ways that cannot be explained fully by Freudian psychology. Their behavior must be understood in terms of the systems they accepted—religion, custom, and pseudo-sciences like astrology, physiognomy, and the theory of the four bodily humors.

If so, Freudian psychology demonstrates the discontinuity, not the continuity, of human nature and the limited validity of all attempts to describe it in universal terms. Apparently, human nature is as undetermined as Schiller understood it to be. Historical scholarship demonstrates the validity of this idea through its descriptions of past cultures. The example of Freud suggests further that whenever a new system of universal truth is announced and widely accepted, it begins to separate the present from the past by creating new patterns of behavior. Things are never quite the same again. Those who know the system become aware of themselves as enlightened "moderns" in contrast to the confused "ancients."

The past, it would seem, refuses to be the present. On the other hand, it will not go away. It is a little like the ghost of Hamlet's father. Is he really the ghost of Hamlet's father? Is he telling the truth? Is he a hallucination? Whatever he is, he exists as an influence that determines the action of the play.

Anthropologists commonly divide the history of culture into a pre-critical and a critical phase. A list of major contributors to the subject over the last half-century would be lengthy and would certainly include such authorities as Henri Frankfort, Carl Jung, Mircea Eliade, Ernst Cassirer, and Claude Lévi-Strauss. Pre-critical thought is typical of primitive societies. Although it was dismissed as childish superstition by the rationalists of the Enlightenment, Giambattista Vico issued a powerful dissenting opinion in his *New Science* (1725). Vico was not himself influential on later thought, but a similar interest in primitive thought appeared in the work of Herder and von Humboldt at the beginning of the Romantic period. It was carried forward in the later nineteenth century by such writers as E. B. Tylor, Andrew Lang, W. Robertson Smith, James Frazer, and Emile Durkheim, and, in the area of philosophy, by Friedrich Nietzsche.

In the words of E. B. Tylor: "Myth is the history of its authors, not its subjects: it records the lives not of superhuman heroes, but of poetic nations." Tylor's suggestion that myth is a projection of human concerns onto the objective world of Nature is doubtless correct from a modern analytical point of view, but it does scant justice to the realities of pre-critical experience. To the pre-critical mind, Nature and the human spirit are equally powerful forces. The shaping influence of Nature is complemented by the influence of divine powers that exist in an invisible world beyond Nature. These divine powers are not indifferent to human life; on the contrary, they intervene in it constantly. They can also be modified by human actions such as incantation, prayer, and religious ceremonies. Properly invoked, they will sustain the conditions on which life depends: seasonal change, climate, fertility, success in warfare, health, and the like. If they are ignored or improperly invoked, they may exert harmful influences.

The gods have their own lives, which are recounted in myth. Creation myths describe the beginnings of things. Cosmological and seasonal myths objectify the movements of heavenly bodies and the annual cycle of the death and rebirth of Nature. Much depends on living in harmony with the forces revealed in these myths. Mircea Eliade describes the myth—common in all pre-critical societies—that society is located at the geographical center of Creation. Its territory is divinely ordained, and certain spots within its territory are sacred because they are passageways between things visible and invisible. Nomadic people carry the center of Creation with them on their travels. Failure to do this can jeopardize survival. In *The Sacred and the Profane* (1957), Eliade cites the tragedy of an Australian tribe that broke the sacred pole representing the axis of the world:

> This pole represents a cosmic axis, for it is around the sacred pole that territory becomes habitable, hence is transformed into a world. The sacred pole consequently plays an important role ritually. During their wanderings the Achilpa always carry it with them and choose the direction they are to take by the direction toward which it bends. This allows them, while being continually on the move, to be always in "their world." . . . For the pole to be broken denotes catastrophe; it is like "the end of the world," reversion to chaos. Spencer and Gillen report that once, when the pole was broken, the entire clan were in consternation; they wandered around aimlessly for a time, and finally lay down on the ground together and waited for death to overtake them.

If space is sacred in pre-critical thought, time is equally so. Linear time is reckoned from a mythic "point of origin," which is commonly established by a momentous eruption of the invisible into the visible world—a miracle, an epiphany, a divine birth, or something similar. "1950" means one thousand, nine hundred and fifty years after the birth of Christ in Palestine. Linear time, however, is less important in pre-critical thought than cyclic time. Cyclic time reproduces the circular movement of the seasons and the constant repetition in the lives of individuals of the unchanging patterns of life established by the gods. In modern America the cycle of the liturgical year preserves this tradition.

There can be no secular knowledge in pre-critical society

because all significant knowledge is religious. Every action partakes of ritual. Things are done in certain ways because they have to be in order to maintain harmony between the visible and invisible worlds. This is true of rites of passage, taboos, marriage ceremonies, funeral and mourning customs, kinship formulas, dietary regulations, and much more. Grace, charm, aesthetic pleasure, individuality—even efficiency—are irrelevant. The pre-critical mind is wrapped in a cocoon of its own making. The image of the universe as a series of concentric spheres with the earth floating at the center like an embryo bathed in amniotic fluid is an apt symbol of this condition.

If any entirely pre-critical society ever existed—which is dubious—all traces of it have vanished. All real societies, including modern society, are mixtures of pre-critical and critical elements. In all real pre-critical societies the holy has limits. Certain activities are indifferent, secularized. They are done because they have to be done, and how they are done is significant only to the doer. No gods have to be invoked, no prayers uttered, no ritual prescriptions followed. Other activities become indifferent because the people who perform them forget their original meanings. Presumably, not every Navajo Indian is thoroughly familiar with Navajo religious symbolism. For a good many Navajos, the traditional tribal designs are probably exactly what they are to the non-Indian: attractive abstractions as empty of symbolism as wallpaper. The divine power has gone out of them. In the same way, agnostics visit cathedrals to admire their stained-glass windows and carved altars without any deep sense of the relation of these objects to the act of worship. Even among devout believers, rituals and customs lose their meaning. The extensive liturgical reforms undertaken by the Catholic and Anglican churches since the Second Vatican Council were made necessary by just this problem. By making the liturgies more comprehensible, the reformers hoped to encourage active participation in worship rather than simply "going through the motions."

Modern life is filled with anachronisms that are legacies of pre-critical stages of culture. The guests at a wedding throw rice because it is the conventional thing to do, not because they believe it will bestow fertility on the newly married couple. The hostess at a dinner party seats the guest of honor on her right because that is a convenient way of identifying the guest of honor, not because she believes, or even knows, that the right side is favored by the gods; and the guest of honor throws spilled salt over his left shoulder automatically. If someone asked whether he thought the sinister powers of the left had to be propitiated, he would probably consider the question impertinent. People knock on wood for luck, indifferent to the fact that they are invoking Pan, the god of trees. They circumcise male children because someone has told them this is the thing to do or because they think the operation is hygienic, not because they believe in ritual scarification.

Critical thought prides itself on confronting the world as it is. It seeks to "buckle and bow the mind to Nature" in Francis Bacon's memorable phrase. Bacon regarded poetry as, at best, a momentary diversion from life's serious occupations. In *The Wisdom of the Ancients* (1619) he came to terms with mythology by deciding that the classical myths are actually allegories of philosophical truth concealed under veils of fiction from the masses by ancient sages. To see things as they are means to divorce them from human concerns. Nature is a machine indifferent to man. The sun ceases to be the chariot of Apollo and becomes an object to be studied by astronomers.

The movement from a basically pre-critical to a basically critical point of view occurs in history long before the emergence of a fully scientific attitude. It is the condition for the emergence of science. When it does occur, every aspect of life is transformed for those who experience it. The world is no longer an assembly of powers that are alternately terrifying and benevolent but a baffling, extremely intricate mechanism. That the mechanism defies explanation does not mean that the task of understanding it is hopeless. The possibility of explanation, in turn, encourages science, and each scientific discovery reinforces the faith that eventually the whole mechanism will be explained. Nature is a complex pattern to be discovered and described. As the effort moves forward there are both gains and losses. The glow the invisible world once cast over life is dimmed, but at the same time the misdirected energies of superstition diminish. Society emerges into daylight that is alternately intoxicating and harsh. The nostalgia for the past that is characteristic of classical humanism is essentially a lament for the loss of pre-critical innocence. Matthew Arnold came close to stating this explicitly in his poem "Dover Beach":

> The Sea of Faith
> Was once, too, at the full, and round earth's shore
> Lay like the folds of a bright girdle furled.
> But now I only hear
> Its melancholy, long, withdrawing roar,
> Retreating, to the breath
> Of the night-wind, down the vast edges drear
> And naked shingles of the world.

Let us now return to the parallel between religion and poetry that Arnold drew in *The Study of Poetry*, for it is a link between classical and modern humanism. The Greeks probably explored the full range of critical thought more thoroughly than any other ancient people. In the two centuries between the pre-Socratic philosophers and the death of Aristotle, the Greeks almost literally remade their world, and the foundations that they constructed were so well built that, two thousand years later, the Renaissance had to master Greek learning before adding to it.

There is a paradox in Greek culture that is very much to the point. In the midst of their astonishing effort to buckle the mind to Nature, the Greeks found time to create works of art that remain permanent glories of the human spirit. All of their art—the pottery, the sculpture, the poems, the drama—has links with religious tradition that are easy to trace. Greek drama, for example, is related to Dionysian festivals celebrating the annual rebirth of Nature in the spring. If Gilbert Murray is correct, these festivals once involved the ritual slayings and eating of a human victim representing the "year daimon."

In *The Birth of Tragedy*, Friedrich Nietzsche argued that as the divine life went out of the Greek religious ceremonies they became historical dramas. Eventually, the dramas became an entirely secular mixture of sensational actions and rhetorical debate. Nietzsche generalized this theory in a book written toward the end of his life, *The Twilight of the Gods*, which, in turn, was influential on the so-called "death of god" theology of the 1960s. Insofar as his theory relates to Greek tragedy, it seems to fit nicely the movement of Greek tragedy from Aeschylus to Euripides and of Greek comedy from Aristophanes to Menander.

But there is another, less rationalistic way of looking at the change. The Greeks credited Thespis with introducing the tragic protagonist and substituting the mask of a human hero for the mask of the god. In other words, the god did not depart—or sink into the twilight—but took on a human disguise. At the same time, the god's liturgy was changed into the plot of an historical drama. In this version of the history of Greek drama, the god does not abandon human society but assumes a more intimate relation to it. He physically enters history rather than staying outside of it. The appearance of representational drama may thus not be a sign that the gods have departed, as Nietzsche believed, but a sign that they have come closer.

Something similar appears to have happened in Greek sculpture. The earliest forms of Greek sculpture are based on Near Eastern and Egyptian models. The statues of the gods are angular, austere, remote from humanity. Gradually, they become humanized. Clearly, the sculptors were beginning to use living models. According to Simonides, Praxiteles used the best features of many different human models to create his statues of gods. Is this process one in which the gods are re-created in the image of man or one in which man's image is discovered in the gods?

Both explanations work. Whichever is right, the canons of physical beauty established by the Greeks assume a close relation between divine beauty and ideal human beauty. Greek portrait busts thus have a radiance, a sense of the eternal fixed in time, that can be understood as the divine archetype shining from the individual human face. Picasso repeated this process—consciously or unconsciously—when, around 1903, he turned to primitive Iberian and African art for ways of introducing a sense of the spiritual behind the physical into his portraits of twentieth-century subjects.

Why is art necessary at all in the critical phase of culture? A rational society ought to find its highest pleasures in the discovery of truth. Plato was troubled by this problem. He explained in the *Republic* that art can be tolerated in a rational society if it reinforces ethical philosophy, but it should be outlawed if it wanders off on eccentric and morally questionable tangents. At the same time, he seems to admit (perhaps ironically) in his dialogue *Ion* that art is a matter of inspiration and that it does not obey the normal rules of logic. Evidently, Plato toyed with the idea that the heart has reasons that the reason knows not of. A completely rational society might be exciting for a day or two but ultimately it would be as dreary as the pebbles of Matthew Arnold's "Dover Beach." Something would be missing that is essential to spiritual life.

As has already been noted, the fear of a completely rational society is an underlying motive of the humanist critique of modern culture. The fear may be in excess of the danger, however. The Greek experience suggests that the old gods never die. As pre-critical shades into critical culture, they assume human form and appear in the epiphanies of artistic experience. The pre-critical sense of the mystery that surrounds existence is recaptured in the apparently secular achievements of painting, sculpture, dance, drama, music, and poetry. To these sources of inspiration the Romantic period added Nature. Wordsworth's *Lines Composed a Few Miles Above Tintern Abbey* offers a moving yet typical Romantic description of the experience of a spiritual reality underlying Nature:

> And I have felt
> . . .
> a sense sublime
> Of something far more deeply interfused,
> Whose dwelling is the light of setting suns,
> And the round ocean and the living air,
> And the blue sky, and in the mind of man:
> A motion and a spirit, that impels
> All thinking things, all objects of all thought,
> And rolls through all things. . . .

Wordsworth's "sense sublime" is like a religious experience, but it is not religious or even pantheistic in the normal sense of those terms. An anthropologist might call it the experience of a "momentary divinity" or an instance of "participation mystique." Whatever it is called, it is evidently the adaptation of a basic spiritual category to the circumstances of critical culture. The adaptation is possible because the human spirit is undetermined and shapes itself in ways that are complementary to whatever realities it encounters. In critical culture, the gods have descended from the sky and are present in the act of perception itself. The kind of knowledge in which they are revealed can be called, for lack of a better term, aesthetic knowledge.

Aesthetic knowledge exists somewhere between religion and science. For most of Western history this was the best definition that could be formulated. The Greeks did not regard aesthetic knowledge as different from other types of knowledge. They placed aesthetics in the category of the useful and taught in their philosophy that it should be the servant of the state. Aristotle probably sided with them. He probably considered tragedy a means of exorcising certain pre-critical superstitions by persuading spectators that they live in a rational world held together by probability and necessity. If someone had informed him that the

Poetics has a strong aesthetic bias (which it does), he probably would not have understood what the statement meant.

There, more or less, the situation rested. In spite of the rich accretion of art, and thus of aesthetic experience, in the two millennia between Plato and the Enlightenment, Boileau, Dryden, Voltaire, and Dr. Johnson seldom went further than Plato in their theories of aesthetics and fell considerably behind Aristotle. The classical humanism of the nineteenth century adopted essentially the same position.

Kantian philosophy changed this situation permanently for those who were willing to learn. Kant's primary question was "How do we know?" His secondary question was "What are the kinds of knowledge that are possible to us?" In the course of answering them, he laid the foundation of a new humanism based on a new concept of the self.

According to Kant, when we consider any phenomenon we have three and only three options. We can assume that it is part of that group of phenomena that follow one another in strict causal sequence, or we can assume that it is undetermined—hence free—or we can assume that it is itself. The first assumption is scientific. The second is moral. That is, since we cannot hold anyone responsible for an action unless he is free not to perform it, freedom must be assumed for moral philosophy to be possible. As Omar Khayyám says in Edward Fitzgerald's translation of *The Rubáiyát*:

> O thou who did'st with pitfall and with gin
> Beset the road I was to wander in,
> Thou wilt not with Predestined Evil round
> Enmesh, and then impute my Fall to Sin!

Kant labeled the third kind of knowledge aesthetic, from the Greek verb *aisthanomai* "perceive." Because we must perceive something before we can decide whether it is a caused phenomenon or a free one, knowledge of the thing itself is more basic than knowledge of pure or practical reason. If we see a tree, the first thing we realize is that we are seeing a tree, and in the act of seeing we simultaneously form a concept of the self that is doing the seeing. Only later do we link the tree to Linnaeus or Darwin or Genesis or our plan to build a garage. Framing and display emphasize the uniqueness of objects, their ability to be, among other things, themselves. These acts tend to make them into art and, by corollary, into means of intensifying the observer's consciousness of self. The display of a Rolls-Royce Silver Cloud in a museum, for example, forces the viewer to see it as itself rather than drift off into a stock fantasy of speed, success, or invincible virility. Shaped stanzas, meter, and irregular lines call attention to the use of language in poetry for artistic effects that go beyond simple communication. They are thus literary equivalents to framing and display.

The idea of a kind of knowledge based on the thing itself is related to the medieval philosophy known as nominalism, which insisted that all generalizations are false because they ignore just those unique qualities of an experience that make it real. A more common modern label for this approach is ontology, the science of being. When John Crowe Ransom surveyed modern techniques of understanding literature in *The New Criticism* (1941), he ended with a chapter asking for a mode of understanding based on direct response: "Wanted: An Ontological Critic." Ransom's basic insights are still suggestive although he is currently out of fashion.

At about the same time that the Ransom school was losing favor in the United States, the phenomenological school of Husserl and Heidegger was gaining favor in Europe. The phenomenological school is explicitly neo-Kantian. Its central preoccupation is how to confront being (*Sein*) and "being in the world" (*Dasein*). How does one confront things in their simple reality without making them something they are not? This, it turns out, is exceedingly difficult. One must pare away the layers of association that have grown around every perceivable thing throughout its history. Whether there is anything at the center, once it is reached, is a nice question which Heidegger never, perhaps, answered with absolute clarity. For him the quest was more important than the conclusion. He developed a method of "destructuralizing" the thing contemplated by systematically reviewing its historical and personal associations in order to eliminate them from consciousness. As he explained: "The concrete possibility of bringing the phenomena of existence into view and specifying them in general conception can manifest itself *only when* the concrete, relevant, and effectively experienced tradition is destructuralized."

This does not sound like John Crowe Ransom. In practice it does not lead to the thing itself but to everything in the world except the thing itself. Since things exist in the mind in a matrix of historical and personal associations, it leads to historicism in one direction and to word-association exercises in another. Since both the history of ideas and the process of discovering the self by examining the relationship among ideas in the mind are fascinating, a Heideggerian analysis of a work of art is also fascinating. But fascination and illumination of a subject are two different things. The chief value of Heidegger's position is its heroic confrontation of the problem of seeing the thing itself rather than its contribution to the understanding of individual things.

A different approach results from concentration on Kant's conclusion that the mind is an information-processing machine. Although Kant did not use those words to express the idea, he suggested that the movement in the mind from data to concept requires a processor, which he called imagination. He believed that the imagination coordinates data by combining them with spiritual "categories." Ideologies and values are culturally determined, but the categories are universal. They are part of the basic equipment of the human mind. Since they adjust to whatever circumstances they encounter, they justify the definition of the spirit as a free and undetermined entity, a potential.

Kant's theory of categories has been adapted across a broad spectrum of disciplines including psychology, neurophysiology, sociology, and linguistics. Carl Jung anticipated this movement with his theory that certain generalized patterns of social response—archetypes—are innate to the human mind. They are "categories of phantasy, activity, ideas *a priori* as it were, the existence of which cannot be ascertained except by experience. In finished or shaped material, they appear only as the regulatory principle of its shaping." The Kantian thrust of this definition is obvious. Jung was led to it by the recurrence in myths and in the dreams of his patients of patterns that could not be explained by cultural conditioning. If they were not produced culturally, they must, he concluded, be part of the basic mental equipment with which we are born. Like the categories, the archetypes are universal and undetermined.

Similar conclusions were reached on the basis of independent research by other important contemporary scientists. Jean Piaget, the great modern theorist of child development, believed that certain patterns of response develop in the structure of the mind either before birth or after birth while the brain is still plastic. Piaget believed with Kant that the concepts of space and time are innate to the mind, but he believed that they are formed during the first years of childhood as a result of the interaction of the mind with its environment.

Claude Lévi-Strauss, who is usually considered a father of modern structuralism, regarded the specifics of behavior and social mores as epiphenomena. The epiphenomena could not be explained directly. They could only be understood as specific and local expressions of a deep structure that is the generalized condition for successful adaptation under any circumstances and that is therefore universal in all human societies, whether "primitive" or "advanced." This concept may be considered an anthropological version of Jung's archetypes. Again, Noam Chomsky concluded at one point in his study of linguistics that the human ability to communicate through language implies a "universal grammar" that is innate (or "hard wired") in the mind and thus the precondition of all natural languages.

That the mind is an information-processing machine is no longer a controversial idea. Until the 1950s, understanding of the way that the processing occurred was based on inference from the facts of psychology, anthropology, linguistics, and the like. In 1953, at least one small part of the processing mechanism was explained. In that year Stephen Kuffler of Johns Hopkins University published an elegant analysis of the optical cells and nerve connections that process incoming visual data in the feline eye. Kuffler's studies were later extended by David Hubel and Torsten Wiesel. The result of this work was a preliminary circuit diagram showing how raw data are converted in one part of the brain into usable information. It is clear that the processing is extensive: that the data are used selectively, that some of them are suppressed and others enhanced, and that the data processed in the nerve system attached to one eye are combined with data processed by the other in order to produce stereoscopic vision. For the first time, Kant's black box became a little less mysterious. Interestingly, this analysis of the feline retina appears to confirm Piaget's theory that the processing machine continues to develop after birth. In other words, parts of it are "hard wired" but other parts do not become fully developed until they interact with the post-natal environment. However the categories of the mind are formed, it appears certain that they are there—that the mind is an information-processing machine and that a given perception contains as much information about the structures that do the processing as about the outside world.

The grand quest of structuralism is for "deep structures" and "universal forms." This quest is both a strength from the scientific point of view and a weakness from the point of view of those to whom diversity is a positive value. Like phenomenology, structuralism explores a central aspect of Kant's legacy, but also like phenomenology, it is inherently reductive. For Kant, on the contrary, and for the tradition that follows this aspect of his thought, a valid philosophy of self must begin with the act of perception, which is always unique. It should therefore be nominalist in contrast to science, which is committed to universals. If there is a sense in which each experience offers itself as a unique, self-referential object of contemplation, then John Crowe Ransom's classified advertisement—"Wanted: An Ontological Critic"—is still needed.

In the Kantian view of perception, man's primary obligation is to be open to experience, and the primary obligation of the state is to encourage this openness through institutions that encourage human freedom. Through direct experience the self is realized and also is progressively enlarged. By nature committed to the objectification and communication of direct experience, art has a special obligation to honesty. The artist is not in business to be a good Rotarian or Presbyterian or biologist or Marxist or Cubist (or even a good Kantian) but to be a good artist. The obligation extends, however, beyond artists to men in general. It is the obligation of man to his potential self.

Classical humanism cannot honor this obligation because it is committed from the beginning to a determined set of values, which it locates in the past, and to a unitary, rather than an undetermined, concept of the self. Because it regards change as a cause of cultural decay, it is sympathetic to authority, and it seeks to make the canon of the classics into an instrument for inculcating its own values, current values, or else for preserving the past in an academic museum.

The humanism that derives from Kant has an almost opposite view of the past. There is no single, universal set of values. The self is undetermined and infinitely adaptable. From the point of view of Kantian humanism, the first value of a canon of classics is that it creates opportunities for the existing self to expand toward the potential self by experiencing of the otherness of the past. The second value is that it defines an identity, even though this identity is admittedly arbitrary.

The two values are parts of a dialectic, a creative tension, between openness on the one hand and closeness on the other.

Is there a way to relate the history of thought to the structure of thought? The fundamental movement in the history of thought is from the pre-critical to the critical mode of consciousness. In a general way, Kant's division of knowledge into moral and scientific categories picks up this historical movement and clarifies it. It is a gradual movement from a world in which everything depends on what is regarded as divine will toward a world in which everything seems to depend on reason in the sense of universals expressed in critical—ultimately, scientific— language. The next step occurs when the universals of science are recognized as human rather than divine or natural constructs, and Nature, having been objectified by reason, is once again regarded as a manifestation of spirit. Thus the progress from will to reason does not end in reason but moves beyond it to a new philosophy of will according to which man is fully responsible for creating both himself and the world.

Will is related to freedom, science to determinism. As the historical process moves forward, the demigod and the hero are replaced by the rational observer, who is joined later by the statistician and poll taker. The oracles cease. The laments of departing gods echo from every abandoned temple. Life seems to lose its divinity. It becomes a matter of getting and spending and facts and schedules.

The Greek experience suggests, however, that the gods may not really have died, no matter what the printout says. Their divinity has entered the world in the idea of beauty and the complementary idea of freedom. At the same time, the idea of beauty has been enlarged to cover the entire spectrum of human experience. It includes the ugly and the painful—as in Shakespeare's *King Lear* or Matthew Brady's photographs of the corpses of Union soldiers—as well as the graceful and the joyful. It includes projections of inner life in the form of the surrealistic and the abstract, as well as representations of the external world. And it includes projections in the form of elegant mathematical equations and the formulas of physics and chemistry and actuarial statistics and the shapes of the artifacts of technology, as well as paintings, statues, and melodies.

Far from having died, the gods first put on human masks and then put on the more subtle masks of Nature and the human psyche. They no longer stand apart in the middle foreground. They have become both the foreground and the self within which the foreground takes shape. The notion of an aesthetic category of experience contains the first hint of why and how this happens and creates the basis for a humanism that is grounded in reality.

Before Kant, the theory of consciousness, and hence the theory of the self, was a confused blend of ethical, religious, and aesthetic motives. The confusion is evident in the venerable misreading of Horace: "Poetry should instruct and delight." "Instruction" in this formula has always been understood to refer to the truths of science and moral philosophy that poetry expresses, and "delight" to the pleasures of meter and poetic imagery. How the two can be reconciled has never been adequately explained.

Since Kant, it has been evident that the formula is a mixture of apples and oranges. Delight refers to perception, and instruction to the uses of perception. Delight is an aspect of freedom, instruction of limitation. In the closing years of the twentieth century, mankind has become accustomed to a world of limits that is long on instruction and short on delight. Yet man was created free. To be human is to use this freedom to seek the possible self that stands beyond the limits of every individual life.

15

Education and Values

The humanities have been the foundation on which education rests in Western culture since the ancient Greeks. They are presently in the midst of a crisis so severe that doubts have been expressed concerning their survival. The apparent causes of the crisis are economic hard times and declining enrollments, but the deeper cause is what was termed in Chapter 7 the triumph of the idea of the useful, a corollary of the imperatives of modern technological society.

Education, however, remains as central to technological society as it was to earlier societies. In addition to teaching skills, it continues to be the chief official means for society to shape the identities of the young, develop their characters, and transmit the values by which they will shape the future. Evidently, education cannot ignore values even if it wants to. Whatever happens to the humanities in the curriculum, education must still confront the questions of what values to express and how to express them.

The solutions to this problem have been innumerable. Some order can be brought into the apparent chaos, however, by reference to two traditions that were examined in the preceding chapter: the tradition of classical humanism, which stems from the Renaissance, and the tradition of the humanism introduced by Kant at the end of the eighteenth century.

As noted in the preceding chapter, Renaissance humanism was a reform movement, a reaction of the intellectuals against what they considered the narrow conservatism, impracticality, and obscurantism of the medieval scholastics. The scholastics themselves had changed the course of education by shifting the emphasis of the curriculum from the literary classics favored in the early Middle Ages to technical subjects like logic and theology, but the Renaissance humanists ignored this historical fact. They equated scholasticism with the Middle Ages in general. Petrarch was crowned laureate in Rome in April of the year 1341. This is as good a symbolic date as any to mark the beginning of Renaissance humanism. In his coronation speech he set the tone for his followers. After acknowledging the difficulty of creating great art, he added: "Some uninspired men toil an entire lifetime, only to produce worthless and meaningless stuff, as the writings of the scholastic philosophers illustrate."

The humanists thought of themselves as realists. They were fascinated with power because they needed it to achieve their reforms. At the same time, and in spite of their stirring manifestos, they were basically scholars and poets and dreamers. They were as eager as modern academicians to give unwanted advice to the government, but they seldom exercised power themselves. When they did, the results could be disasterous. Cola di Rienzi brought his followers to ruin by attempting to set up a republic in Rome in the middle of the fourteenth century, and Petrarch was very nearly involved in the catastrophe. Some two hundred years later, Sir Thomas More accepted the Lord Chancellorship of England from Henry VIII only to discover that the office led not to sweeping social reforms but to the executioner's block.

The real key to power, many humanists concluded, was

education. If rulers tended to practice *Realpolitik* in total indifference to the noble ideals of Demosthenes, their children might still be taught otherwise. Under the tutelage of the humanists, these children could be trained to be the philosopher-statesmen, perhaps even the philosopher-kings, of the future. Teaching could be understood from this point of view as an exciting, almost revolutionary, calling.

The humanists saw their task as the preparation of future leaders. Today they would be considered elitists. In their own age they considered themselves servants of the *res publica* and hence benefactors of all levels of society. Although they trained children of the upper classes, they also supported the establishment of scholarships for talented but needy students. They took as their motto the definition of the ideal orator attributed to the Elder Cato: *vir bonus peritus dicendi,* "a good man skilled in the art of speaking."

The definition has two components, goodness and the art of speaking. The art of speaking relates to the ability to communicate effectively, which was considered necessary for leadership. It involves both skillful use of language and the general knowledge needed to communicate to diverse groups and in diverse circumstances. The art of speaking was understood to be a useful accomplishment, much like knowledge of law or medicine or electronics today, in spite of the fact that it required exposure to a select list of literary and moral masterpieces.

By goodness the humanists meant the ethical and political values that they traced to both pagan and Christian sources. In practice the emphasis was on pagan sources. To the degree that the humanists were committed to making their students good as well as eloquent, they were therefore committed directly and explicitly to the teaching of values. Putting aside for the moment the question of what these values were, it is useful to consider how they were taught. First, the humanist educator considered himself an authority and a custodian of values. Students were assembled in his classroom to learn, and the process of learning was, itself, part of the lesson since it taught the virtues of hard work, respect for authority, and self-discipline, and, incidentally, the swift retribution to be expected if those virtues were ignored. Second, the values were derived from the same works that were used to teach the art of speaking. These works were chosen for their exemplary morality as well as for their literary polish, and many classical works that were considered stylistically brilliant but morally questionable were simply ignored. We once again confront the canon of classics. Because the classics were carefully screened, they gave the impression of a uniform and generally consistent system of values—a distorted image of classical culture. These values, in turn, were thought to define the ideal identity of Western man.

In the early phase of humanism, the values it taught were new in the sense that they were opposed to typical medieval values. They were the values of action rather than contemplation and of the building of nations rather than the cultivation of the saints. Later, the coalition between humanist educators and the governing elite modified the idea of goodness. Republican values tended to become imperial, and the Socratic ideal of absolute personal integrity gave way to the Platonic ideal of service to the state. Eventually, goodness lost its challenge. It came to mean whatever the governing class considered important: religious conformity, unquestioning patriotism, obedience to authority, and willingness to die on the battlefield for the Crown and to bend with the prevailing wind in court. Perhaps humanism was always tainted. Realization that the humanist ideal had been coopted by the ruling class does not become a recurrent theme in literature, however, until the sixteenth century in Italy and the seventeenth century in England in the black humor of Donne's satires and the drama of Jonson, Webster, and Tourneur.

By the eighteenth century the image of the revolutionary humanist had dwindled into the image of the bigoted pedant. This image is fixed forever in the pages of Henry Fielding's *Tom Jones* in the person of Thwackum, the narrow-minded, sour disciplinarian for whom the classical heritage is no longer a glorious spiritual adventure but a set of facts and moral clichés to be beaten into sullen students with a cane. The characterization dramatizes the fact that what had been the forward edge of a revolution in the fifteenth century had become, three hundred years later, as dry and reactionary as the scholasticism against which the humanists had originally rebelled.

The search for the classical heritage did not end with Henry Fielding. In many ways, nineteenth-century education was able to revive the ideal of the classics. It did so, however, at a price. On the one hand, it opened the canon of the classics to vernacular literature and in this single action robbed classical antiquity of much of its influence as a stabilizing and centering force in modern culture. On the other, it surrounded the classics with a halo of nostalgia. They were no longer revolutionary influences as they had been, at least intermittently, in the Renaissance. They were relics of a departed glory, objects to be venerated like the Elgin Marbles in the British Museum. They were still regarded as sources of permanent values, but the effort to make those values relevant became increasingly strained. Their otherness was an embarrassment rather than an asset. Their primary justification was that they provided a convenient and attractive means of social indoctrination. Their secondary justifications were that they taught the meaning of hard work and provided the raw materials of historical scholarship.

In spite of its weaknesses, humanist education has virtues that are real and permanent. The first of these are minor virtues culturally but important for those who pay the cost of education. The humanist curriculum taught students to communicate, gave them a general understanding of the world around them, and instilled a sense—quixotic at times but still real—of commitment to honesty, service, and nation. By and large, it also equipped them for leadership. These virtues are not, after all, so commonplace that they can be dismissed today either in Europe or in the United States.

The second is a major virtue culturally though of little immediate practical value. In the nineteenth century, American education prided itself on being a melting pot in which members of different races, classes, and language groups were made over into Americans. The function of the primary school was to equip students with an understanding of the common language, the basic principles of citizenship, and skills like reading and computation that were necessary for economic viability. The humanities curriculum of the secondary schools and the colleges offered a higher type of integration. Until comparatively recently—the early 1960s—this curriculum was similar in its function and much of its content to the curriculum of the Renaissance humanists. It existed to teach goodness, with goodness generally interpreted as a specific set of ethical and political values characteristic of Western culture in general and American culture in particular. Its deeper function was to provide a common experience and a common set of attitudes. It was in effect a culture myth, a definition of identity both historically and in terms of direct involvement with historical and cultural documents. In this way it created a community whose members shared an understanding of where they had come from, who they were, and what they lived for it: it defined their center.

This central identity appears from a contemporary vantage point to be the chief contribution of the traditional humanities curriculum to education, and as it threatens to disappear there seems to be nothing to take its place. No one knows how effective it has been, but it is at least a force, and perhaps a truly powerful force, working against the tendency of America to divide into ethnic groups, racial groups, sexual groups, regional groups, class groups, religious groups, and various other factions. Before it is abandoned, it should be evaluated very carefully. Whatever its faults, it has, like Othello, done the state some service.

Humanist educational theory was challenged in the eighteenth century by new ideas about human psychology. The prophet of these new ideas was Jean-Jacques Rousseau. Rousseau was profoundly and viscerally disenchanted with his age. He was also capable of an exceptional degree of self-analysis, a talent that makes his *Confessions* a living (if faintly repellant) document today. His great insight, based partly on his own miserable childhood, was that man is born good and then is corrupted by society. This contradicts the Christian idea of original sin. It also places education in a new light. From Rousseau's point of view, if teaching is a method of preparing students for leadership by indoctrinating them in approved social values, it is committed by definition to destroying their goodness as speedily and efficiently as possible. If the child is good and society depraved, instead of teaching official social values, the conscientious educator will shield his charges from those values with every ounce of his energy. By concentrating on the child's innate goodness, the educator will bring him up to be a constructive influence on society rather than an accomplice in its hypocrisy.

Rousseau's ideas were more intuitive than practical. They were converted into a usable theory of education by a succession of educational theorists who drew their inspiration from Kantian philosophy as well as from *Émile*.

They were able to do this because Kant's substitution of imagination for reason or will as the central human faculty had introduced a new element into educational thought. Until Kant, it had been assumed that the mind was essentially a container to be filled with a substance called knowledge; or, in the formulation of John Locke, a *tabula rasa* that experience, including the experience of education, gradually covers with indelible inscriptions. In this view the mind is passive, which accords well with an emphasis in education on authority and memorization.

Kant, however, regarded the mind as active. Its basic faculty is imagination, which shapes the material it receives in the process of recording it. The imagination is a pure potential at birth and hence is untouched by evil—a parallel to Rousseau. Eighteenth-century psychology believed that mental activity was determined by the association of ideas (an anticipation of modern behaviorism), and traditional Protestantism taught that it was enslaved by original sin. The Kantian imagination, conversely, is initially undetermined and in this sense free. During childhood, it hardens into a shape dictated by its environment. At this point, the association of ideas enters the picture. The child grows up male or female, French rather than German or Chinese, an eighteenth-century coachman rather than a Roman senator or a Victorian ironmonger, an amateur gardener rather than a discus thrower or a golfer.

In this analysis of mind the function of education is to remove the limits imposed on the child's imagination by circumstance, not to reinforce them. In doing so, it restores to the child a measure of the potential self he was born with. Education can thus be understood as a removing of barriers—an elimination of mental inhibitions—rather than a filling of empty containers with official information. The essential value which this kind of education has to offer is liberation.

To a generation intoxicated by Rousseau, Kant's theory pointed the way toward a new and deeply human understanding of education. The first work to explore this understanding is one that has been cited in the preceding chapter as a seminal book in the history of modern humanism: Friedrich Schillers *Letters on the Aesthetic Education of Man.* The epigraph at the beginning of the *Letters* is a quotation from Rousseau: "Si c'est la raison, que fait l'homme, c'est le sentiment, que le conduit." What Rousseau calls "sentiment" in *La Nouvelle Héloise* becomes in Schiller's *Letters* a kind of existential experience, experience unmediated by conditioning.

For Schiller the key element of education is imaginative experience. In this kind of experience we confront reality directly, without preconceptions or prejudices. It therefore exposes us not to what we know already but to what we do not know. Classical humanism typically wants to convert something distant and alien —a poem by Horace, for example—into something familiar by reducing it to a moral commonplace of which the poem then becomes an example. It cannot communicate in a meaningful way with the past because it refuses to acknowledge that the past exists, and the community that it establishes is therefore a community only of contemporaries. Schiller's aesthetic humanism, conversely, demands the surrender of the present to the past. It is not interested in Horace because he is like contemporary men but because he is different. Full appreciation of the difference has two effects. First, it permits us to transcend the limits of our identities. And second, it creates a community of the spirit that extends across time as well as space.

This is not to say that Schiller was indifferent to ethical values in education. He was, in fact, passionately interested in them. Although the *Letters* is not a formal treatise on educational theory, the point of Schiller's argument is that to respond to art in terms of already established values—and worse, for the educational system to teach such a response—is to miss the principal benefits that both experience and education have to offer. It confirms people in their prejudices and reinforces the limits of their mental worlds. On the other hand, an educational system that encourages aesthetic response will, from Schiller's point of view, broaden the mental worlds of its students. It increases understanding of the real world and hence encourages such ethical values as tolerance, sensitivity, and the sense of wonder.

Three concepts are closely associated with Schiller's aesthetic education: liberation, play, and community.

Liberation is the freedom gained from being taken out of the local habitation and identity that one inherits from one's culture. Imaginative experience is liberating because it demands the surrender of the self to the object or event contemplated. Schiller called this kind of liberation *Freiheit in der Erscheinung*, "freedom in the world of appearance." It is an inner freedom, and it has its correlative in the freedom of the individual to accept it or not. The classroom implicit in Schiller's theory of education is so informal that it hardly exists at all, and the teacher is not an authority figure, but—at his most explicit—a guide or advisor or, in a modest way, a non-directive therapist. This sort of a classroom is the ideal of much contemporary progressive education.

Play is associated with aesthetic education because imaginative experience, being healthy and typically human, is enjoyable. When not forced to do so, we enjoy going to plays and concerts and looking at paintings. Learning is equally natural, and when not done under compulsion, should be equally enjoyable. Schiller called the aesthetic impulse the *Spieltrieb*, "the play impulse." Play is an activity entered freely for the immediate satisfaction that it offers. It is opposed to work, which is done under compulsion and for the sake of compensation. (Of course, the ideal situation is one in which the individual does something for pay that is enjoyable under any circumstances.) According to Schiller's *Letters*, education should be more like play than work. Great effort should be exerted, but it should be more like the effort expended in a game of tennis than the grudging and painful effort of a laborer whose only motive is the need to pay the grocer.

The sense of community that aesthetic education seeks to create has already been mentioned. It is achieved by departing from, rather than affirming, the familiar. Schiller was conscious, even at the end of the eighteenth century, of the increasing fragmentation of society into nations, races, classes, and occupations. He felt that aesthetic experience could counter this trend by creating means of communication across barriers that threatened to become impenetrable otherwise. His argument remains valid today, and, in fact, the provisions of the 1975 Helsinki Conference for increased international cultural exchange in the interests of increased international understanding show that his argument is accepted by modern politicians as well as educators.

The sense being part of a community that extends beyond

one's class or nation or culture or period of history is unquestionably a positive and very precious value. As has been noted, it is liberating to the individual and affirms the wholeness of humanity. At the same time, however, it requires a kind of surrender of individual and social identity. Such a surrender is risky. As was noted in Chapter 3, too much openness is as destructive as too little. Every tribe needs a sacred pole to mark its center. If the pole is broken the tribe perishes.

This brings us back to the sort of community that is implicit in the educational theories of classical humanism. The humanities curriculum that is defined, or at least symbolized, by a canon of classics, is an assertion of cultural identity. It does not define human identity through qualities that define humanity in general. Instead, it identifies specific traditions and specific groups in their separateness from other traditions and groups. The canon of Western classics defines the unique identity of European man while asserting the kinship of all those who share the Western tradition. The specific adaptation of that canon to American education defines an American identity that is part of Western tradition but also in some ways unique. The process of creating such a canon is political. It can be extended beyond states to ethnic groups (Chicano classics), classes (proletarian classics), and sexes (feminist classics) depending on who is in charge. It is arbitrary—a necessary fiction—not absolute. At its best, however, it does what it promises. It authenticates a community. Horatio Greenough's statue of George Washington attempted to do this through art. American education has done it better through its humanities curriculum.

The problem is that the specific virtues of the humanities curriculum do not seem to be separable from its inadequacies from the point of view of the sort of humanistic education foreshadowed in Schiller's *Letters*. To define a center it must (apparently) wrap the surrounding space around itself. Instead of liberating the self it seems to imprison the self. In place of play it offers a kind of civic obligation, and its community is local rather than global. Is there an escape from this dilemma?

The conflicts between the classical and the aesthetic concepts are evident today across the whole spectrum of contemporary educational thought. Should textbooks and school libraries be examined for their Americanism or their morality or their lack of these values? Should the schools teach the basics in structured classrooms, with periodic examinations to determine whether the students have mastered standard requirements, or should classrooms be open and students be encouraged to proceed at their own pace? Are students in fact damaged by regimentation? Is grading a useful kind of evaluation or a form of intimidation? Should the humanities be retained as a central element of the curriculum and their influence be assured through core requirements, or should they be allowed to survive or perish in the curricular marketplace? Can knowledge be compartmentalized into schools and departments, or do such divisions force it into predetermined forms? Should teachers lecture or lead discussion groups, or attempt to act as tutors? Should programs of study be formalized and move from least to most advanced subject, or should they be task- or subject-oriented as in schools of the performing arts and architecture and in the "case study" method found in many lawschools? Are degrees meaningful documents, or useless pieces of paper, or tickets of admission to good jobs? Should the study of French Renaissance art concentrate on the political, social, and critical influences that shaped the art, or should it concentrate on individual paintings?

Though these questions only skim the surface of the debate, they suggest its range. The debate extends beyond the academy. It is carried on with varying degrees of understanding among trustees, legislators, patrons, and voters in society at large. Time and again it involves positions that are corollaries of the older and the newer humanism.

It is a true debate because it seems to require choosing between two goods. In fact, it is impossible to choose between the two goods. They both have values that are essential for modern education, and somehow they both must be preserved. If the older tradition is threatened it must be supported by a conscious —and a political—act. But is not a decision to do nothing a political act too? The decision required in the present case is the reestablishment of a curriculum organized around a canon of responsibly chosen classics. This is, of course, easier to propose than accomplish, given the fragmentation of modern society in general and of the educational establishment in particular, but it is possible.

At the same time, the core curriculum must not be allowed to revert to the indoctrination and pedantry that characterized the humanities curriculum of the nineteenth and early twentieth century. This is where the point of view of Schiller's *Letters* is useful, even essential, both as a means of presenting the works that make up the curriculum and as a way of structuring the presentation itself. A canon of classics can and should define a common experience and a common identity. These are important values, and America needs them today. However, the works that comprise a canon cannot all be forced to speak the same language and yield the same message. They, too, demand a degree of surrender if they are to speak as eloquently as possible.

In 1972 the government of Alberta, Canada, appointed a commission to study the future of higher education in the province. The report that the commission submitted was called *A Choice of Futures, a Future of Choices.* Its first assumption was that the province of Alberta was changing rapidly and that the pace of change would accelerate in the future. Having made this assumption, the commissioners argued that Alberta's students would need a larger humanistic component in their education. They argued that if change is a centripetal force tending to social division, humanistic education—education in common values—

can be a force that brings citizens together—an echo of the idea of community.

The next twenty years will bring intense social stress to the United States as well as Alberta, Canada. The idea of education as a center around which Americans can arrange their diversities and in terms of which they can sense each other's common humanity is attractive. As the preceding observations should have made clear, it is not a novel idea, but it is not for that reason, inconsequential. It is one of the threads that still connect us to the entrance of the maze we have entered.

16

The Future of Poetry

By standard definition, the First World is the world of the industralized West, with major outposts in Israel, South Africa, Australia, Japan, Taiwan, and South Korea. The Second World is a child of the First. The idea of the Second World was first conceived by Karl Marx at the British Museum out of an unlikely union between Hegel and Jeremy Bentham. For its first half-century it was considered relevant only to industrialized societies, which is to say that Russia was the last place most nineteenth-century socialists considered ripe for a workers' revolution. But history has a way of ignoring probability, and Russia rather than Germany or France became the first great socialist state. Today, the Second World consists of the Soviet Union and its satellites. These nations reveal their generalized relation to the First World in their dedication to the ideal of material progress, which is the same ideal that dominates the First World, and in their imperialistic ambitions, which are the mirror image of Western imperialism.

What can be said about the Third World? To many it is the gentle world typified by Gandhi and Zen Buddhism. It might be considered a world quietly preaching sanity at a time when the first two worlds appear to be running neck and neck in a race toward annihilation.

The Third World is also a victim. The first two worlds have one-third of the earth's population and consume over two-thirds of its resources. This leaves the inhabitants of the Third World, in Franz Fanon's memorable phrase, "the wretched of the earth." Wretched because while the rich nations grow richer the poor nations become inexorably poorer. And wretched because they live on a precarious balance between life and starvation, at the mercy of the slightest variations in climate and the world economy.

But is Fanon's phrase appropriate for all of the Third World? Within the Third World there are nations as rich as Nigeria, Iran, and Saudi Arabia and nations as poor as Bangladesh and the Sudan. There are nations as ancient and as complex as Ethiopia and India and nations as young and wracked by unresolved tensions as Indonesia and Zimbabwe. And there is the People's Republic of China, which is a giant balanced precariously between the Second and Third worlds.

A few Third World nations are democracies. Most, probably, are socialist and are controlled by a strong ruling elite. Several are dictatorships varying from benign to brutal. And some are misshapen survivals of colonial or other political arrangements divided by religious and regional differences. The official policy of the Third World is non-alignment, but every Third World nation constantly modifies its foreign policy in relation to the world demand for its resources, its need for capital, its geographical location, and the pressures created by its own internal factions. The 1979 Third World Congress in Havana, Cuba, demonstrated, if demonstration is needed, that many Third World nations are in reality clients of the First or Second World.

There was once a widespread hope, shared by many in the First World, that the Third World had a vision of human life on a human scale that would teach the First and Second worlds how to live together in peace. This hope has not disappeared, but it has faded. In retrospect it looks like a modern version of the ancient myth of the pastoral, the idea that somewhere, anywhere but where we are, there is a breed of men more innocent, more truly noble, less cruelly materialistic than ourselves.

Poets have always been especially fond of pastoral themes, not because poets are dreamers and escapists but because poetry is an expression of value. To express even the simplest experience in poetry is to express it from the poet's angle of vision, and that angle of vision is an implicit value. In pastoral, the point of view is emphasized, not latent. The pastoral image is an image of human potential, of what humans might become given ideal circumstances, which is at the same time a criticism of what humans actually are in present circumstances.

To imagine what human beings might be and to express that image in language is to define a goal. Human beings may not reach the imagined goal, but once it is defined it gives them a sense of direction. They know whether they are approaching it or moving away. It might therefore be said that the idea of the moral superiority of the Third World is an important pastoral theme in modern art. Whether or not it is true in a way that is acceptable to the economist or the political scientist (and it is probably a very complicated mixture of truth and falsehood) it is a creative and life-enhancing idea for all three worlds. By defining a goal, it exemplifies the truth of Shelley's definition of poets as the unacknowledged legislators of mankind.

There is a Fourth World, one not of nations but of individuals. The center of this world is beauty, and specifically the beauty expressed in art. Benedetto Croce used to say that beauty is one, indivisible and entire. He meant that a truly beautiful creation is beautiful to anyone who can respond to it directly. Its beauty is not peculiar to the artist. Rather, its beauty is a quality the artist finds in his own experience, which is common to the experience of others. To say that beauty is one, indivisible and entire is to say that it exists outside of normal time and space. This is why people can be moved by a statue thousands of years old, produced by a lost civilization for ceremonial purposes that cannot even be imagined today. It is also why beauty leaps across barriers of nationality, race, and culture—why an American bureaucrat can be reduced to silent awe before an African face mask, and a Japanese schoolchild can be captivated by the music of Beethoven.

To say that beauty is one, indivisible, and entire, is not to say that there is a formula for making it, or that the more beautiful two objects are the more alike they will be, or that beauty can be defined in terms of a universal ideology. Quite the opposite. Whether it is as utilitarian as a woven basket or as ponderously and self-consciously artistic as a Wagnerian opera, each artwork is born out of the special circumstances of the artist who produces it: his culture, the function the artwork is intended to serve within that culture, the artistic conventions the artist followed, his own personality as shaped by his family, his social class, and his profession, and the sum of all the experiences that have given him an identity different from that of other men. This is why for every work of art that the artist creates there are innumerable works of art that he did not create, and why art itself is inexhaustible and perpetually new.

Nor is beauty beautiful in any standardized sense of the term. In the first of the *Duinese Elegies* (1923), Rilke asked, "What is beauty but the beginning of terror that we only barely endure?" Beauty is sometimes terrifying because it takes us out of ourselves into the infinite world that is not ourselves. The world of the self is a refuge, and we need it in order to retain our identiy. But it is also a prison that we need to break out of to enlarge our identities. To surrender the self is an adventure under the best of circumstances. It is always an adventure to leave what is familiar with the knowledge that the experience will change us in such a way that we will never be able to return to precisely the point from which we began.

Such an adventure becomes terrifying if the unknown wears a mask we have been taught to fear. We attack this kind of beauty and attempt to defend ourselves against it by calling it ugly or offensive or subversive and by using all of our resources of ridicule and vilification to keep it at bay. Societies do the same thing. They reject artists whose vision of beauty violates approved standards. Often they express their fear of beauty in their laws and deprive the artist of his freedom to create, or deprive him of his freedom to communicate with others, or, if all else fails, deprive him of life itself.

Rightly understood, the extreme measures taken to suppress beauty are the best evidence of its terrible power. What is harmless does not need to be suppressed. Hence, too, the failure of those bureaucrats of art who are allowed to prosper because they create according to the rules of the censor, the directives of the ministry of propaganda, the formulas of the schools. Alfred North Whitehead once observed, "It takes an exceptional intelligence to contemplate the obvious." That is why so few men are artists. It also takes an exceptional society to allow men to contemplate the obvious. That is why there have been so few periods in history when the arts have flourished. In fact, for men and societies, there are probably only different degrees of failure, but the degrees exist and are plain to anyone who cares to look for them.

To say this is to define the Fourth World. It is the world of artists and those willing to open themselves to art. It is timeless because it unites the past with the present, and it is universal because it unites the tribal craftsman in Nairobi with the symphony conductor in Tokyo and the insurance executive in Hartford, Connecticut. It is a world, in other words, that regards infinite diversity as a means to discover an essential unity. Actually, "discover" is probably too strong a word. Since the diversity of art is truly infinite, we can never know more than a small part of it. What we achieve through our knowledge is more accurately described as an intuition or a faith validated by experience than a discovery.

On the other hand, this kind of intuition is neither vague nor —in spite of appearances to the contrary—impractical. It is practical in the most fundamental meaning of the term. It helps us to live. It has always done so, and one way of understanding the history of art is to see it as the reverse side of the coin of man's struggle for survival. Art authenticates the forms that a society uses to transact its essential business; it articulates society by giving groups and individuals their identities; and, at the same time, it prevents differences from becoming destructive by creating means of communication among different and potentially hostile groups.

Art thus has enormous practical consequences, and it may be that art has never been a more powerful force in human history than it is today. This claim may seem excessive, since artists often think of themselves as ineffectual and neglected, but it is offered seriously. In the twentieth century, photography, phonograph and tape recordings, radio, film, and television have created an international culture—a unified human consciousness—that is unique in human history. This international culture is radical in that it can draw elements from all the cultures of world, and it is subversive in that by humanizing the peoples of the world to one another, it undermines forces of political and economic nationalism. Because of this culture, we are more aware than at any earlier time in history that we are part of one world and that, to echo John Donne, one man's suffering—or death— diminishes us all.

This is not to say that either the present or the future is rosy. The emerging international consciousness is new and consequently fragile, whereas vanity, greed, and aggression are as old as history. We have a long way to go before war becomes impossible simply because it seems absurd to those who are asked to plan it; and a still longer way to go before we recognize that we have a collective responsibility for the life of every person on this planet. Long before art has completed its work, we may be swept into irreversible catastrophe. But if such a catastrophe can be avoided, art may eventually (and perhaps more rapidly than anyone can now imagine) help society to turn in a creative and life-enhancing direction.

But what about poetry? The medium of poetry is language, and this fact creates problems that do not seem to exist for music and the visual arts. Poetry has to be translated, and translation is at best an inadequate device. The best translations of poems tend to be free variations on what is allegedly being translated, while more typical translations stand as testimonials to the old definition: "Poetry is what gets left out of a translation."

The diversity of poetry is simply not as accessible as the diversity of film or television, in which meaning is carried by images as well as by language, not to mention such nearly transparent—hence universal—forms of art as costume, architecture, music, and painting. Poetry is opaque. There are over three hundred major languages out of a known total of around three thousand, and each creates a separate form of the self, a separate way of giving shape to reality, which is to say that each language is, in Ernst Cassirer's phrase, a separate symbolic form, a separate way of putting the world together.

Because of this, poetry may be considered from two points of view. The poetry of languages other than our own is a continuous challenge. To learn a new language can be a transforming experience. At the same time, it is an experience that has to be purchased with considerable effort. Few people learn more than three or four foreign languages well. It is exceptional, in fact, to find someone who is fluent in two languages other than his own. Translating prose is difficult, but poetry, in which every nuance is significant, is the most severe taskmaster of any of the arts. It speaks more directly and more precisely than any other art, but it speaks only to those who understand. The first lesson it teaches is that no one can experience more than a tiny fraction of what it offers. The concept of poetry is therefore, even more than the concept of art in general, an intuition, or a kind of faith, rather than a discrete idea.

Within a given language, poetry has another function. Because language is the medium of consciousness, poetry objectifies the texture of consciousness. The body of poetry in a given language expresses, cumulatively, the range and coloring of conscious experience possible within the language, and every new poem extends the range a little farther. Collectively, poetry may be considered the objectified consciousness of the language in which it is written. At the same time, each poem is a precisely objectified moment in the consciousness of its creator.

Since the Romantic period the consciousness objectified in poetry has been understood historically. In the major reference works and in the schools, poetry is usually studied by periods, from the earliest to the most modern. The Romantic period, which developed this approach, was also an age of intense nationalism. When set in a nationalist framework, the historical approach to poetry tends to convert it from the study of beauty to the study of the origin and evolution of the national consciousness. In other words, Romantic nationalism enlisted poetry in the service of the state. Used in this way, poetry no longer testifies to the unity of human experience but to its diversity.

In his 1937 essay *La Poesia*, Benedetto Croce called attention to this problem. He complained that beauty was being mutilated, and that its unity was being carved into separate and hostile territories, one bearing a Union Jack, another a tricolor, another a hammer and sickle, another a swastika, and so forth. Croce regarded this progressive fragmentation as a betrayal of beauty, and he pointed out that its practical result was to ratify those bloody impulses that led Europe, only two years after his essay was published, into the most destructive war in history, a war in which an estimated twenty million people died. The dismemberment of beauty did not cause the war, but once dismembered, beauty was powerless, and her disciples were unable to escape becoming servants of the politicians. The psychological anguish that resulted from this dismemberment of beauty had its practical complement in the physical anguish of World War II, and also, perhaps, in the pervasive sense of impotence and isolation that characterized post-war existentialism.

It is a tragic story, but it points to the major theme of these observations. The tradition of poetry is not that of the First, Second, or Third World. It is a tradition linking each of us through language to a place, a society, and a history, and through these, to all other inhabitants of this anguished planet. It is the tradition of the Fourth World, the world of art, that encompasses the first three worlds and remains one of their brightest hopes.